XML:

A Beginner's Guide

XML:
A Beginner's Guide

Dave Mercer

Osborne/**McGraw-Hill**

New York   Chicago   San Francisco
Lisbon   London   Madrid   Mexico City   Milan
New Delhi   San Juan   Seoul   Singapore   Sydney   Toronto

Osborne/McGraw-Hill
2600 Tenth Street
Berkeley, California 94710
U.S.A.

To arrange bulk purchase discounts for sales promotions, premiums, or fund-raisers, please contact Osborne/**McGraw-Hill** at the above address. For information on translations or book distributors outside the U.S.A., please see the International Contact Information page immediately following the index of this book.

XML: A Beginner's Guide

1234567890 CUS CUS 01987654321

ISBN 0-07-212740-6

Publisher   Brandon A. Nordin
Vice President & Associate Publisher   Scott Rogers
Acquisitions Editor   Ann Sellers
Project Editors   Lisa Theobald, Patty Mon
Acquisitions Coordinator   Tim Madrid
Technical Editor   Robert J. Brunner
Copy Editor   Marcia Baker
Proofreader   Pat Mannion
Indexer   Jack Lewis
Computer Designers   Roberta Steele, Tara Davis, Jean Butterfield
Illustrator   Beth E. Young, Lyssa Sieben-Wald, Michael Mueller
Series Design   Gary Corrigan
Cover Design   Greg Scott
Cover Illustration   Kevin Curry

This book was composed with Corel VENTURA™ Publisher.

About the Author

Dave Mercer has been building databases professionally since 1993, and he built his first Web site in 1995. He has a diverse background, including 15 years as an industrial engineer; he has a degree in business from San Diego State University; and he has worked on Web sites for everything from flower shops to car dealerships to real estate appraiser directories. He's been teaching Web site design and development classes since 1996 and has been writing books for the computer market since 1998.

Dave is currently CTO of a Web site design and database development company and is helping to create the new Internet economy all of us are gradually coming to live and work in. His latest projects include both non-profit and commercial Web sites, and a wireless application service provider at **www.e4free.com**.

Contents at a Glance

PART III
Extending XML

PART IV
Appendixes

Contents

PART III
Extending XML

Acknowledgments

Thanks to Ann, Lisa, Tim, Marcia, Patty, and Robert for the wonderful job you did with this material. Thanks to Michael for the work on the examples in Module 12. And thanks to the XML community for the excellent standards work that will make the new economy real.

Introduction

The other day, I was with a client working on his Web site, and I had my laptop with me. It was convenient, but I still had to run cables for my trackball, power supply, and network connection. I remarked that soon I'd be able to attach a high-speed wireless modem and surf from anywhere. My point is that the wireless information age is finally dawning, and in the future, XML-based wireless Web sites are going to be the norm, rather than the exception.

The whole concept of XML and related languages/specifications is to separate data from presentation and to provide a standard format that describes itself in a language both machines and people are comfortable with. This is a tall order, but the W3C and all the contributors to these standards have been quite successful, if industry acceptance is any measure. XML and all its language variants increasingly seem to be the solution whenever data must be exchanged.

It doesn't really matter what format your data is in, how you store it, or how you work with it internally. Insiders know the real power for the next century is in the rapid, efficient, and effortless communication of selected data between parties, whether B2B, B2C, or any variation on the theme.

We've all seen the ups and downs of the Internet phenomenon, and we've heard outrageous numbers relating to ecommerce. But we're not even halfway "there" yet, and even with the recent market downturn there's no avoiding the fact that new economical ways of doing business are going to outdo old ways of doing business, many times over.

If you're just getting started with XML, take the time to review the HTML and XHTML stuff in this book, because those languages are not going away anytime soon. But, for now, XML is the way to go, so be sure to learn all you can about the technology. It really is the wave of the future.

If you've just picked this book up and want to learn XML, that's great. But I should warn you that the languages that make Web sites work are many and varied, and you'll want to expose yourself to all of them. Osborne/McGraw-Hill has been publishing computer books for years, and many resources are available to fill you in on the other languages. Even so, we cover in very basic terms about 10 of them in this book alone. And just let me add that some awesome reference material is also available online, at the Osborne Web site (**www.osborne.com**) and at the Web sites of the big guys like Microsoft, Oracle, Sun, and others.

Unlike many technologies you'll learn, XML is not a programming language—or a database, a markup language, or an application. Instead, it is a *specification* for creating your *own* markup languages. By writing your own DTDs of XML schemas, you are literally creating a new vocabulary for your particular needs, whether Web-related or not. Don't be afraid to experiment!

Who Should Read This Book

Welcome to *XML: A Beginner's Guide*. As the name suggests, this book is for everyone—from raw programming trainees to programming professionals breaking into XML for the first time. If you intend to use XML or related languages, this book is for you. If you intend to manage those who write XML documents, this book is for you. If you own a business and wish to understand one of the primary technologies by which developers will create data exchange mechanisms for you, this book is for you.

We hope you'll find the material interesting, well rounded, clear, concise, comprehensive, and fast-moving. Once you understand how it works, you'll find yourself seeing applications for XML everywhere. It's a remarkably powerful tool, in the right hands.

What This Book Covers

This book is broken into 12 modules and two appendixes, the first appendix being an answers guide and the 12 modules being pretty much all you need to know to begin creating and transforming XML documents and converting data to and from databases—all the way from simple DTDs to XML schemas to database manipulation to wireless applications. Today's Web sites are built from many different languages, technologies, and components, so this book uses XHTML for some examples, as well as CSS2, Active Server Pages, SQL, and common database design techniques.

At the back of the book is another appendix that details some common XML DTD and XML Schema examples and operators. It should come in handy as you write your first DTDs, and on the Web site (**www.osborne.com**) all the code is available for easy download and insertion into your own site or application. If you follow along with the examples written in the book and produce code and databases to match, you can use the samples to add powerful functionality to any Web site or application.

- **Module 1, "The History of XML"**   In this module, we discuss the roots of XML, why it was needed, and how it fits in with other Web and data-storage technologies. We also compare it with HTML and XHTML, as many of you will be already familiar with these two languages (and you're going to have to know them well anyway).

- **Module 2, "XML Basics, Syntax, and DTDs"**   As XML is not a language but a specification for writing extensible markup languages, we cover the construction of Document Type Definitions (DTDs) in this module. All the components that may be included in an XML document, such as elements, attributes, comments, processing instructions, and so on, are covered from the standpoint of their definition in a DTD. We also cover how to connect an XML document to a DTD.

- **Module 3, "XML Schema"**   The W3C language for creating XML vocabulary definitions as schemas is covered in this module. An XML Schema performs the same type of function as a DTD but is more flexible and capable and includes data types for finer definitions.

- **Module 4, "XML Namespaces and Advanced Schemas"** This module reviews the Namespaces recommendation, a key part of XML technology that allows reuse and mixing of DTDs and schemas. We also cover XML Schema usage with namespaces.

- **Module 5, "XML Graphics Basics and SMIL"** Graphics can be incorporated into XML documents, and in this module we cover graphics basics, inserting graphics in XHTML and XML documents, and Synchronized Multimedia Integration Language (SMIL). SMIL documents are XML documents based on the SMIL XML vocabulary, and the project constructing a SMIL document is quite fun.

- **Module 6, "XML Applications, XLink, XPath, and XPointer"** Creating and working with XML documents means using processing applications and scripting languages. In this module, we cover some of the popular application programs for validating and rendering XML documents and the specifications for tapping into XML documents with them. The XPath language in particular is important for transforming XML documents into a format that can be rendered on browsers and other end devices.

- **Module 7, "XML and the Web"** Although not a requirement, many of your XML documents will end up on the Web, and in this module we cover typical Web site construction related to XML documents. We also provide background data on XML Signature, Platform for Privacy (P3P), and XForms, each of which may come in handy during the construction of your Web-based XML documents.

- **Module 8, "The Document Object Model"** The DOM is used for many W3C languages, not just XML. Because it is particularly useful for the manipulation of XML documents programmatically, we give it in-depth coverage in this module. We compare using it with XHTML to using it with XML and provide examples for working with XML documents (in DOM form) using Active Server Pages and VBScript.

- **Module 9, "Designing Data Models for XML"** XML is a great format for the exchange of data, but what about data storage? Vast quantities of data are currently found in traditional databases, and in this module we cover how to design data models for XML documents along the same lines as data models for traditional databases, including the Entity-Relationship (ER) model and the Parent-Child Relationship (PCR) model.

- **Module 10, "Databases and XML"**   In this module we cover the basics of designing common relational databases, including Microsoft Access and SQL Server, with a little coverage of the Structured Query Language (SQL) as well. We also examine XQuery, the W3C query language for XML that is currently under development.

- **Module 11, "XML Presentation and XSL"**   The basic functions for changing XML documents into finished, renderable documents are covered in this module, starting with an examination of traditional style-sheet languages (such as CSS2) and proceeding to XML style-sheet creation, XSL, and XSLT using XPath.

- **Module 12, "XML, WAP, and Ecommerce"**   This module includes a short introduction to ecommerce, followed by an introduction to the Wireless Markup Language (WML), an XML vocabulary well suited and commonly used for the creation of wireless Web sites. The module finishes with an example of creating and using XML documents and transforming them into wireless documents using ASP and VBScript.

- **Appendix A, "Answers to Mastery Checks"**   Each module contains questions at the end (called Mastery Checks) that help you make sure you've absorbed the basics, and Appendix A provides the answers to these questions.

- **Appendix B, "XML Schema and DTD Syntax"**   This is a quick reference to common XML DTD and Schema coding and element examples.

How To Read This Book

This book can be read from beginning to end, and you can also open any module for an easy-to-follow introduction to the specific XML recommendations and specifications you are interested in. Each module provides code and projects to help you understand the subject. Please review the material on the Web site whenever working with examples, as the code is available so you can avoid rewriting everything by hand.

Special Features

Throughout each module are *Hints, Tips,* and *Notes,* as well as *detailed code listings* (the code can be downloaded from the Web site in full). The *1-Minute Drills* check to make sure you're retaining what you've read (and help focus your attention on the more important points). The *Ask the Expert* question-and-answer sections give in-depth explanations about the current subject. Included with the book and on the Web site are *Projects* that help you put what you've learned into working applications. At the end of each module is a *Mastery Check* that gives you another opportunity for review, and the answers are contained in Appendix A. The actual DTDs for many of the languages/recommendations reviewed may be found at the Web sites noted in the book, such as the W3C and the WAP forum sites. While detailed explanations are provided for the subjects covered, the best approach is to try out the code with the appropriate platforms so you'll get up to speed quickly.

Quite a bit of additional information is available at the Web sites mentioned within the modules, from the Microsoft corporate Web site to the W3C Web site to third-party XML Web sites. You can also visit the Osborne Web site to access links to Zip files that have all the code and projects found in the book, so you can visit and download what you need rather than copying from the book. You can find the filename for each module's projects listed next to the project headings.

So let's get started. XML is a big part of the future of Web site design, as well as application design in general, and you'll find that it's not that difficult after you've run some of the examples in this book. Tally-ho!

Part I

XML Basics

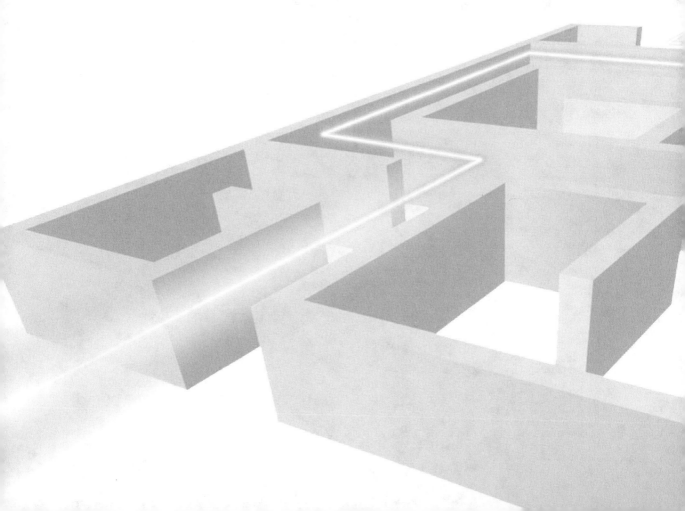

Module 1

The History of XML

The Goals of This Module

- Understand markup languages
- Understand XML as a language development technology
- Explore SGML, HTML, and XHTML and their relationships with XML
- Create a simple HTML document
- Learn how the HTML DTD was built
- Dissect the HTML DTD
- Learn the differences between HTML and XHTML
- Convert an HTML document into an XHTML document
- Examine XML components

Welcome to eXtensible Markup Language (XML) and to *XML: A Beginner's Guide*. If you have an interest in the Internet, the Web, and Web page design, you've probably heard of XML, because it is "the next big thing." In fact, XML is the next logical step in developing the full potential of the Internet and the Web. Just as HyperText Markup Language (HTML), HyperText Transfer Protocol (HTTP), and Web browsers paved the way for exciting new methods of communications between networked computers and people, XML and its associated technologies open new avenues of electronic communications between people and machines. In the case of XML, however, the promise is for both human-machine and machine-machine communications, with XML as the "lowest-common-denominator" language that all other systems, proprietary or open, can use. Because this book is for beginners, we'll start in Module 1 with some of the most basic concepts, but be prepared to do your homework because the field is rapidly changing, advancing, developing new technologies, and morphing into an ever more useful set of tools.

Note

The World Wide Web Consortium (W3C), at **www.w3.org**, maintains drafts and recommendations for XML and its related technologies (as well as HTML and XHTML). Although the information on this site is rather dry, it is the source of XML specifications and should be referred to whenever you need to find out the latest news. Since the working groups attached to this organization are the official authors of XML technologies as open standards, these standards should be followed as you create your own XML applications.

A Simple XML Document

Before we get into the intricate details of XML, let's examine a very simple XML document to see how it is related to SGML (Standard Generalized Markup Language) and HTML. Hopefully this will provide you with the foundation for understanding XML. All the parts and components of XML are described throughout the book. XML and SGML are similar in terms of what they can do, but XML is a subset of SGML. HTML, and languages like it, are defined in terms of SGML, just like XML languages are defined by XML. The following illustration should make it a little clearer:

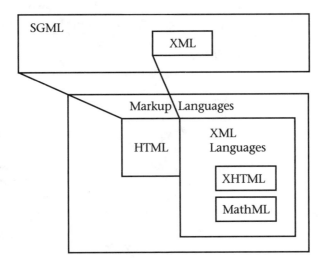

Writing an XML document is pretty straightforward. For example, let's say you want to write a simple document that conforms to the basic rules of XML, and you want to make a statement. The following bit of code would be acceptable:

```
<?xml version 1.0 ?>
<statement>A statement in an XML document</statement>
```

The first line specifies the XML version the document complies with, and the second line uses an element that contains a statement. How do we know it contains a statement? The element itself is named <statement>, and as such, it describes the content it holds. The ability to use any elements and attributes the author desires is fundamental to the power of XML.

The Origins of XML

If you're already a Web designer, you're likely familiar with HTML. Most Web pages you see are made from HTML elements (often called *tags*, although this term actually refers to the HTML commands that begin and end HTML elements). HTML, in turn, was derived from SGML, which was developed as a framework for defining documents and the data within them in a standard way. In this module, we will cover HTML basics as a way of giving you something recognizable (such as elements, attributes, and DTDs—Document Type Definitions) to compare to XML later on.

Note

What are DTDs, elements, and attributes? Think of Lego blocks. A DTD is a written specification defining the building blocks you can use to make a document—whether HTML, XHTML, or XML, or any of the other SGML-related languages. *Elements* are the "things" in the document, such as paragraphs, tables, forms, and images (but keep in mind that with XML, you can define as many of your own "things" as you want). *Attributes* provide elements with properties such as width, height, or number of rows. Again, with XML you can define whatever attributes you want to define your elements.

Standards are important with computers, because a lack of across-the-board standards makes communication difficult or impossible. Communication depends on understanding, and understanding depends on agreement as to the meaning of the terms used to communicate. Although philosophers may debate the essence of the word *meaning*, people can usually agree at some level, and from that basis, common terms can be established and communication can take place.

SGML is an international standard (ISO 8879) for the definition of device-independent, system-independent methods of representing information, both human and machine readable. Languages conforming to the rules in SGML are called *applications*, and HTML is an SGML application. SGML has played (and still plays) an important role in defining documents to a consistent communications standard, but it is considered rather complex for most Internet-related purposes. At the same time, HTML has no provisions for extending itself in a standard way into new tags, attributes, data structures, or content types, and so is too limited. XML, however, rather than being a predefined language like HTML, is a predefined way of defining new languages while avoiding the overly complex nature of SGML. Technically, XML includes a subset of the capabilities found in SGML.

1-Minute Drill

● What is SGML?

● What is HTML in relationship to SGML?

● What is XML in relationship to SGML?

Markup Languages

A *markup language* is a set of commands that tell a program how to display content. *Content* is words, pictures, and other digitized data. Markup language commands are written in plain text that people can read and write fairly easily. Imagine the following scenario, and you'll get a good idea of how a markup language works.

A manager hand writes a memo, and then asks the administrative assistant to type it (yes, that's actually the way it used to be done). The administrative assistant types it and brings it to the manager. The manager then reviews the typewritten document and marks it up with corrections, symbols that indicate what is to be bold and italicized, and where the charts and graphs should go. Then the administrative assistant makes the changes and retypes the document, delivering the final version for approval before distributing it.

In this scenario, the original contains most of the content, and when the first typewritten draft is marked up, those symbols are roughly equivalent to the commands used in a markup language. However, modern markup languages have a fairly precise syntax for markup, and a program (such as a browser) is usually doing the interpretation of the markup commands and displaying the final results.

● SGML is the Standard Generalized Markup Language, a specification for creating markup languages in a standard way.

● HTML is a markup language constructed according to the SGML standard. Thus, it is an SGML application.

● XML is a subset of SGML that is particularly suited to creating markup languages for the Internet. Thus, it is not a markup language but a specification for creating markup languages for the Internet.

One of the best examples of a markup language is HTML. HTML documents are a single file of markup commands and content in many cases, although there are exceptions that employ JavaScript, server-side include files, and so forth. You can view the HTML markup commands in your Internet Explorer browser window by choosing View | Source (Netscape has similar menu commands).

In an HTML document, you'll see a series of HTML commands (tags) that are used to define the elements in the document. For example, <HTML> is the tag for the main element for an HTML document. Because the nature of markup languages is that they are made up of elements that contain other elements, attributes, and content, all other content in an HTML document is contained within the starting and ending <HTML> tags (<HTML> is the starting tag, and </HTML> is the ending tag).

Attributes are modifiers for HTML elements (and they play the same role in many other markup languages as well). They consist of a *name-value pair*: the name of the attribute, an equal sign, and then the value of the attribute. For example, the BGCOLOR attribute may be included in the starting <BODY> tag of an HTML document. It could look like this:

```
<BODY BGCOLOR="white">
All content appearing in the main screen of the
browser goes here, including other elements, such
as the <IMG SRC="myimage.gif"> element for images.
</BODY>
```

In this example, the BGCOLOR attribute modifies the BODY element, indicating that the background color of the BODY element is white. In the next section, we'll review HTML documents and the HTML language in more detail, so that you can compare it to XML and XML documents.

A Basic HTML Document

To lead us into XML, let's review the basics of HTML. HTML came before XML, and the limitations of HTML spurred development of XML, so HTML is a good starting point because the constructs and processing of HTML documents are similar to those used in XML languages. In fact, the latest version of HTML is XHTML, an XML language for HTML that conforms to XML standards, but here we use HTML 4.01 as a reference, because many of you are probably already familiar with HTML.

First, here's some HTML code that forms a simple page:

```
<HTML>
<HEAD>
<TITLE>The Title</TITLE>
</HEAD>
<BODY BGCOLOR="#CCFFFF">
Here is the content of the page
</BODY>
</HTML>
```

HTML is written as a plain text file (that is, it can be written with Notepad or any simple text editor). Generally, one file equals one Web page, although it is possible to combine several files into one Web page using server-side includes and so forth (which we'll get to later). HTML Web pages consist of elements that are defined by tags. Tags are delimited (marked off) by angle brackets— the less-than and greater-than signs (< and >). In the example code, the Web page opens and closes with an HTML element. The starting tag is <HTML>, and the ending tag is </HTML>. The HTML element is considered the *root* element of the document, because all other elements in the document are contained within it.

Other elements may be *nested* inside the HTML element, and some of these elements may have more elements nested inside them. Nested means that the starting tag of the containing element (the parent element) occurs before the starting tag of the child element (the one being contained), and the ending tag of the parent element occurs after the ending tag of the child element. For example, in the preceding code, the HEAD element tags are inside the HTML element tags, and the TITLE element tags are inside the HEAD element tags. An interesting thing about the TITLE element is that text content (the words "The Title") is contained between the beginning and ending <TITLE> tags. And although all of the elements in the example code are written in uppercase, this is not required. In fact, HTML elements can be written in uppercase, lowercase, or a mixture of cases.

Notice the BODY element in the example code. Not only does it have starting and ending tags and text content, there is something additional inside the starting tag—the BGCOLOR attribute. The default color for the background of a Web page is a light gray. The BGCOLOR attribute is set to light blue using the HTML color code #CCFFFF, so the background of the BODY element (the BODY element's attribute) will be light blue.

Using Attributes in HTML

In HTML, attributes always appear in a name-value pair (as shown in the first example that follows), unless the attributes are minimized (as shown in the second example that follows, in which SELECTED is a minimized attribute). Attributes that are minimized create their effect when only the name of the attribute is included in the tag—with no value. For example, a radio button created with an INPUT element on a page appears in the selected state upon opening the page in a browser when the *selected* attribute is included, so no value needs to be set for the attribute. The following code examples show how this works.

In the first example, two INPUT elements are included in a form, each with its TYPE attribute set to "radio" for radio button, its NAME attribute set to "CCType" for credit card type, and the VALUE attribute for the first one set to "Visa" and the second one set to "MC":

```
<FORM METHOD="POST" ACTION="myscript.asp">
Please choose a Credit Card Type for your order
<INPUT TYPE="radio" NAME="CCType" VALUE="Visa">◄——— NAME and
<INPUT TYPE="radio" NAME="CCType" VALUE="MC">              VALUE attributes
</FORM>
```

Because these two INPUT elements are both of type "radio" and have the same NAME attribute value ("CCType"), only the radio button chosen by the Web user will be returned as data consisting of a name-value pair: the name being "CCType" and the value being the data in the VALUE attribute of the chosen radio button (that is, Visa or MC).

The next example uses the same code, but the minimized *selected* attribute is included in the first element. The difference here is that the first button will be displayed on the Web page as selected when the page is first loaded.

```
                                        selected is minimized
<FORM METHOD="POST" ACTION="myscript.asp">
Please choose a Credit Card Type for your order    │
<INPUT TYPE="radio" NAME="CCType" VALUE="Visa" SELECTED>
<INPUT TYPE="radio" NAME="CCType" VALUE="MC">
</FORM>
```

1

Publishing HTML Documents

To make Web pages using HTML, an author writes plain text files with HTML elements and attributes, adds text content, and then copies the file to a published area on a Web server. When a request is made (usually over the Internet) for that Web page, the Web server copies (transmits) the text file to the requesting application (usually a Web browser such as Internet Explorer). The Web browser has the job of reading through the HTML commands and content and reconstructing (interpreting) the Web page for user viewing onscreen.

You should be aware of two additional points about HTML. First, it is possible to set a reference within a Web page for other content, such as images or small applications. For example, the IMG element contains a reference to an image file. This means that within the starting IMG element tag (this element has no ending tag, because all the data required to make the element work is contained in the first tag) is a URL pointing to the image file. When the page is loaded, the image file is requested, and when the image is received, it is placed inside the page according to the settings of the IMG element's attributes.

Second, it is possible to create hypertext links with HTML. The A element is named *A* because it stands for *Anchor*: this element creates an anchor for hypertext links. Using the A element, the *href* attribute can be set to reference another Web page anywhere on the Internet, so that a click of the mouse will instantly request that page. The *href* attribute is set equal to the URL where the user will be taken when he clicks the link (like this: <A HREF="http://www.e4free.com">*Here's the link*</A>). Together, these capabilities provide HTML with much of its power as a communications technology.

Proj1-1.zip

Project 1-1: Create a Simple HTML Document

In this project, you'll use a basic text editor to write a simple HTML document by hand, using HTML 4.01 and earlier tags. You'll be surprised how easy it is to construct documents using a markup language.

Step-by-Step

1. Use Notepad if you're working on a Windows machine, or use any plain text editor, such as SimpleText for the Mac. Open your text editor to a new, blank file (this happens automatically when you open Notepad). You can open Notepad by choosing Start | Programs | Accessories | Notepad.

2. Type **<HTML>** on the first line. Press the ENTER key to move to the next line, and then type **<HEAD>**. Now you've started your HTML document with the HTML element's starting tag (<HTML>), and you've started the HEAD section of the document with the starting tag for the HEAD element (<HEAD>). By the way, as mentioned, HTML is not case sensitive, so you can type these tags in uppercase or lowercase.

3. Type **<TITLE>** to start the title section of your document. Then enter a short line describing what your page is about, such as "My First Web Page". This will be the title of your HTML document. In the finished page, the title will appear in the dark blue title bar at the top of the browser window.

4. After entering your title, type **</TITLE>**. This is the ending tag of the TITLE element. Notice that it looks the same as the starting title tag, but it includes a forward slash. This convention is followed by most markup languages, including XHTML and XML.

5. Now you can end the HEAD section of the document by typing in the ending TITLE tag: **</TITLE>**. Then start the BODY element by typing **<BODY>**.

6. Of course, you may want to use a few attributes in your BODY element, such as a background color and perhaps some text colors. If so, enter these attributes as shown in the following code example:

```
<BODY BGCOLOR="white" TEXT="black" LINK="red">
```

This code example sets the BODY element attribute so that the background color on the screen will be white, the text will be black, and links will be shown in red.

Note that the available attributes aren't just thought up arbitrarily; they are specifically defined in the three DTDs for HTML, and you can't change them or give them different values other than what is specified in the DTD. The DTD is discussed further in the next section.

7. Now it's time to enter the content for your HTML document that appears in the main screen of the browser. You can add paragraphs (text separated by the <P> and </P> tags), you can create lines, or rules, that stretch across the screen with the HR element, you can make text bold or italicized (the <B> and </B> tags and the <I> and </I> tags), and so on, until you have a complete document.

1

8. To end your document, type the **</BODY>** tag to end the BODY section, and then type the **</HTML>** tag to end the entire document. What you've created might look like this (and is shown in the illustration that follows):

```
<HTML>
<HEAD>
<TITLE>My First Web Page</TITLE>
</HEAD>
<BODY BGCOLOR="white" TEXT="black" LINK="red">
<P>Here are my paragraphs, and some of the words
are <B>bold</B>, some of the words are
<I>italicized</I>, and I also have an occasional line
across the screen, made with the HR element.</P>
<HR>
</BODY>
</HTML>
```

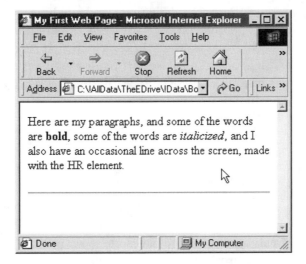

Formal HTML Specifications

The HTML code examples shown so far cover creation of a basic Web page and a very simple form, but they do not show all the formal specifications for HTML. Because the display of HTML Web pages depends upon browsers, and because browsers are made by commercial and noncommercial software companies, organizations, and individuals, each browser can interpret the same HTML in a slightly different manner. Therefore, not all browsers require that all the formal HTML specifications be met in order to display HTML Web pages.

Document Type Definitions

You know that HTML is an SGML application, or a markup language conforming to the rules in SGML that specify how such a language should be constructed. What determines the elements and attributes allowed in HTML, and the possible values they may assume? It's called the Document Type Definition (DTD), and several DTDs are available to use with HTML 4.01 (you can find out more at **www.w3.org**).

- **The Strict DTD** This DTD contains all elements and attributes that have not been *deprecated*. Deprecated elements and attributes are obsolete (that is, they were used in earlier versions of HTML but are no longer needed). While they may still be supported, these elements and attributes are being phased out, and it is best not to use them unless you absolutely have to. This DTD also supports elements and attributes that do not appear in the Frameset DTD, which is covered shortly.

- **The Transitional DTD** This DTD includes everything in the Strict DTD, plus all elements and attributes that have been deprecated. It is useful to use in creating HTML documents that are compatible with older browsers (that's why it's called *transitional*).

- **The Frameset DTD** This DTD includes everything in the Transitional DTD as well as elements and attributes required to support frames. *Frames* are a method of breaking single Web pages into a set of Web pages, each of which appear in the browser screen as an integrated set of individually scrollable screens.

1

?Ask the Expert

Question: Why are we spending time on HTML? I want to learn about XML!

Answer: Many of the constructs used in XML are similar to those found in HTML. For example, elements and attributes are used throughout HTML and form the basis for XML as well. Understanding clearly how HTML is made will give you a good idea where XML came from, and understanding this relationship will be helpful later on when we get into the more complex aspects of XML. Plus, a lot of your XML will likely end up rendered as HTML/XHTML Web pages.

Question: Why is it important to understand DTDs? I've never used them when I've made Web pages, and popular HTML editors and browsers don't seem to require them.

Answer: DTDs are part of the basic HTML specification, but the browsers already know what HTML code they understand, so they don't require the DOCTYPE declaration. However, DTDs are very important in XML; they tell XML processors how to appropriately process XML elements in your XML documents. Understanding the HTML DTD is the first step in learning how to write XML DTDs, as well as other methods (such as XML Schemas) for specifying XML document components. Remember, you may be writing entire XML languages, or mixing and matching parts of existing XML languages, so you need to understand DTDs.

Formally, an HTML document should have as its first line a DOCTYPE declaration showing which DTD it uses. A DOCTYPE for a Frameset DTD declaration looks like this:

```
<!DOCTYPE HTML
 PUBLIC "-//W3C//DTD HTML 4.01 Frameset//EN"
 "http://www.w3.org/TR/html4/frameset.dtd">
<HTML>
<HEAD> And so on
```

The purpose of the DOCTYPE declaration is to inform the browser (or whatever user agent is displaying or rendering the document) of the version of HTML and the DTD being used in the document.

Note

Although technically required by the specification, popular browsers will accept HTML documents without the DOCTYPE declaration, because they already know what HTML elements they support. Moreover, browser makers often add support for their own, proprietary HTML elements (called *HTML extensions*), making for the infamous (and annoying) incompatibilities between browsers. Even separate versions of browsers by the same maker may not support the same HTML elements in the same ways. The flexible properties of XML languages will alleviate some of these problems.

From HTML to XHTML

Now that you're pretty familiar with the technical specifications for HTML 4.01, let's move on to extensible HTML (XHTML). XHTML 1.0 is the next version of HTML, and it is completely XML compliant, so learning how XHTML works will not only help you understand the next iteration of HTML, but it is a great way to introduce you to the XML standard in general. Much of what you'll learn in this section will follow right through to any XML language you write or use.

You can find out plenty about XHTML at **www.w3.org**; just look for XHTML in the sidebar. Of course, since you probably already have plenty of HTML Web pages to work with, you may be most interested in converting existing HTML documents to XHTML. You'll find plenty of tools to help you perform this function pretty reliably, but it is important to understand what these tools are doing and to begin to change your HTML coding habits so you automatically write good XHTML.

Comparing HTML and XHTML

The W3C organization writes and maintains the HTML standard, and it's interesting to note that the standard is called a *recommendation* rather than a *specification*. That's because W3C realizes that no one is *forced* to use the standard as is. How it is interpreted in a browser depends upon what the browser maker decides, and browser makers have long chosen to deviate from the standard for about 10 percent of what their browsers recognize.

As a consequence, how browsers interpret HTML varies from one browser to the next, as well as how "sticky" the browsers are about differences in the way HTML code is written. For example, some browsers will forgive you if you leave off quotation marks when specifying an image file (more on this later). Some browsers will also complete a table for you if you forget to include the closing table tag; others, however, just display a blank screen.

For example, in HTML, if you let your tags overlap, it doesn't matter; they still work. Overlapping tags? That's when you start one element, start another element, and then place the content and finish the first element before you finish the second element, like this:

```
<B><I>This text is bold and italicized</B></I>
```

You can use tools that will look for poorly written or nonconforming HTML and convert it for you (more on these tools in just a bit). But before we get too far off track, let's look specifically at how HTML and XHTML differ. You can't always rely on a tool to convert everything for you (what if the HTML is embedded in JavaScript?). Reviewing the differences between the two languages will also clue you in about how good XML-conforming documents must be written.

One thing you'll often hear in relation to XML is that documents must be *well formed,* which means that they conform to the basic XML syntax and a few other rules. XHTML is the same way. Specific rules must be followed for XHTML documents to be considered well formed.

Here are the rules that make XHTML documents well formed:

- All documents must include a DOCTYPE declaration.

- The root element of the document must be <HTML>.

- Elements and attributes must be lowercase.

- Attribute values must be enclosed in quotation marks and not minimized.

- Leading and trailing spaces in attribute values will be stripped.

- Only the *id* attribute can be used to identify an element uniquely.

- Nonempty elements must be terminated or have an ending tag.

- Nested elements must be properly nested, not overlapping.

- SCRIPT and STYLE elements must be marked as CDATA areas.

Now let's examine what each of these points means.

DOCTYPE Declarations

We've already discussed the DOCTYPE declaration for HTML, and you know it can be left off HTML documents. However, this declaration must be present in XHTML documents (and in XML documents as well).

Here's an example DOCTYPE declaration for the Frameset DTD:

```
<!DOCTYPE html
  PUBLIC "-//W3C//DTD XHTML 1.0 Frameset//EN"
"http://www.w3.org/TR/xhtml1/DTD/frameset.dtd">
```

The three DTDs that were listed previously (Strict, Transitional, and Frameset) are available (but of course they have been modified to suit XHTML, and therefore have slightly different URLs to reference them). To reference them, you need to exchange the words *Strict*, *Transitional*, and *Frameset* in the code example.

Here, then, is the Transitional DTD DOCTYPE declaration:

```
<!DOCTYPE html
  PUBLIC "-//W3C//DTD XHTML 1.0 Transitional//EN"
"http://www.w3.org/TR/xhtml1/DTD/transitional.dtd">
```

And here's the Strict DTD DOCTYPE declaration:

```
<!DOCTYPE html
  PUBLIC "-//W3C//DTD XHTML 1.0 Strict//EN"
"http://www.w3.org/TR/xhtml1/DTD/strict.dtd">
```

The <html> Root Element

The <html> starting tag must follow the DOCTYPE declaration because the html element must be the root element of the document. You see, XML has a strict requirement about elements (and this is related to overlapping elements, as we will discuss). Each element must be a parent or a child element of some other element, but at the top of the heap (for XHTML documents) is the <html> element. Always.

1

The starting tag must also contain a reference to the XML namespace the document uses. A *namespace* is a closed set of names that identify tags from a particular DTD. Module 4 will tell you more about namespaces, so for now you can satisfy your curiosity with an example of what a reference to a namespace looks like. Here is an example of the coding for the HTML element in XHTML:

```
<html xmlns="http://www.w3.org/1999/xhtml">
```

Lowercase Elements and Attributes

Unlike HTML, XML is case sensitive, and all XHTML elements and attributes are written in lowercase. I always write the html element lowercase when I'm writing XHTML documents, but uppercase HTML when I'm writing HTML documents. If I wrote the tag <HTML> in an XHTML document, it wouldn't be interpreted as an XHTML element.

Popular HTML editors, such as Macromedia DreamWeaver, can be set to write tags and attributes in lowercase, so it's not difficult to change or convert case if you're using a particular type of authoring program. For example, the following two code examples show a simple HTML document as it might have been written and the XHTML it has been transformed into.

First, here's the plain HTML (by convention, the DTD does not need to be included, even though strictly speaking it should be):

```
<HTML>
<HEAD>
<TITLE>The title</TITLE>
</HEAD>
<BODY BGCOLOR="#000000" TEXT="#FFFFFF">
This body section has a black background and white text.
</BODY>
</HTML>
```

The XHTML would read like this:

```
<!DOCTYPE html
PUBLIC "-//W3C//DTD XHTML 1.0 Transitional//EN"
"http://www.w3.org/TR/xhtml1/DTD/transitional.dtd">
<html xmlns="http://www.w3.org/1999/xhtml">
<head>
<title>The title</title>
</head>
```

Notice the DOCTYPE declaration and the lowercase element names

```
<body bgcolor="#000000" text="#FFFFFF">
This body section has a black background and white text.
</body>
</html>
```

Attribute values (for example, the white and black color codes for the body bgcolor and text attributes) are excluded from the case rule. Filenames in URLs may be uppercase or lowercase and can't be restricted to lowercase.

Adding Quotation Marks and Minimizing

We've already discussed minimized attributes for HTML. In XHTML, attributes must all be fully assigned, so the selected attribute, instead of just appearing as the word selected, must be written inside quotation marks, like so: selected="selected". Learning to write all attribute values in quotation marks is a good habit anyway, as it will help you as you make the transition to XHTML.

Stripping Spaces in Attribute Values

This rule is pretty self explanatory. Extra white spaces (more than one between words) will be stripped in XML documents, so XHTML simply strips them. Another important aspect of this rule is that more than one space between words in an attribute value will also be mapped to a single white space character.

Elements and the *id* Attribute

This is a pretty big change for HTML authors. Sometimes you need to identify an element by name. Here's an example. When you are using a form, each form control needs to have its own name, so you can differentiate between phone numbers and fax numbers when the data in the form gets sent back to you. Also, when you are changing elements on a Web page with a JavaScript, you need to identify the exact object on the screen that gets changed by the script.

In XHTML, instead of using the *name* attribute to identify an element as you do in HTML, you use the *id* attribute. The *id* attribute is more restrictive in the values it can assume, and only one instance of a given *id* attribute value can exist per document.

A *name* attribute value, on the other hand, can be used as many times in a document as necessary. (For backward compatibility, the XHTML recommendation suggests using both the *id* and *name* attributes but also notes that the *name* attribute is deprecated in XHTML 1.0 and will be removed from future versions.)

1

Terminating Nonempty Elements

Any HTML elements that have both a starting and ending tag must use both
of them in XHTML. Unlike HTML, XHTML won't help you out by assuming an
ending tag. In HTML, for example, a paragraph could include a starting <P> tag
without an ending </P> tag, and this would be properly interpreted by the browser.
In XHTML, however, both the starting and ending tags must be present for the
paragraph to be interpreted correctly.

For elements with an EMPTY content model, the end symbol (/) preceded
by a space must be used, as shown here for the line-break tag (in HTML <BR>):

```
<br />
```

In addition, when a nonempty element contains no content (so that it
appears empty), both the starting and ending tags must be used, like this:

```
<p></p>
```

Nesting and Overlapping

In HTML, if a heading (H) element of size 3 is italicized, for example, the
author can write it like so:

```
<H3><I>An italicized heading</H3></I>
```

These elements overlap, but HTML can cope with this just fine. In XHTML,
these elements must be written so they nest properly and in order, as
shown here:

```
<h3><i>An italicized heading</i></h3>
```

XML is set up so that there is no way to exclude nesting an element within
another. However, some elements should never be nested:

- The A element (used to indicate a hyperlink, or anchor) should not
  contain other A elements.

- The PRE element should not contain the IMG, OBJECT, BIG, SMALL,
  SUB, or SUP element.

- The BUTTON element should not contain the INPUT, SELECT, TEXTAREA, LABEL, BUTTON, FORM, FIELDSET, IFRAME, or ISINDEX element.

- The LABEL element should not contain LABEL elements.

- The FORM element should not contain FORM elements.

Note

You'll learn more about these elements in Module 7.

Delimiting with CDATA Symbols

If you've ever written JavaScript code or style sheet code into a Web page, you know how different they are from HTML code. You also know that you often need to insert HTML comment delimiters around your script or style sheet code so the browser doesn't make the mistake of including the special script or style sheet commands as plain text on your page. Using the HTML comment delimiters (<!-- and -->) is a *hack*, but it seemed to be the only way to exclude script and style sheet code from the browser. XHTML, however, makes an explicit declaration of script and style sheet code using the CDATA (character data) delimiters, as shown here:

```
<script language="Javascript">
<![CDATA[
function clickme() {
alert("Hi")
}
 ]]>
</script>
```

Note

If you are using external style sheets or references to external scripts, you don't have to include a CDATA section.

1-Minute Drill

- What is XHTML?
- Why is learning XHTML important?
- What are some of the differences between HTML and XHTML?

The Development of XML

Many of the restrictions XHTML places on HTML are the result of XHTML being compatible with the rules of XML. As a matter of fact, XHTML is a language specifically set up to conform to XML. Now it's time to trace XML from its first working drafts to today's more mature XML recommendations. All the draft, notes, and recommendations discussed can be found at the W3C's Web site.

The oldest working draft regarding XML currently listed at the W3C is called "Extensible Markup Language (XML)," dated November 14, 1996. It says XML is to be an extremely simple version of SGML that will allow generic SGML to be served, received, and processed on the Web like HTML. XML documents are considered data objects stored on computers, made up of entities (in this context, *entities* refers to storage units, analogous to files).

The draft goes on to say that entities may contain either text or binary data, and the text entities may contain content text and markup. In simple terms, *content text* is character data that can be read, such as the content you might see on a Web page, while *markup* is the tags, elements, and attributes that tell the browser how to arrange the content text and where to put the links.

- XHTML is an XML-compatible version of HTML. It includes all the HTML elements and attributes, and is the newest version of HTML.
- Learning XHTML now is important because new Web pages should be written in XHTML, and many old Web pages will need to be converted to XHTML format.
- In XHTML, all elements and attributes are written in lowercase, they must include proper closing tags, and they must be properly nested (not overlapping), among other things.

The draft states that an XML processor is required to work with XML documents, and it points out the assumption that the XML processor is a separate application that will provide what it interprets from an XML document to another application (the way the XML processor for Internet Explorer works).

Another interesting document is "XML, Java, and the Future," by Jan Bosak of Sun Microsystems, dated March 10, 1997. It discusses XML and Java applications, and defines several of the advantages of XML over HTML. For example, this paper says XML

● Allows information providers to create new tags (elements) and attributes

● Allows documents to have nested levels of complexity to any level

● Allows real-time validation of structure

The document also goes on to say that XML will find uses on the Web in which XML is superior where

● Browsers have to work with different databases (or other information sources) at once.

● The Web site must expect the client (browser) to do more of the processing work.

● The rendered document will be displayed differently on different platforms.

The remainder of the document discusses in more detail each of the ways in which XML is superior to HTML.

Another step in the development of XML was the development of an XML application (language) named Web Interface Definition Language (WIDL), termed a "NOTE" dated September 22, 1997. Although only a note submitted by a company called webMethods, Inc. (which indicates that no support may be provided from the W3C), it points to a serious limitation of HTML. As you may know if you are already a Web developer, it is possible to write scripting code that will make requests for database searches from a Web site; you can set it up so that this code runs automatically whenever someone goes to a particular page on your Web site. Unfortunately, if the receiving party changes his HTML interface to his database, the code you've made will probably not run anymore and may give no reasonable error messages in that case. WIDL is designed to correct these limitations by defining interactions with Web servers as functional interfaces that can be accessed by remote systems over standard Web protocols. Essentially, what this means is that any programming language could be used to connect to any Web server capable of interpreting the WIDL language, even without using a browser or HTML interface.

On December 8, 1997, the W3C issued XML 1.0 as a Proposed Recommendation. In July 1998, the Internet Engineering Task Force (IEFT) issued an informational Request For Comment, RFC 2376, calling for two new XML media types: text/xml and application/xml. In August 1998, "XML-QL: A Query Language for XML" was submitted as a note to the W3C specifying a query language applicable to XML. On July 31, 1998, the note "Document Content Description for XML" was submitted to the W3C, and it appears to be a precursor to XML Schemas. In September 1998, "Extensible Forms Description Language (XFDL) 4.0," a note to the W3C concerning digital representation of complex business forms (including electronic signatures) was submitted. The XML page at W3C also lists a number of other footnotes, milestones, and activities related to the development of XML that have taken place over the years.

The end result is that XML is now a formally accepted recommendation (as of October 6, 2000, it is in its second edition but still called XML version 1.0), and a number of related technologies are (or are soon to be) formally defined as recommendations. These related technologies and their functions are described here (and many are discussed in detail in this book):

- **XHTML 1.0**   A W3C recommendation as of January 26, 2000, it reformulates HTML into an XML-compatible application.

- **eXtensible Stylesheet Language (XSL) version 1.0**   A W3C candidate recommendation as of November 21, 2000, the purpose of this language is to express style sheets for XML documents. It is the main topic of Module 11.

- **XSL Transformations (XSLT) version 1.0**   A W3C recommendation as of November 16, 1999, the purpose of XSLT is to describe specifically how an XML document is transformed into the finished product for a particular platform, with particular emphasis on XSL formatting elements.

- **XML Pointer (XPointer), XML Base, and XML Linking Language (XLink)**   XPointer is a W3C candidate recommendation as of June 7, 2000. XML Base is a candidate recommendation as of September 8, 2000; and

XLink is a candidate recommendation as of July 3, 2000. All are concerned with defining a means of creating links and navigating through and across XML documents and are discussed in greater detail in Module 7.

● **XML Path Language (XPath)**   A W3C recommendation as of November 16, 1999, this language provides a means of specifying a path through XML documents, in much the same way that a file on a hard drive can be specified by a path statement (like C:\ mydocuments\myimages\, and so forth).

● **XML Schemas**   A W3C candidate recommendation as of October 24, 2000, this is an alternative method for designing XML applications, allowing authors to specify elements, attributes, data types, and constraints in much the same way that these parameters would be specified for a database (similar features, not similar syntax). XML Schemas are discussed thoroughly in Module 3.

● **Working Drafts**   Under the heading "XML Query" can be found "XML Query Requirements," "XML Query Data Model," and "The XML Query Algebra" on the W3C site. These three working drafts are all related to the effort to produce a workable query language for XML documents and are covered in Module 10.

● **XML Protocols**   This area focuses on developing machine-machine communication protocols for XML documents and has just begun the formalization process. The only document currently available is the working draft of XML Protocol requirements, dated December 19, 2000.

● **XForms 1.0**   A W3C working draft as of December 19, 2000, this document deals specifically with the problems of forms development and presentation across the Internet as well as other platforms. It is addressed in Module 5.

● **XML Signature Syntax and Processing**   A W3C candidate recommendation as of October 31, 2000, this proposes XML syntax and processing rules for creating digital signatures and makes the point that these rules can be applied to any digital object, not just XML documents. XML signatures and the related Platform for Privacy Preferences (P3P) are discussed in Module 5.

● **Miscellaneous**   Documents about Resource Description Framework (RDF), Synchronized Multimedia (SMIL), Scalable Vector Graphics (SVG), MathML, and other useful and common XML languages are also found at the W3C Web site, and some of these are discussed in detail in Modules 6 and 12.

Setting Up for XML

Before you can begin the development of XML applications (languages) and documents, you'll need a few software tools to help you write and debug your applications, and you'll need still others to help parse and validate your documents. You'll also need viewers (browsers) to view the results of your efforts. We'll start our discussion with the tools you'll need to write XML applications.

Writing XML Applications

Because XML applications are created by writing a DTD (or perhaps a schema), and because DTDs and schemas are composed of plain text, you can use plain text editors to write them, such as Notepad, SimpleText (for the Mac), or Programmer's File Editor (a text editing utility suited for programmers; for more information go to **www.lancs.ac.uk/people/cpaap/pfe**).

Notepad is a simple and lightweight text-editing tool that is supplied with all usual installations of Windows, as part of the Accessories group. It is capable of creating and saving text files and searching for text strings, and it produces ASCII text, plus carriage-return and line-feed characters. However, almost no automated functions are included with Notepad. SimpleText for the Mac works in much the same way.

Programmer's File Editor is a bit more sophisticated than Notepad or SimpleText, in that it has tools that relieve the programmer of common, repetitive tasks. One feature I especially like is that it allows you to display line numbers whenever you like, which is helpful when error messages happen to include line numbers but the source code doesn't.

Automated Development

In contrast with plain vanilla text editors, automated development environments provide a rich set of tools that make the task of developing XML languages and documents easier, faster, less error-prone, and more intuitive. A quick search of your favorite search engine, using terms such as "XML Development Tools" will bring up a nice list of available automated development tools.

XML Spy, made by Icon Information Systems (find it at **www.xmlspy.com**) seems to have just about all the features a professional XML developer could want, including four separate views of your XML documents (grid, table, text, and project) and niceties such as color-coded code and editing help. The main limitation is that it is available for Windows systems only. However, this means that the XML processor built into Internet Explorer is always available, making it easy to validate your XML documents against the DTDs or schemas. It also includes the ability to read, create, and convert between all the major schema languages (DCD, XML-Data, XDR, and so forth).

Ask the Expert

Question: It seems to me that HTML is written in a pretty standard way. Aren't there automated tools that convert HTML directly to XHTML, without my having to know XHTML?

Answer: There are tools, such as HTML Tidy at the W3C site. These tools use a two-step process to convert HTML to XHTML. First, the tool cleans up the HTML so it conforms to the HTML standard (plenty of code out there doesn't actually conform to the standard but still renders in a browser because the browsers tend to be forgiving of coding errors). Second, it converts HTML code to XHTML code. This is not a big step because coding HTML and XHTML is very similar.

However, it is a good idea to get plenty of practice manually writing XHTML, because site developers often need to hand-code sections of pages within JavaScript, Active Server Pages, or some other scripting or programming languages.

Question: There seem to have been a lot of steps in the development of XML, and some of them seem redundant. Also, some of the standards seem to have started out as notes from third parties. What's the process used for standards development at the W3C, and how do I know when standards are stable enough to use?

Answer: There is no pat answer to this question, but there are some general rules. The W3C can only recommend, not enforce. Like most of the Internet, the languages and protocols of the Web are not take-it-or-leave-it propositions. A company can use any languages or protocols, or any combination of languages and protocols. What makes companies and people tend toward a particular language or protocol is *the number of other companies or people using those same languages or protocols*. It's like the English language. Why do we speak English in the United States? Because so many of us speak English.

1

Therefore, introducing new Internet languages and protocols involves much discussion and is a pretty messy process. Everyone gets a chance to make comments and submit suggestions, and eventually some standards body or another declares the proposal stable enough to use. By itself this is not enough, though; the proposal must be adopted by a significant percentage of users to be considered a standard.

The notes listed in the section about XML development are often proposals from companies wanting their proprietary languages or protocols adopted as a standard (there are benefits to this for the company doing the submitting) or from individuals either working independently (often academics) or directly for the W3C. Sometimes these notes go directly to the proposal phase, and sometimes they are picked apart for the best ideas and return as a proposal named something else.

Here's how it works in a nutshell: Ideas get submitted or are generated by the W3C and, if they are considered to have merit, are made into working draft. From there they may become candidate recommendations (after much discussion and perhaps modification), and when they are fairly complete, they may become recommendations. Recommendations are the finished product, but if not generally adopted, they may fall by the wayside even then. And there's nothing to stop people or companies from adding to (extending) languages and recommendations on their own. In fact, one of the driving forces behind the development of XML was the desire to make it easy for people to extend, in a standard way, the languages and protocols they use across the Internet.

Question: There seem to be a lot of XML-related languages and technologies. How do they fit together?

Answer: The next section and the rest of the book devote quite a bit more discussion to this subject as we discuss XML and its relations in each module. For now, here's a quick explanation:

- SGML is the parent technology of XML, HTML, XHTML, and so on. It is a standard way of creating document languages.

- XML, as a subset of SGML, contains many of the same capabilities as SGML (call it *mini-SGML*, perhaps), and XML is specifically suited to the Internet.

- XHTML is the XML version of HTML, especially suited for Web pages.

- XSL and XSLT are used to add style to XML documents (as well as transforming them into a format suitable for a particular media).

- XLink, XPointer, and XML Base are used for making links in XML documents.

- XForms is used for making forms in XML documents.

- XQuery is used for making queries in XML documents.

- XML Schema is used for building structure into XML documents (it is related to the basic method of adding structure to XML documents with DTDs).

- XML Namespaces are used for identifying a particular DTD or schema for use with some or all elements and attributes within your XML documents.

- XML Signature is used for making electronic signatures for XML documents.

- Math Markup Language (MathML), Wireless Markup Language (WML), Synchronized Multimedia Integration Language (SMIL), and Scalable Vector Graphics (SVG) are XML languages (applications) that may or may not have use in your XML documents.

Proj1-2.zip

Project 1-2: Write/Convert an XHTML Document

This project takes you through all the steps of the initial design phase of an XHTML document that fully conforms to XML. It covers the DOCTYPE declaration and XML namespace, and it includes all the differences you'll find between HTML and XHTML. By properly converting an existing HTML document by hand, you'll gain enough code-writing experience to form the habits that will be useful whenever you create HTML or XHTML documents in the future.

1

Step-by-Step

1. Determine which XHTML DTD your document will conform to. Write the first line of your XHTML document. For the sake of simplicity, let's assume your XML document will have frames:

```
<!DOCTYPE html
  PUBLIC "-//W3C//DTD XHTML 1.0 Frameset//EN"
"http://www.w3.org/TR/xhtml1/DTD/frameset.dtd">
```

2. Add the root element for the page: **<html>**. Since all XHTML documents must have <html> as the root (top-level) element, you know the next thing you'll be doing is writing a line of code for this element, immediately following the DOCTYPE declaration. Don't forget to include the reference to the XHTML namespace, like this:

```
<html xmlns="http://www.w3.org/1999/xhtml">
```

3. Convert the following HTML code to properly formatted XHTML code, step-by-step:

```
<TITLE>Here is the Title</TITLE>
<META NAME="keywords" CONTENT="XML, XHTML, HTML, SGML">
```

This HTML code has elements and attributes written in uppercase, and the optional HEAD element tags are missing. When converted to XHTML, it looks like this:

```
<head>
<title>Here is the Title</title>
<meta name="keywords" content="XML, XHTML, HTML, SGML">
</head>
```

4. Convert the following HTML code into properly formatted XHTML code:

```
<SCRIPT LANGUAGE="Javascript">
<!--
function pushbutton() {
alert("This is an XHTML document")
}
-->
</SCRIPT>
```

This HTML SCRIPT element is written in uppercase and is missing the CDATA delimiters required by XHTML. When converted to XHTML, it looks like this:

```
<script language="Javascript">
<![CDATA[
function pushbutton() {
alert("This is an XHTML document")
}
 ]]>
</script>
```

5. Convert the following HTML code to properly formatted XHTML code:

```
<BODY BGCOLOR="#FFFFFF" TEXT="#000000">
 <CENTER>
<TABLE WIDTH=400><TR><TD VALIGN=top>
</TD></TR>
<TR><TD><FORM METHOD="POST" ACTION="sendcomments.asp">
Please choose:<P>
<UL>
<LI><IMPUT TYPE="radio" SELECTED NAME="answerchoice"
 VALUE="email">Send an Email
<LI><IMPUT TYPE="radio" NAME="answerchoice" VALUE="form">
Fill Out the Form
</UL>
<DIV ALIGN="center">
<TABLE WIDTH=96% BORDER=1 CELLPADDING=6 CELLSPACING=6
 BORDERCOLORLIGHT="#CCFFFF" BORDERCOLORDARK="#CCFFFF"
 BORDERCOLOR="#CCFFFF">
<TR><TD><DIV ALIGN="LEFT">
<FONT FACE="ARIAL, HELVETICA, SANS-SERIF">
<B><I><FONT SIZE=-1>
PLEASE FILL OUT THIS FORM:</FONT></B></I></FONT></DIV>
</TD></TR>
<TR><TD WIDTH="54%"><DIV ALIGN="RIGHT">
<FONT FACE="ARIAL, HELVETICA, SANS-SERIF">
<B><FONT SIZE="-1">
NAME</FONT></B></FONT></DIV></TD>
<TD COLSPAN="2" WIDTH="46%">
<INPUT TYPE="TEXT" NAME="NAME"></TD></TR>
<TR><TD WIDTH="54%"><DIV ALIGN="RIGHT">
<FONT FACE="ARIAL, HELVETICA, SANS-SERIF">
<B><FONT SIZE="-1">
```

```
EMAIL ADDRESS</FONT></B></FONT></DIV></TD>
<TD COLSPAN="2" WIDTH="46%">
<INPUT TYPE="TEXT" NAME="EMAIL"></TD></TR>
<TR><TD COLSPAN="3"><DIV ALIGN="CENTER">
<TEXTAREA NAME="COMMENTS" COLS="50" ROWS="4">
PLEASE PUT YOUR COMMENTS HERE</TEXTAREA>
</DIV></TD></TR>
<TR><TD WIDTH="54%"><DIV ALIGN="RIGHT">
<INPUT TYPE="SUBMIT" NAME="SUBMIT" VALUE="INQUIRE">
</DIV></TD>
<TD COLSPAN="2" WIDTH="46%">
<INPUT TYPE="RESET" NAME="SUBMIT2" VALUE="CLEAR">
</TD></TR></TABLE></DIV>
</FORM></TABLE>
```

This HTML code contains elements and attributes written in uppercase, minimized attributes, use of the NAME attribute rather than the ID attribute, overlapping elements, and nonempty elements without an ending tag. Converted to XHTML, here it is:

```
<body bgcolor="#FFFFFF" text="#000000">
<center>
<table width="400"><tr><td valign="top">
</td></tr>
<tr><td><form method="POST" action="sendcomments.asp">
Please choose:<p>
<ul>
<li><imput type="radio" selected="selected"
 id="answerchoice1" name="answerchoice" value="email">
Send an Email</li>
<li><imput type="radio" id="answerchoice2"
 name="answerchoice" value="form">Fill Out the Form</li>
</ul>
<div align="center">
<table width="96%" border="1" cellpadding="6"
 cellspacing="6" bordercolorlight="#CCFFFF"
 bordercolordark="#CCFFFF" bordercolor="#CCFFFF">
<tr><td><div align="left">
<font face="arial, helvetica, sans-serif">
<b><i><font size="-1">
Please fill out this form:</font></i></b></font></div>
</td></tr>
<tr><td width="54%"><div align="right">
```

```
<font face="arial, helvetica, sans-serif">
<b><font size="-1">
Name</font></b></font></div></td>
<td colspan="2" width="46%">
<input type="text" id="thename" name="name"></td></tr>
<tr><td width="54%"><div align="right">
<font face="arial, helvetica, sans-serif">
<b><font size="-1">
Email Address</font></b></font></div></td>
<td colspan="2" width="46%">
<input type="text" id="theemail" name="email">
</td></tr>
<tr><td colspan="3"><div align="center">
<textarea id="thecomments" name="comments"
 cols="50" rows="4">
Please put your comments here</textarea>
</div></td></tr>
<tr><td width="54%"><div align="right">
<input type="submit" id="submit" value="inquire">
</div></td>
<td colspan="2" width="46%">
<input type="reset" id="reset" value="Clear">
</td></tr></table></div>
</form></table>
</body></html>
```

Designing XML Applications and XML Documents

We've given a fair amount of discussion to HTML and XHTML to get you primed for XML overall. This section covers, from start to finish, the process you would use to design any given XML application and documents from that application. This section gives you an overview, and the following modules take you through each part of the process in detail.

Determine XML Application Requirements

Any XML document includes two parts: the DTDs or schemas from which its elements and attributes are created, and the document itself. Of course, many other components may be included, but for broad, top-level categories, these two

1

are sufficient. Therefore, the first task in designing an XML document is to either write or find the DTDs or schemas that will support the documents required. But before you can write DTDs or schemas, you must complete two steps.

1. From a description of the elements and attributes required, research existing XML DTDs and schemas to see what portions may be reused in your XML documents.

2. Determine what requirements must be supported by the XML documents you intend to write. For example, suppose you need to make inventory update forms. You might determine the need for elements such as raw material, part, label, and so forth.

Research XML Applications

You can easily research existing XML applications by going to your favorite search engine and entering terms such as "XML DTDs" or "XML schemas." You may have to poke around a bit, but you're sure to come up with some winning hits. For example, each of the following is an XML language already in existence (or under development):

- XBEL (Bookmark Exchange Language)

- AIML (Astronomical Instrument Markup Language)

- AML (Astronomical Markup Language)

- CML (Chemical Markup Language)

- DCML (Dental Charting Markup Language)

- DSML (Directory Services Markup Language)

- GEML (Gene Expression Markup Language)

- IRML (Investment Research Markup Language)

- MathML (Mathematical Markup Language)

- NewsML (News Markup Language)

- OMF (Weather Observation Definition Format)

- PetroXML (Petroleum XML)

- ThML (Theological Markup Language)

- UDDI (Universal Description Discovery Integration)

- VIML (Virtual Instruments Markup Language)

- WSDL (Web Services Description Language)

- XAML (Transaction Authority Markup Language)

While not all XML applications are going to be freely available to everyone at all times; some are "open source" and are competing to become industry standards. For example, MathML is a creation of the W3C, and the MathML 2.0 DTD is available at the W3C, as well as complete documentation of all elements and attributes within it. It is straightforward to review them to see whether they suit your requirements.

Define New XML Applications

Having reviewed XML DTDs in existence (and remember, the company you are working for may have created some DTDs of its own, as well, so don't forget to research internally), you may find that you need to create additional elements and attributes to support your requirements fully. If so, it is time to begin writing your own XML DTDs or schemas. The first step in writing your own DTDs or schemas is similar to an early step in designing a database—that is, the creation of the data model for your DTD or schema.

Create a Data Model

A *data model* is a conceptual representation of the "things" your application must track or account for. The data model may describe the "things," their relationship to each other, and any constraints on the values they may assume. For example, if your application will provide a means of taking inventory, and you need to track parts, you may decide to include an element named "part," and a child element named "sub-part" with a one-to-many relationship (we'll discuss relationships in more detail in Module 9). You may also decide that the element "part" has an attribute named "quantityinstock" that may assume a value no lower than 0 and no higher than 100,000.

Create the DTD or Schema

Now that you know how your data model works, it's time to write the DTD or schema. A number of tools are available for this, and of course you'll want to decide whether to use the traditional DTD or one of the more recent (and more flexible and powerful) schema languages. Either choice should work fine, but if your application is likely to be data intensive, you might best use a schema language such as XML Schemas.

Create a Sample Document for Testing

After you've written the DTD or schema, give it a quick run-through by writing a sample document referencing the DTD or schema. Then open the document using Internet Explorer or some other browser that includes a functional XML processor. You'll know right away whether your document is properly written, and seeing it displayed may give you some clues as to whether the DTD or schema you've written will provide the performance you require. If not, go back to the drawing board to modify and improve your DTD or schema.

Write Your XML Documents

The next step, of course, is to write some "real" XML documents. Write the basic documents supporting your application, and write some XSL style sheets so more finished looking styling will be added to your documents when they are viewed on a variety of platforms.

Test Your XML Documents

In the same way that you would view finished Web pages on a number of platforms to make sure they render properly, view your finished XML documents on a number of platforms and under a variety of conditions to determine whether they render and perform properly.

☑ *Mastery Check*

1. How does XML differ from HTML?

    A. XML is the same as HTML, but more powerful.

    B. HTML is a language; XML is a technology for making languages.

    C. XML is the next version of HTML.

    D. All of the above.

    E. None of the above.

2. What components do HTML and XML languages have in common?

3. Name four differences between XHTML and HTML.

4. What is the relationship of a DTD to an XML document, if the document references the DTD?

    A. The DTD defines the namespace for the document.

    B. The DTD defines some or all of the allowable elements and attributes for the document.

    C. The DTD replaces the schema for the document.

    D. None of the above.

5. What is the process by which XML documents are transformed into a finished product for rendering in a browser?

6. What signs mark the beginning and ending of an HTML command; and what are the signs called?

    A. The start and end tags; a tag

    B. The greater-than and less-than signs; a tag

    C. Dashes; a tag

    D. None of the above

✓ Mastery Check

7. What two parts always make up an attribute?

    A. The name of the element and the name of the attribute

    B. The name of the element and the value of the attribute

    C. The name of the attribute and the value of the attribute

    D. None of the above

8. When an attribute is minimized, what does that mean? How is it different from an attribute that is not minimized?

9. What is a new XML application?

    A. A new XML language

    B. A new XML DTD or schema

    C. A new XML document

    D. Possibly all of the above

    E. None of the above

10. Who may create new XML applications?

    A. Anyone

    B. Only the World Wide Web Consortium (W3C)

    C. Only major companies like Microsoft and Netscape

    D. None of the above

11. In what case must HTML elements and attributes be written?

    A. Uppercase

    B. Lowercase

    C. It doesn't matter

    D. None of the above

☑ Mastery Check

12. What are elements and attributes in XML documents?

    A. Elements are text content, and attributes are the values that quantify or qualify the content.

    B. Elements are tags, and attributes are element modifiers.

    C. Elements are important parts of a document, and attributes represent properties of those elements.

    D. None of the above.

13. What does it mean that elements may not overlap?

    A. The start tag of an element that is inside another element must be written after the start tag of the element it is inside, and the end tag of the inside element must be written before the end tag of the outside element.

    B. Each element can have only one child element inside it.

    C. Two elements must never have the same ID attribute value.

    D. None of the above

14. What is a CDATA section, in XHTML?

    A. CDATA stands for Character Data, and it refers to a section of content defined by the CDATA delimiters, in which scripting content is placed. Within a CDATA section, scripting commands that would not ordinarily be unprocessed by the browser are left alone.

    B. CDATA stands for Content Data, and it is used to delimit areas of scripting languages so that browsers can process them.

    C. CDATA sections are reserved for the "C" programming language commands.

    D. None of the above

15. What is a data model?

    A. A description of the problem you are trying to solve with an XML application

☑ Mastery Check

B. A conceptual representation of the way data flows and interacts in your problem area

C. An illustration of the things that need to be tracked in your problem area

D. All of the above may be descriptions of a data model

Module 2

XML Basics, Syntax, and DTDs

The Goals of This Module

- Learn XML document components
- Define and understand XML application structures
- Explore the HTML Strict DTD
- Learn how XML DTDs are written
- Explore entities, elements, and attributes
- Learn basic XML syntax
- Create a DTD
- Create a basic XML document

Now that we've seen a bit of XML, where it came from, and how it relates to HTML and XHTML, it's time to get into the internal workings of XML itself. This module explores the basic structures of XML: XML vocabularies, entities, elements, attributes, DTDs, schemas, and the structure of XML documents. These items form the foundation for any XML application.

XML Basics

As mentioned in Module 1, XML, like HTML, consists of elements and attributes, but authors may add to or create new elements and attributes without changing the XML standard. This makes XML extensible—but still a standard. Another aspect of XML is that authors may create XML documents to any degree of complexity, even millions of instances of elements and attributes in a single document (although for processing purposes, a smaller size is almost always going to work better). For example, if a relational database was converted to XML format, there could be millions of elements representing the millions of records in the database.

XML is ideal for use on the Internet because the data in an XML document, like HTML, is encoded with tags made of plain text. Most operating systems can easily handle plain text, and it is therefore easier to build processors and browsers to handle XML. And because XML elements and attributes may be defined in DTDs and schemas that are available to any person or machine, whenever extensions are made, they may be immediately recognized (as long as they conform to the XML standards).

In fact, the XML method of marking up data goes a long way toward solving the problem of explicitly defining information in a standard way that machines can understand. For example, in an HTML document, information about a customer's age may be written in this way:

```
<P>Customer = <B>John Smith</B></P>
<P>Age = <B>35</B></P>
```

This tells a user reading the page that the customer is 35 years old, but it does nothing for a machine scanning the document—at least as far as the elements go. In an XML document, however, it could be coded like this:

```
<customer>
<name>John Smith</name>
<age>35</age>
</customer>
```

Since there is an age element (a child element of the customer element), a machine processing the XML document would be able to deduce that this element refers to the customer's age, rather than having to infer this fact from the proximity, in HTML, to the line showing the customer's name.

In an XML schema, the age element could include a constraint, such that age could not be less than zero or more than 200 and must always be an integer calculated as the number of years since the customer's birth date, rounded down. These additional instructions allow fairly precise definition of the element age, to the point that little ambiguity exists concerning the meaning of the element age.

Reducing ambiguity is desirable in that communication depends on a high degree of agreement among communicating parties, especially among machines, most of which have little capability for detecting erroneous data (such as an age showing as 210, which we humans would automatically suspect as an error but machines would blithely pass on).

XML Document Components

One term you'll see used constantly in reference to XML documents is *well formed*. XML documents must follow a number of rules to be considered well formed, and if a document is not well formed, it will likely raise error conditions upon processing. Of course, your job is to make sure your documents are well formed in every respect before they are published, so you'll want to make sure you follow the rules. These rules will be covered in each section that describes XML document components. By the way, it's also important to note that XML documents may be well formed but still not valid. A valid document conforms to rules and limitations set up in its DTD or schema, while a well-formed document conforms only to the rules of XML in general.

XML Entities and Data

XML documents are composed of units called *entities*. Think of these as files or other sources of XML data. An XML document may be composed of one or more of these units, in the same way that an HTML document might be derived from an HTML file plus a server-side include file, plus some data retrieved from a database. Entities are identified by their names, and they can either contain all their data in their own declaration or reference their data via a URL.

Data that is a part of an XML document consists of parsed and unparsed entities. *Unparsed* entities contain data that may or may not be text; if text, it may or may not be text that is allowed in parsed XML entities. Unparsed entities, therefore, are often used to include binary data (such as image data) or code that cannot be parsed without blowing up the XML document (that is, text that is not allowed). Unparsed entities must have an associated notation, and the notation must be identified with a proper XML name. *Notations* are XML document components, like elements and attributes, and they are defined in a DTD as being of a particular type, perhaps image/jpg, for example. They are used to identify the type of unparsed data in XML documents.

Parsed entities are content and/or markup that are well formed according to the rules of XML, and so only allowable content and markup may be included. Parsed entities are referenced within a DTD or document by a proper XML name, and during processing, their names are replaced by the content and markup they represent. Parsed entities can be further broken down into *general entities* (used in XML documents) and *parameter entities* (used in DTDs). All these entity types are discussed further as we review XML document components later in this module.

Ask the Expert

Question: What's the difference between an URL, a URI, and a URN?

Answer: In the HTML, XHTML, and XML recommendations published by the World Wide Web Consortium (W3C), URL references are often written *URI*, and a distinction should be made between a URI and a URL. URI stands for Universal Resource Identifier, while URL stands for Universal Resource Locator. The difference is that a URL is the familiar *protocol–domain name–path–filename* construction, such as **www.e4free.com**, that we all know, and URI can be this or any other kind of identifier that works. Throughout this book you'll see the common term URL, but keep in mind that it can just as easily be a URN or URI. Here is what the W3C has to say about the subject: The URI, Uniform Resource Identifier, is the generic set of all names/addresses that are short strings that refer to resources. The URL, Uniform Resource Locator, is the set of URI schemes that have explicit instructions on how to access the resource on the Internet. The URN, Uniform Resource Name, is a URI that has an institutional commitment to persistence, availability, etc. (Note that this sort of URI may also be a URL. See, for example, PURLs. A particular scheme, urn:, specified by RFC2141 and related documents, is intended to serve as persistent, location-independent, resource identifiers.)

XML Vocabularies

Module 1 offered a short list of some prebuilt XML languages (applications) that are available for use by anyone. Anyone can develop an XML language based on anything; and in some industries, two or more groups are trying to develop XML languages they hope will become the standard for the industry. In addition, some groups are trying to develop proprietary XML languages for use only by members. Without examining the merits and drawbacks of standard or proprietary XML languages, the one common factor is that these languages are called *vocabularies*.

An XML vocabulary is a set of elements and attributes that pertain to a specific industry, field-of-study, or some other category that makes sense. An analogous term is *jargon*, as in *technical jargon*. The vocabulary used within a particular DTD or schema identifies it as applicable to a particular discipline, group, culture, and so forth. And of course, the DTD (or DTDs or schema or schemas) used is an important component of an XML document.

XML Characters

Most everyone is familiar with ASCII characters, which are supported by XML. However, XML also supports the entire Unicode character set. You can find information about Unicode at **www.unicode.org**. This site features the latest version of Unicode (3.0 at this writing) and includes technical documentation that explains that Unicode consists of all ASCII characters plus thousands of other scientific, language, punctuation, and mathematical characters. In all, more than a million characters are supported by Unicode, with quite a few reserved for private use and future needs.

The XML 1.0 recommendation at W3C defines XML characters as being from the group defined by ISO 10646-1:2000, the same set of characters used in Unicode. Although the standards are currently the same, there is no guarantee that this will be the case in the future, so it would be a good idea to check once in a while.

XML Names

Like attributes and other XML structures, elements have XML names. Naturally, the XML recommendation places some limitations on the format of these names. For example, all XML names must begin with a letter (but not a number), an underscore, or a colon, but from the second character on, any Unicode characters that are letters, digits, hyphens, or periods may be used. The main exception to this rule is that no XML name may begin with the letters *x*, *m*, and *l*, in any combination of cases. So XML names may not start with *XML*,

xml, *Xml*, *xmL*, and so on. And even though it is permissible to use the colon, you should never do so, because it is used to separate namespace names from basic XML element and attribute names. (More on namespaces in Module 4.)

Here are some acceptable XML name examples: *_123*, *OneTwoThree*. Unacceptable XML names are *123*, *_123%*, *xmlOneTwoThree*. Acceptable names that shouldn't be used are *:123* and *:OneTwoThree*.

1-Minute Drill

- Give three examples of XML names that include the string *xml* but are acceptable.

- Give an example of an acceptable XML name that includes the ampersand (&).

XML Document Sections

A well-formed XML document may have three sections: a prolog (optional), a body, and an epilog (also optional). Although the prolog is optional, it is a good idea to include it because it can contain some important information. For example, it contains the XML declaration:

```
<?xml version="1.0"?>
```

The XML declaration should be the first line in the prolog, and no white space or comments should appear before it.

This declaration may also contain the *encoding* and *standalone* attributes. The *encoding* attribute specifies the character-encoding method, while the *standalone* attribute specifies whether or not the document contains all required entity declarations (if not, an external DTD will be used). Here is an example of the code for an XML declaration with these two optional attributes:

```
<?xml version="1.0" encoding="UTF-16" standalone="yes"?>
```

Character encoding refers to the method used to store the Unicode character set for a particular system. There are a number of character-encoding methods (such as UTF-8, UTF-16, ISO 8859-1, and so forth), and signaling the encoding

---

- Three examples are *_xml*, *axml*, and *a-xml*.
- The ampersand may not be included in an XML name.

2

method is considered good form, since some systems trying to read the document may not understand the encoding system used, even if they would recognize the unencoded characters. If this attribute is not used, the processor will assume UTF-8 or UTF-16, based on the encoding found in the first few characters of the document (*<?xml...*, for example).

The next optional part of the prolog is the Document Type Declaration. Although it has the same initials as the Document Type Definition (DTD), this part refers to a line in the document making *reference* to the DTD. A well-formed XML document may omit this declaration, but to be valid, your XML document must include it.

Note

Confused about well formed versus valid? A well-formed document means that it contains properly written XML tags; they nest properly, don't overlap, and so forth. Being well formed doesn't mean the tags have any special meaning; it just means they follow the basic XML syntax rules. Valid is another story. An XML document can't be valid if it is not well formed (it also can't be parsed properly). Plus, if you as the author want to specify the elements and attributes (among other components) that can be present in the document, and the characteristics they can assume (such as values and number of occurrences), the document must reference a DTD or schema that supplies that kind of information. If the document is read by an XML processor that checks for well-formedness as well as for validity, the processor will generate an error if it finds the document not well formed. It will also review the information in the DTD or schema and generate errors if the elements and attributes in the document do not follow the rules specified there.

Internal and External DTDs   The Document Type Declaration may make a reference to an external DTD or an internal DTD. An *external DTD* is referenced by a URL or by an internally recognized name for a DTD. If only a URL is referenced, it is labeled with the term *SYSTEM*, while referencing both a URL and a DTD means the reference is labeled with the term *PUBLIC*. This means that the DTD may simply be somewhere on the Internet (referenced by a URL) or somewhere in the path of the internal network or the operating system of the computer on which the XML document will be processed (kind of like a Data Source Name, DSN). Just for good measure, you can write the DTD entirely inside the XML document, and this is called an *internal DTD* (don't confuse this with the reference to a DTD using an internally recognized name). An internal DTD reference means that the DTD is coded as part of the Document Type Declaration. In either case, the syntax is shown in the following examples.

Here's an external DTD referenced only by a URL:

```
<?xml version="1.0" encoding="UTF-8" standalone="yes"?>
<!DOCTYPE Customer SYSTEM
"http://www.e4free.com/XMLBeginnersGuide/Module02/DTD01">
```

Here's an external DTD referenced by both an internally recognized name and a URL:

```
<?xml version="1.0" encoding="UTF-8" standalone="yes"?>
<!DOCTYPE Customer PUBLIC "DTD01.dtd"
"http://www.e4free.com/XMLBeginnersGuide/Module02/DTD01">
```

Here's an internal DTD with an entity declaration:

```
<?xml version="1.0" encoding="UTF-8" standalone="yes"?>
<!DOCTYPE Customer [
<!ENTITY XMLBG "XML Beginner's Guide">
]>
```

Undoubtedly you will have questions as to what an "entity" is. You've already learned about parsed and unparsed entities, and next you'll learn even more. For now, you should know that an entity is one of the things that can be defined in the DTD (whether external or internal); These particular entity types will be covered in more detail in the section entitled "XML Entity References," later in this module.

Also, note that the word *Customer* appears in the DOCTYPE declaration. This word denotes the name of the root element of the document. In this case, the root element of our XML document is *Customer*, as we will be building a retail XML application during the course of this book. Speaking of elements, that is the subject of the next section. Elements, attributes, entities, and more are defined in the DTD (or DTDs) and exist in the body of the XML document, so we will discuss the contents of the epilog after we cover these XML document parts.

XML Elements

XML elements represent the "things" the XML document is concerned with. For example, if you are creating a document that will keep track of customers and their orders, one of the elements included should be Customers and another should be Orders. Naturally, within the *Customers* element, there might be many individual *Customer* elements, and within the *Orders* element, there might be many individual *Order* elements. Since a single customer may have one or more orders, the *Orders* element will be a child of one of the *Customer* elements within the main *Customers* element.

And in a single *Order* element, there might be an *OrderDetails* element and an *OrderItems* element. Inside these elements, there might be attributes such as *OrderNumber*, *OrderDate*, *OrderTotal*, *ItemName*, *Quantity*, and so forth. Figure 2-1 shows the relationships among these elements:

XML elements contain all the data of an XML document. This data, known as *element content*, may include other elements, character data, character references, entity references, and other information. (All these types of data will be discussed in detail later in this module.) If attributes are present, they are always included in the starting tag of the element.

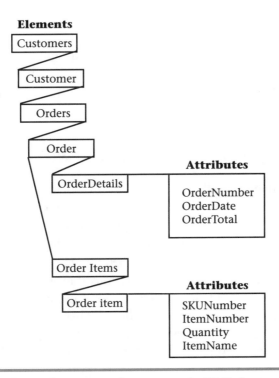

Figure 2-1   The relationship among elements in the XML document

As in HTML, XML elements are *delimited* (marked) by tags. Tags come in starting and ending pairs, unless the element is empty (contains no content), in which case, the starting and ending tags are combined into a single tag with an ending indicator built-in. A single tag is delimited by the angle brackets (< and >). These are positioned around the name of the element and also contain any attributes of the element. The ending tag can be recognized by the slash (/) before the element name—unless the element is empty, in which case, the slash is placed just before the > signs at the end of the tag. Following are some examples.

Here's the starting tag of the nonempty Customer element, with no attributes:

```
<Customer>
```

Here's the ending tag of the nonempty Customer element:

```
</Customer>
```

Notice the slash preceding the element name in this ending tag. Any element content would fall between the starting and ending tags of this element.

An empty element with a single attribute needs only a starting tag with a slash in it at the end:

```
<CurrentTime
  thetime="http://www.thetime.com/currenttime"/>
```

This made-up element would get the current time from the fictitious Web site (thetime.com) and would contain no content. (Notice the slash before the greater-than sign at the end of the starting tag in this empty element. The slash makes this tag serve as both the starting tag and the ending tag.)

XML Element Rules   XML is more rigorous than HTML in that ending tags may never be left off, and all elements must be properly nested (that is, not overlapping). Elements must have an ending tag because XML wants an explicit beginning and ending for every tag so there are no ambiguities, and elements must be properly nested so the definition of a parent and child element is never confused.

The root of an XML document is called the *document entity* or *document root* (not to be confused with the root element), and from this root springs the main components of the document: the prolog, epilog, and document element. The document element is the root element of the document from which all other elements in the document spring. Therefore, all elements in an XML document are child elements of the root element. In our previous Customer example, the Customers element is the root element of the document and all other elements in the document are its children.

As a practical matter, everything in the Customers XML document must be related to customers. But suppose you wanted a system that would track employees as well. In that case, you would create another XML document called Employees, and you might query it for a particular employee number in case you wanted to track which employee took a customer's order.

XML Attributes

Figure 2-1 showed a number of elements as parents and children, and the final elements in two cases show some attributes. For example, OrderItem is a child element of the element OrderItems, but SKUNumber is an attribute of the element OrderItem. If you've ever seen an order form, you know that order items are often listed individually, and it is common for an order item to have a Stock Keeping Unit (SKU) number.

So how is the decision made as to what is an element and what is an attribute? Here are some general guidelines:

- Elements often include other elements within them. For example, the Customer, Orders, and OrderItems elements all have child elements.

- Elements frequently have attributes, but attributes do not have their own attributes. For example, while the OrderItem element has several attributes (SKUNumber, ItemName, Quantity), it's hard to imagine what attributes the name or SKU number of an item could have.

Attributes may be included for any element (they are defined in the DTD or schema), whether or not the element is an empty element; the attributes always take the form of a name-value pair (*name="value"* or *name='value'*). An attribute may be included in an element only once, and the order in which attributes are included makes no difference.

XML Reserved Attributes   Although an author can usually devise any name for an element or attribute in XML, some names are reserved (remember, no element may begin with *xml*). A number of attributes have been defined (so far) as reserved in XML, including the *xml:space* and *xml:lang* attributes.

The *xml:space* attribute causes the white space in the element within which it resides, and all the child elements of that element, to be preserved. It operates in a manner similar to the PRE element in HTML, which preserves white spaces and tabs in text it contains. The *xml:space* attribute must be declared in the DTD if you intend to use it, and it may take only *preserve* and *default* as its values. *default* means that the XML processor is free to handle white space as it chooses, while *preserve* means the processor should respect all white space. However, there really is no guarantee that the processor and application using the XML document will process this attribute according to its intentions.

Note

Handling white space in HTML documents is different from the way it's handled in ordinary word-processing documents, in that browsers remove all white space except one space between words. For example, if you press the SPACEBAR several times in Notepad to create white space between words, the browser ignores all the space characters except one. To make more spaces in an HTML document, you must use the character reference   (which means nonbreaking space) for each space or use the PRE element to preserve your white spaces. In XML, all white-space characters in content (such as text) are preserved, but white space in element tags and attribute values is removed when the document is processed. So why the need for the *xml:space* attribute? The *xml:space* attribute gives directions to the final application receiving the processed XML document, such as Internet Explorer. That application can use the directions to decide whether to preserve white space in content.

The *xml:lang* attribute is used to denote the language and country in which the content of the document is written. It must be declared in the DTD if used, and it can use only one of three types of language codes: ISO 639, RFC 1766, or a user-defined language code. ISO 639 language codes may consist of two characters (such as *en* for English and *fr* for French). A subcode may also be attached by a hyphen (such as *en-US* for English in the United States). If the language code begins with an uppercase *I* or lowercase *i*, it may be followed by a hyphen and the name of a language registered with IANA (see **www.ietf.org/ rfc/rfc1766.txt**). If the language code begins with an *X*, it is for private use and may represent any language the author chooses.

XML Strings and Character Data

If you've ever done any programming, you already have a good idea of what strings are. Strings, numbers, dates, and the like are all types of data, and the term *data type* refers to how a chunk of data is stored and what can be done with it. In computing terms, a *string* is simply characters in a row, and in XML, attribute values are strings.

A string can represent anything, but a string is not a number for computing purposes. For example, if an attribute named *year* is in your XML document, you could set it equal to "1999", like so: *year="1999"*. However, this value is not considered a number for computing purposes; it can't be added to another number. It is also not a date value. You see, behind the scenes, the *number* 1999 and the *string* 1999 are stored differently. Of course, this doesn't mean that an application couldn't immediately change the value from a string data type to a date data type, and then process it as a date. In fact, you might not even be aware this has happened.

Bottom line is that all XML attribute values defined by a DTD are strings when they are assigned, and what happens to them after that depends on the application using the data. This is one of the reasons XML schemas are so popular. In an XML schema, data types may be assigned, so the application doesn't have to assume a data type based on the name of the element or attribute in which it finds the data.

Character data in an XML document is defined as all text, not part of the markup of the document. Character data consists of the allowed Unicode characters discussed earlier in the module. As you'll recall, the only restrictions are that you may not use the ampersand or the less-than sign in the characters data as is. You must escape these characters using the numeric character references (discussed in the next section) or the strings *&* and *<*.

Tip

Don't confuse character data with CDATA (Character Data) sections; CDATA are special sections for including scripting code and so forth in XML documents, and the text (including special characters such as the ampersand and less-than sign) is passed through as is. We'll discuss CDATA sections in more detail later in this module.

Parsed character data (PCDATA) is simply data that is to be parsed, meaning it contains character data and markup; you will often see the content of an element defined as PCDATA, which means that it can contain other elements and text data.

XML Character References

In HTML, if you want to include the < sign as a displayed character on a Web page, you must use the character reference for it. Why? Because the browser will assume that this character is part of the markup, rather than displayable text characters, and will try to process it as an HTML tag rather than display it.

A similar mechanism (also called *character references*) exists in XML for displaying characters that are reserved or not part of the ASCII character set. To write a character reference, start with the ampersand; then put a decimal, hexadecimal, or string literal for the character; and end with the semicolon. It works the same way as character references in HTML, so that the < sign may be displayed (rather than processed) when it is written as *<* (the decimal numeric), *<* (the hexadecimal numeric), or *<* (the string literal). Notice that the pound sign (#) must precede the decimal numeric, while the hexadecimal numeric must be preceded by the pound sign and a lowercase x.

XML Entity References

Technically, a character reference using a string literal is a predefined *entity reference*. Entity references are quite useful in XML; they make it easy to insert large amounts of string characters into a document with just a few short characters, preceded by the ampersand and ended by the semicolon. General entity references must be defined in the DTD (either internally or externally), and several reserved entity references are used as escape characters in XML. For example, the *<* and *>* entity references are reserved for escaping these characters in XML because they would ordinarily be misinterpreted as the tag delimiters. Three other reserved entity references are *&* (for the ampersand), *'* (for the apostrophe), and *"* (for the quote).

In addition to being used for character references, entity references can be used in XML to insert any string into an XML document. If they are used solely in the DTD, they are called *parameter entities*. For example, if you wish to insert the statement "All Rights Reserved" into an XML document, you could define the entity reference *&rights;* in the DTD as follows:

```
<!ENTITY    rights "All Rights Reserved">
```

Anywhere in the XML document that this entity reference (&rights;) is placed would make it so that the whole string "All Rights Reserved" would appear when the document is processed. You'll read more about DTDs and the construction of entity references in the section "Inside the HTML Strict DTD—Entities," later in this module.

XML Processing Instructions

XML Processing Instructions (PIs) are the mechanism provided by the W3C for passing indications to an application about how to handle elements, attributes, and content. PIs are written like this:

```
<?target instruction ?>
```

In this code example, the word `target` refers to the application to which instructions are being passed, while `instruction` refers to the commands you are sending to the application. Obviously, you as the author expect a particular application to be used with your document; otherwise, the processing instructions may not work properly.

The target can be any valid XML name, but nothing starting with *xml*, except for a deliberate exception created by the W3C, the xml-stylesheet PI. This exception is documented at **www.w3.org/TR/xml-stylesheet**, and we'll discuss it in detail in Module 11.

XML Comments

Like HTML, XML allows comments, and the syntax is exactly the same. For example, a comment may be written like this:

```
<!--This is my comment text -->
```

Comments cannot be included inside other markup and the content of comments cannot include two hyphens in a row because that would look like the end of the comment. In addition, the content of comments cannot end with a hyphen because that may also confuse the processor. Although entities may be written into comments, they are not expanded to their defined form; they are left as is.

XML CDATA Sections

As mentioned in Module 1 during the discussion of XHTML, scripts and other kinds of code can be included in CDATA (Character Data) sections in XML documents. The purpose of these sections is to enable you to include text that contains characters that would otherwise be interpreted as markup. For example, suppose you wrote a short JavaScript that passed out HTML markup as part of its function. The markup characters would have to be included in the code, but if they weren't identified as part of a CDATA section, the processor would attempt to process those characters, blowing up the script. Using a CDATA section prevents this from happening.

Tip

Here's a good way to remember when to use CDATA sections: Use them whenever you need to include code that should not be directly processed by the XML processor.

CDATA sections are written using the syntax covered in Module 1, and here it is again:

```
<![CDATA[
function clickme() {
alert("This is a Javascript function")
}
]]>
```

As you can see from the code, a CDATA section begins with the < sign, continues with the exclamation point (!), a square bracket ([), the characters *CDATA*, and then a closing square bracket (]). Next comes the character data we wish to contain, and finally two closing square brackets are followed by a greater-than (>) sign.

The Epilog

The epilog in an XML document may contain comments, PIs, and white space, but it should probably not be included because it may not be processed the same way by all applications. At this time, it's not clear what it should be used for, if anything, and the latest version of the standard doesn't seem to mention it. It's good to know that it's there, but that's about it.

1-Minute Drill

● What does DTD stand for, and how is it related to an XML document?

● What kind of DTDs can be used with XML documents, and how do they work?

● DTD stands for Document Type Definition, and all the elements, attributes, entities, and so forth that may be used with an XML document are defined in it.

● DTDs can be internal or external to an XML document. An internal DTD is written directly into the XML document itself, while an external DTD is written as a separate file and referenced from the XML document.

Document Type Definitions (DTDs)

DTDs are a very important part of XML because they form the basis for any XML document not relying on an XML schema. DTDs and schemas are roughly equivalent in the work they do to support XML documents, but schemas are considered to be a better way to go. However, you will probably use DTDs in many cases when creating or maintaining XML documents, simply because DTDs were invented first. The next section gives you all the basics and background you'll need to move on to the discussion of schemas in Module 3.

To give you a proper start, you'll use the HTML DTD (you can find it at the W3C site), in which the elements and attributes are familiar to many of you. Then you'll construct our own XML DTD and, from that, an XML document.

Inside the HTML Strict DTD—Entities

As you may recall, both HTML and XHTML draw their elements, attributes, and so forth from one of three predefined DTDs. To get an idea how DTDs are made (this is pertinent for both HTML and XML DTDs), let's take a look at the HTML Strict DTD. We'll break it down into sections, starting with the specifications for ENTITY. Although we will discuss only ENTITY for text, a number of entities are defined in the beginning of the DTD (after the introduction and notes about the authors). Here is the DTD code specifying the ENTITY for text:

```
<!ENTITY % Text "CDATA">
```

The code starts with a < sign, continues with the exclamation point and the word *ENTITY*, a percent sign (%) followed by the word *Text*, a space, and then within quotes the designation "CDATA". Formally, this is called a *parameter entity definition*. A parameter entity definition provides a kind of shorthand throughout the DTD for larger strings that will be reused repeatedly. So wherever the entity *%text* appears, the string "CDATA" will be inserted when the DTD is read by machine. CDATA is an SGML data type meaning character data and can include any characters from the allowed character set for the language the HTML document uses.

As another example of parameter entity definitions, here is the declaration from the HTML DTD for the heading ENTITY:

```
<!ENTITY % heading "H1|H2|H3|H4|H5|H6">
```

In this case, it is easy to see why a parameter entity is used, because it would be cumbersome to have to write out "H1|H2|H3|H4|H5|H6" every time these values are appropriate in the DTD, rather than writing just "%heading".

DTD Elements and Attributes

Elements and attributes are also declared in the DTD, using syntax such as this:

```
<!ELEMENT A - - (%inline;)* -(A)        -- anchor -->
<!ATTLIST A
%attrs;                                 -- %coreattrs,
 %i18n, %events --
charset       %Charset;     #IMPLIED  -- char encoding
 of linked resource --
type          %ContentType; #IMPLIED  -- advisory
 content type --
name          CDATA         #IMPLIED  -- named link end --
href          %URI;         #IMPLIED  -- URI for
 linked resource --
hreflang      %LanguageCode; #IMPLIED  -- language
 code --
rel           %LinkTypes;   #IMPLIED  -- forward
 link types --
rev           %LinkTypes;   #IMPLIED  -- reverse
 link types --
>
```

This ELEMENT declaration defines the *A* element, which makes hypertext links in HTML. The declaration starts with the < sign, followed by an exclamation point and the word *ELEMENT*, a space, and then the name of the element (*A*). Next comes code specifying whether starting or ending tags are required (-- means both are required, –O means the starting tag is required and the ending tag may be omitted, and so forth).

The parameter entity %*inline* in the element declaration means that inline elements may appear in an *A* element, but the –(*A*) following that means that no *A* elements may appear inside another *A* element. That makes sense, because while you could have text, images, whole paragraphs, and so on inside a

2

hypertext link, you can't have a link inside a link. The text at the end of the first line of this element declaration is just a DTD comment telling us what type of element the *A* element makes (-- *anchor* -->).

The attributes supported by the *A* element are listed following the <*!ATTLIST* line, and the list of attributes includes those referenced by the parameter entity *%attrs;*. Without going into all the attributes supported (and the *A* or anchor DTD shown here is not complete, by the way), it is sufficient to say that each attribute is defined with a name, a data type (text, URL, content type, and so forth) for its value, and how the default value of the attribute is supplied (IMPLIED means the default value is supplied by the browser, REQUIRED means it must be supplied by the author, and so forth).

DTD Comments
Comments in the DTD are written with a pair of dashes (--) at each end (as described in the paragraph about the *A* element). Comments in HTML are written with <*!--* at the beginning and --> at the end. HTML elements, as mentioned, may have starting and ending tags, although for some element, one or both may be omitted, and in some cases, ending tags are forbidden (such as the IMG element). If an HTML element has no ending tag, it is said to be an EMPTY element. *EMPTY* refers to the content model. *Content model* is just a technical way of describing what content is allowed within an element, if any. For example, the *P* element has beginning and ending tags, and any text between them is content. Therefore, the *P* element is not an EMPTY element.

DTD Character References
Another component of HTML documents is the character reference. Like their XML counterparts (discussed previously), character references are numeric or symbolic names for characters that would ordinarily not be properly displayed in a browser or might not be supported by your keyboard. For example, if you want to display the characters <*HTML*> directly in a page (rather than having the browser interpret it as an HTML tag), you must use character references for the < and > signs. Instead of <HTML>, you would write <HTML>, where < is the symbolic character reference for the < sign, and > is the symbolic character reference for the > sign. Note that character references always begin with an ampersand and end with a semicolon, and that the numeric character references for these two signs are < and > (note also that the pound sign must be included when using numeric character references).

Project 2-1: Dissect and Discuss an HTML DTD Element

This project involves reading through the DTD for an HTML element, identifying the function of each line and its components, and discussing what it means in general. We'll use the DTD for the IMG element, as it may be found on the W3C Web site in the DTD for HTML 4.01.

The IMG element DTD begins with the element declaration, shown here with a starting tag required and an ending tag forbidden and an empty content model:

```
<!ELEMENT IMG - O EMPTY                    -- Embedded image -->
```

Next is a list of attributes for the IMG element, including the %attrs; entity and the %coreattrs entity, as well as intrinsic events supported by the element (in the %events entity). The attributes of the IMG element that are not core attirubtes are *src* (URI, required), *alt* (text, required), *longdesc* (URI, implied), *name* (CDATA, implied), *height* (length, implied), *width* (length, implied), *usemap* (URI, implied), and *ismap* (ismap, implied).

Step-by-Step

1. Find the DTD at the W3C Web site and read the first line. It begins with <! and then the word *ELEMENT*, so we know it is the declaration of an HTML element. It is followed by the characters *IMG*, so we know the name of the element is IMG, and it is easy enough to understand that this element is an image element. This assumption is further reinforced by the DTD comment (surrounded by dashes) -- *Embedded image* — at the end of the line. Prior to the end of the line, the – O characters indicate the start tag is required; and the end tag is omitted, followed by the word *EMPTY*, which indicates that this element has no content (no text content or other elements may be contained in the IMG element).

2. Read the second line. This line begins with *ATTLIST*, telling us it is a list of attributes. Then *IMG* tells us it applies to the IMG element.

2

3. Read the third line. It says *%attrs;* and because it starts with a percent sign, we know it is a parameter entity. Going back to the HTML 4.01 recommendation, we go to the HTML DTD and find that this parameter entity is defined as including three other parameter entities (*%coreattrs;*, *%i18n;*, and *%events;*). These parameter entities, in turn, refer to attributes present across the board in HTML elements (core attributes such as *id*, *class*, *style*, and *title*), language attributes (*lang* and *dir*), and events (onmouseover, onclick, and so forth). What this means is that all the attributes specified in the parameter entities apply to the IMG element as well as any specifically listed.

4. Read the next eight lines. These lines spell out any additional attributes that apply to the IMG element, such as *src* and *alt*. For example, the *src* attribute is denoted by the name *src* in the DTD. That name is followed by the data type (*%URI;*) specified as a parameter entity meaning any resolvable URL. The data type is followed by the word *REQUIRED*, meaning that a reference to an image file must be included (no automatic default value is supplied for this attribute by the browser). At the end of the *src* attribute line is a comment telling us that this attribute is for the URL of the image file.

Ask the Expert

Question: With all the XML parts we've covered, I'm a little confused as to what each part does and how it is related to the others. Can you sort them out a bit for me?

Answer: Sure! Here's a concise description of the parts and how they are related:

- **The DTD or schema**   Before you can create a valid XML document, you must find or build your own DTD or schema. The DTD or schema tells validating XML processors which elements, attributes, and so forth are allowed in your XML document. Keep in mind that the DTD may be external (contained in a separate file) or internal (written into the XML document itself, in its own special section).

- **The XML document prolog**   This beginning section of an XML document may contain the XML version to which the document conforms, the DOCTYPE declaration, comments, and PIs.

- **The XML document body**   This section contains the elements, attributes, and content of the XML document.

- **The XML document epilog**   This section may contain comments and processing instructions, but it is better not to use it because it may not be processed correctly.

- **Entity references**   Entities are defined in the DTD as a way of creating a small bit of code that represents a larger chunk of text. Character references refer to characters that will not ordinarily display properly (because they refer to reserved coding characters in XML), while plain entity references may refer to any sizable chunk of text to insert.

- **Elements**   Elements are defined in the DTD or schema and are the main structure in XML documents. They represent "things" the document is meant to work with, such as customers, orders, musical notes, mathematical symbols, and so forth. An XML document is made up of a hierarchy of elements, and the hierarchy must be properly constructed. Tags for an element that is the parent of another element must begin before and end after the tags of the child element.

- **Attributes**   Attributes are defined in the DTD or schema and are meant to modify or set properties for elements. Attributes always come in a name-value pair written inside an element, in any order. Two predefined attributes are *xml:space* and *xml:lang*.

- **Comments and Processing Instructions (PIs)**   Comments are written using the XML comment delimiters and are useful for reminding yourself (or other programmers) of the purpose and meaning of commands, tags, attributes, and structures. Comments are not processed. Processing instructions are special commands for the application after the XML code has been processed.

- **Strings, Character data, white space, and CDATA sections**   Strings are simply strings of characters enclosed in double or single quotation marks. They are used for the value of attributes and entities and are considered part of the character data

2

of the document. Character data (as opposed to CDATA sections) is the text in your document that isn't markup, meaning it is content. CDATA sections are for character data that includes characters that may not be parsed, such as the ampersand and the less-than and greater-than signs (and as we mentioned, PCDATA is for data that is going to be parsed, such as child elements with content). White space is simply any white space character (such as would be produced by pressing the SPACEBAR or the TAB key), and XML passes white space through the processor to the application on the other end. Note that white space inside element tags or attribute values will be removed.

Question: I noticed in the HTML IMG DTD a reference to events supported by the IMG element. I have a pretty good feeling for what attributes are, but what are events?

Answer: You have a sharp eye, and that's good. Everything in the DTD means something, and learning to read it carefully will do wonders when you're picking one to create XML documents.

Some attributes in HTML occur over and over again, applying to most elements in the entire HTML DTD. Therefore, these are called the *core attributes*, and they are listed only once in the DTD. From then on, they are referenced by the entity *%coresttrs*.

In the same way, there are events that apply to almost all HTML elements. They are listed once in the DTD and then referred to by the entity *%events*. So what are events? Well, that gets to the nature of the way HTML, XHTML, and XML documents are structured.

In Module 8, we'll cover the Document Object Model (DOM) in detail, but for now, we'll briefly describe it. The DOM is a way of looking at the elements and attributes within a document and structuring them in a format that makes them easy to address and work with. In HTML, elements are arranged in this structure so that the document is the parent of other elements, which are parents of other elements, and so on down the line to the smallest element on the page. For example, a button on a form is a child element of that form, and the form itself is a child element of the document.

When a button on a form is clicked, an event takes place (called the *onclick event*), and this event can be detected. When the event takes place, it travels through the elements in the DOM, and so can be used to trigger scripting functions that may modify elements and their attributes or to perform other functions. Since the button element supports the main events (and perhaps a few special ones), it is possible to make HTML pages perform functions programmatically, by using scripting languages, the DOM, and built-in events.

Building XML DTDs

The HTML DTD is pretty much static, as defined by the W3C. Some major companies add their own extensions to HTML to the HTML DTD, but in some cases, no one else follows along (such is the case with the MARQUEE element, which is supported by Internet Explorer but not by Netscape). One of the main reasons XML was developed was so that there would be a standard way for anyone to create, and for any processor to understand, extensions to a markup language. XML allows this because it is not a markup language but a standard way of defining markup languages.

Quite a few XML DTDs are in existence already, and some of them are available for anyone to use. In some industries, an industry standards group has already created an XML DTD that supposedly has all the correct elements, attributes, and other structures needed to describe and work with "things" common in that industry. However, in many cases, you'll find that even though an industry standard XML DTD or schema exists, you still need to create a few additional elements and attributes (or even a whole new DTD) to describe the "things" your company or organization is interested in.

Fortunately, XML allows you to use multiple DTDs in a single document, via namespaces, which are discussed further in Module 4. For now, let's concentrate on how XML DTDs are built.

Using Internal and External DTDs

As mentioned, the elements, attributes, and other components of a DTD can be defined as part of the XML document (internal) or in a separate file (external). Both types of DTDs are called *declaration subsets*, implying that either or both may contain only some of the total set of element and attribute declarations the document is based on.

Since internal DTD are part of the XML document, users don't have to retrieve the DTD from some universally available location. Using an internal

DTD is appropriate when only a few declarations are included, but one of the drawbacks is that the declarations must be repeated (and possibly maintained) for every document. When declarations are made in an internal DTD, they override declarations made in an external DTD used with the document, if an element or attribute in the internal DTD is also declared in the external DTD.

External DTDs, of course, have the advantage of being widely available (assuming you have posted them where people can get to them), and maintenance to the DTD need be performed only once, no matter how many documents are supported by the DTD.

DTD Markup Declarations

Within a DTD, four types of declarations can be made. Although we frequently refer only to elements and attributes when describing DTD components, all four of these declarations are permissible, but you'll probably use elements and attributes most frequently. Here are the four declaration types:

- **ELEMENT**   Defines the "things" your XML documents pertain to, such as customers, orders, buildings, cars, patients, and so forth.

- **ATTLIST**   Defines the attributes and specifics about the values those attributes may assume for a given element.

- **ENTITY**   Defines a name that represents a larger string for insertion wherever the entity name is written.

- **NOTATION**   Defines a name for data other than XML data and associates it with the appropriate application to process the data. For example, we can define a notation with a name of avi and associate it with a player such as the Windows Media Player.

1-Minute Drill

- What is an entity?
- What is a notation?

- An entity, defined in a DTD, is a programming construct designed to make it easier to write and read the DTD. The entity is a defined name for a string of text, and when the DTD is read, wherever in the DTD the entity is found the text string replaces it.
- A notation, defined in a DTD, associates a particular name with a file type and an application to handle that type of data.

Project 2-2: Create an XML DTD

This project walks through the creation from scratch of a simple but comprehensive external XML DTD file. You'll use and expand upon the elements and attributes we examined in the section "XML Elements," earlier in this module. However, you'll save the more complex questions concerning relationships and data models for Modules 3 and 9.

In this project, you'll use Notepad to create both the external DTD file and the XML document, and you'll use Internet Explorer (4.0 or above) to view your processed XML document. You will also use the program XML Spy to view what you've done and begin exploring the capabilities of XML Spy.

You will declare entities, elements, attributes, and notations and then use them in the coming project to create an XML document from them. In the XML document, we'll also write in a couple declarations to form an internal DTD as well, just for good measure.

Step-by-Step

1. Open Notepad to a blank, new file. If a blank file does not appear, click File | New. Save the file in an appropriate folder as **Project2-2DTD.dtd**.

2. Begin writing your DTD. It's a good idea to place some explanatory comments at the top, so it will be easier to identify which DTD you're working with and what its purpose is. Your comments should be something like this:

```
<!-- Customer version 1.0 DTD
This DTD is an example for the book
 XML Beginner's Guide, and builds a customers
 and orders management system.
Copyright Dave Mercer 2001, 2002
-->
```

This DTD is not really going to be long or complex enough to contain entities or notation. However, entities must be declared before they are used elsewhere in the DTD, and because you are going to create some entities in this exercise, they should appear in the DTD at this point.

3. Begin declaring the elements and attributes of your DTD. To define elements, type **<!ELEMENT**, and then add the name of the element, **Customers**. (Remember that the name of an element must conform to XML naming rules, so it cannot start with *xml* (in either uppercase or lowercase)

and it can't start with a number.) The element definition for our first element looks like this:

```
<!ELEMENT Customers
```

4. Now add the content model. Element content refers to the data an element may contain, and it comes in four types: EMPTY, ANY, MIXED, and CHILDREN. An element designated as EMPTY has no content and therefore has no content model. It can have no text data or other elements inside it, but it can have attributes. An element designated as having a CHILDREN content model may have child elements within it, and it can have attributes, but no text data. An element with a MIXED content model may contain child elements, text data, and attributes. Both CHILDREN and MIXED content model designations are used when the author wishes to place restrictions on the child elements or text data that can appear within an element. Instead of simply using the terms MIXED or CHILDREN, special syntax specifically states what data and elements may appear. If no restrictions will be included, use the content model ANY. For the *Customers* element, since it is going to be the main element in any XML documents you produce, give it the content model designation **ANY** and close it off with the > sign, like this:

```
<!ELEMENT Customers ANY>
```

5. There are no attributes for the Customers element, so you can go on to the next elements in your DTD. The next two are Customer, signifying a single customer among a group of potential customers, and Orders, signifying a group of orders that a single customer may have. The Customer element may include the customer's name as PCDATA, but each customer would also have to be associated with attributes for contact and billing information, such as phone number, e-mail address, street address, and so forth. In addition, each customer should have a unique CustomerID number. Now you will expand upon the simple outline of elements and attributes shown in Figure 2-1 and add some representative attributes for contact information to the Customer element. Write the Customer element as follows:

```
<!ELEMENT Customer (#PCDATA | Orders )* )
<!ATTLIST Customer
    customerid      ID        #REQUIRED
    phone           CDATA     #IMPLIED
    email           CDATA     #REQUIRED
    fulladdress     CDATA     #IMPLIED >
```

Before going on to the next element, let's discuss how the Customer element was structured. Following its name (*Customer*) is the content model. The content model is written within parentheses, spelling out a mixture of PCDATA plus the Orders element. This qualifies as a content model of MIXED. Notice that whenever the content model is mixed, #PCDATA must appear first in the list, and all components of the content model must be inside parentheses followed by the zero or more indicator.

Note that the special syntax described here includes a number of powerful ways to restrict the types, order, and number of elements appearing inside an element. For example, if element names appear with commas separating them as in the following code example, they must appear strictly in that order inside the element being declared.

```
<!ELEMENT myelement
  (firstchild, secondchild, thirdchild)>
```

If elements appear with pipes (|) between them, they may appear in any order in the element being declared:

```
<!ELEMENT myelement
  (secondchild | firstchild | thirdchild)>
```

Also, merely appearing in the list means that an element must be included once as a child of the element being declared. The number of times an element appears is called the *cardinality of the element*, and *cardinality operators* specify this condition: the question mark (?), the asterisk (*), and the plus sign (+). If an element name has the question mark next to its name, however, its appearance is optional. If an element has an asterisk next to its name, it may appear zero or more times, and if an element has the plus sign next to its name, it must appear one or more times, as shown in the following code example:

```
<!ELEMENT myelement
  (appearsonce, mayappear?, zeroormore*, oneormore+)>
```

The attribute declarations listed in Step 5 begin much like the element declaration, with a < sign and an exclamation point, followed by the term *ATTLIST*, the name of the element the list applies to, and then a list of attribute names, attribute types, and attribute values. Here, your attribute names are *customerid*, *phone*, *email*, and *fulladdress*—each one a good, descriptive name for an attribute of the customer element.

Attribute types are similar to data types, except that data types such as date and number have not been included in the XML specification (XML schemas, covered in Module 3, address data types quite effectively). The allowable types for attributes are shown here:

- **CDATA**   Character data
- **ID**   A name that is unique across the entire document
- **IDREF**   A reference to another element with an ID attribute carrying the same value as the attribute with IDREF
- **IDREFS**   A series of IDREFs separated by white space
- **ENTITY**   The name of an external entity
- **ENTITIES**   A series of ENTITY names separated by white space
- **NMTOKEN**   A valid name
- **NMTOKENS**   A series of NMTOKENs separated by white space
- **NOTATION**   The name of a NOTATION declaration
- **An enumerated value**   Rather than a specific name, this is a list of values the attribute may assume, within parentheses and separated by the pipe symbol.

Following the attribute types comes the default value type. Four types of default values may be assigned, and like attribute types, they offer some powerful control over the structure of a document. The four types are

- **#REQUIRED**   If the attribute is required to appear every time the element appears (such as the customerid and email attributes), the default value is set to #REQUIRED. This doesn't specify what the value of the attribute should be, just that it must be there in every instance.
- **#IMPLIED**   If the attribute may or may not appear, the default value is set to #IMPLIED.
- **#FIXED and the specific value**   If the attribute must always have a fixed value, whether or not it appears in the element, the default value is set to #FIXED with the default value appended to it.
- **The specific value itself**   Using a specific value means if the attribute is not present, it will default to that value, but if it is present, it may assume valid value.

6. Write the Orders and Order elements. The Orders element has no attributes and only Order elements within it (occurring zero or more times), so it has a CHILDREN content model, while the Order element has both text content and child elements within it (the child elements must appear in a specific order), so it has a MIXED content model, like so:

```
<!ELEMENT Orders (Order*)>
<!ELEMENT Order (OrderDetails, OrderItems)>
```

The Order element may occur zero or more times, so the asterisk appears next to it, but the OrderDetails and OrderItems elements occur only once per order, so no cardinality symbol appears next to them. However, they occur in a specific sequence in the Order element and are therefore written with commas separating them.

7. Now write the OrderDetails, OrderItems, and OrderItem elements. The OrderDetails element has no child elements, but it carries attributes specifying the OrderNumber, OrderDate, and OrderTotal, so its content model may be empty. The OrderItems element has only OrderItem elements as child elements, and the Order Item element carries attributes for SKUNumber, ItemNumber, Quantity, and ItemName. Add ItemCost and ItemPrice as child elements for OrderItem elements, and a ForOrder attribute to connect each OrderItem element to a specific OrderDetails element. These elements should be coded as follows:

```
<!ELEMENT OrderDetails EMPTY>
<!ATTLIST OrderDetails
    OrderNumber ID      #REQUIRED
    OrderDate   CDATA   #REQUIRED
    OrderTotal  CDATA   "0.00" >
<!ELEMENT OrderItems (OrderItem+)>
<!ELEMENT OrderItem (ItemCost,ItemPrice)>
<!ATTLIST OrderItem
    SKUNumber   CDATA       #REQUIRED
    ItemNumber  CDATA       #REQUIRED
    Quantity    CDATA       "0"
    ItemName    CDATA       #IMPLIED
    ForOrder    IDREF       #REQUIRED >
<!ELEMENT ItemCost (#PCDATA)>
<!ELEMENT ItemPrice (#PCDATA)>
```

Since the OrderDetails element has no content and no child elements, its content model designation is EMPTY. The *OrderNumber* attribute of the OrderDetails element is of the type ID, since each Order in the document must be unique, and of course this attribute is required. The *OrderDate* attribute is also required, but since there is no Date data type, the attribute must be made of character data (CDATA). The *OrderTotal* attribute must appear with at least a default value of 0.00 (but could be some other value), so only the default value is given. And remember that all values in attributes are produced as strings, even when they look just like numbers.

Note

In the content of elements, character data is any string of characters that does not contain the start-delimiter of any markup. In a CDATA section, character data is any string of characters not including the CDATA-section-close delimiter, the two closing brackets and greater-than sign:]] >.

The OrderItems element also has no text content, but it does have a single child element named OrderItem that can occur one or more times (every order should have at least one ordered item), and so this element is written inside parentheses followed by a plus sign.

The OrderItem element has no text content, but it has attributes and two child elements that must occur in a specific sequence, so its content model is CHILDREN. The two child elements each consist of parsed character data (PCDATA). All the attributes are types as CDATA except for the ForOrder attribute, whose type is IDREF. The value of this attribute would be set to the same value as the OrderNumber attribute found in the OrderDetails element for the Order element in which both reside, thereby linking all OrderItem elements to their proper OrderDetails element, and from there (by virtue of the fact that only one OrderDetails element may occur for a given Order element) to the appropriate Order element in the document. The ItemName default value is set as #IMPLIED because there may be items without formal names (identified by item number only), and the Quantity attribute default value is set to zero but may take other values. All other attributes are #REQUIRED. The entire DTD, together, should look like this:

```
<!-- Customer version 1.0 DTD
This DTD is an example for the book
 XML Beginner's Guide, and builds a
 customers and orders management system.
Copyright Dave Mercer 2001, 2002
-->
<!ELEMENT Customers ANY>
<!ELEMENT Customer (#PCDATA | Orders+ )>
<!ATTLIST Customer
   customerid          ID          #REQUIRED
```

```
   phone               CDATA          #IMPLIED
   email               CDATA          #REQUIRED
   fulladdress         CDATA          #IMPLIED >
<!ELEMENT Orders (Order*)>
<!ELEMENT Order (OrderDetails, OrderItems)>
<!ELEMENT OrderDetails EMPTY>
<!ATTLIST OrderDetails
   OrderNumber         ID             #REQUIRED
   OrderDate           CDATA          #REQUIRED
   OrderTotal          CDATA          "0.00" >
<!ELEMENT OrderItems (OrderItem+)>
<!ELEMENT OrderItem (ItemCost,ItemPrice)>
<!ATTLIST OrderItem
   SKUNumber           CDATA          #REQUIRED
   ItemNumber          CDATA          #REQUIRED
   Quantity            CDATA          "0"
   ItemName            CDATA          #IMPLIED
   ForOrder            IDREF          #REQUIRED>
<!ELEMENT ItemCost (#PCDATA)>
<!ELEMENT ItemPrice (#PCDATA)>
```

When this DTD is viewed in XML Spy, it looks like this:

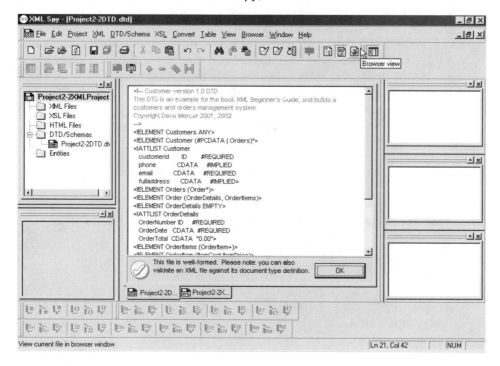

9. Now that you've got a valid DTD to work with, you can write an XML document and validate the XML document against the DTD. Practice writing XML code by hand in Notepad, and you can check our work afterward with XML Spy. In Notepad, choose File | New to open a new file. Choose File | Save As to save it in the same folder as the DTD. Name your XML document **Project2-2XMLDoc.xml**.

10. The first line of code for your XML document is the version line, like so:

```
<?xml version="1.0" encoding="UTF-8"?>
```

This, of course, states that your XML document conforms to XML version 1.0 and is encoded using UTF-8 character encoding.

11. The next line will be an internal comment stating the purpose of this XML document, as follows:

```
<!--This document tracks Customers and their orders-->
```

12. The next line in the document is the DOCTYPE statement. It includes a SYSTEM reference showing where on the system the DTD may be found, as well as a PUBLIC reference to the DTD on a Web site, like so:

```
<!DOCTYPE Customers PUBLIC "Project2-2DTD.dtd"
"http://www.e4free.com/XMLBeginnersGuide/Module02/
Project2-2DTD/Project2-2DTD.dtd">
```

This DOCTYPE declaration uses the PUBLIC keyword to denote the use of both an internally recognized name for finding the DTD and a fully qualified URL for finding the DTD.

13. The next line in the document begins the root element named Customers, and it also has a little text data describing the contents of the element, as shown here:

```
<Customers>Here are our customers
```

14. Next begin a single Customer element and add text data for the customer's name and attributes for other data associated with the customer:

```
<Customer customerid="cid111" email=jd@e4free.com
 fulladdress="123 MyStreet MyCity, MyState, 90000">
John Doe
```

As usual, the Customer element starts with the name of the element, and the attributes associated with the element each appear as name-value pairs separated by a white space. Notice that the customer number must start with a letter, not a number, because ID attribute values must conform to the rules for XML names. This is a good fact to remember if using XML documents in conjunction with relational databases, which allow the use of numbers as primary keys (which, in turn, are often used for ID numbering schemes).

The *email* and *fulladdress* attributes are merely strings of character data, and in a real-life document, you would probably want to separate the address components into their own attributes, such as street, city, state, and zip. Following everything else is a short string of PCDATA for the name of the customer. Again, in a real-life document, you would probably want to give the first, middle, and last names their own elements, so that it would be easier to set up searches down the road.

15. The next few lines start the Orders element and proceed to include child elements called Orders, and an OrderDetails child element in the Order element. The Orders element is just a container for Orders and therefore requires no content of its own, except for individual Order elements. The Order element is just a container for OrderDetails, which holds data and elements peculiar to a single Order. The OrderDetails element is included as an element because your finished document might end up including another section, so you break out the Order Details into their own element rather than having this data be attributes of the Order element, or individual child elements of the Order element.

```
<Orders>
<Order>
<OrderDetails OrderNumber="onid111"
 OrderDate="1/12/01" OrderTotal="0.00"/>
```

Notice that the OrderDetails element, because it is EMPTY and has no content, is closed using the slash within the starting tag; therefore, it requires no ending tag.

16. The next lines of the document begin the OrderItems and OrderItem elements. Once again, the OrderItems element is just a container for the OrderItem elements, and the only content of the OrderItem element is the two child elements ItemCost and ItemPrice, as shown here:

```
<OrderItems>
<OrderItem SKUNumber="1212"
 ItemNumber="1212-1" ForOrder="onid111">
```

```
<ItemCost>500</ItemCost>
<ItemPrice>1500</ItemPrice>
</OrderItem>
</OrderItems>
</Order>
</Orders>
</Customer>
```

This order contains only one order item; in many cases, an order would include quite a few item lines. Note that each order item is linked back to the correct order by the IDREF type attribute *ForOrder*. Also, the *ItemCost* and *ItemPrice* attributes do contain what look like numbers, but they are actually PCDATA strings, so they would have to be converted for processing as actual dollar values. The last five lines simply close off the OrderItem, OrderItems, Order, Orders, and Customer elements using the appropriate ending tags.

17. The next set of elements and attributes in the document repeats the process for a new customer and a new order, and ends with the closing tag for the entire document </Customers>:

```
<Customer customerid="cid222"
 email=js@e4free.com
 fulladdress="234 Your Street,
 Your City, YourState, 90000">Jane Smith
<Orders>
<Order>
<OrderDetails OrderNumber="onid222"
 OrderDate="1/12/01"/>
<OrderItems>
<OrderItem SKUNumber="2121" ItemNumber="2121-2"
 ForOrder="onid222">
<ItemCost>200</ItemCost>
<ItemPrice>1200</ItemPrice>
</OrderItem>
</OrderItems>
</Order>
</Orders>
</Customer>
</Customers>
```

18. To see what you've done, you can view the XML document in Internet Explorer, because IE 5.0 and above has a built-in XML parser. However, even though the document parses just fine, Internet Explorer displays the document as XML elements rather than a finished Web page because you haven't included any transformations of style information. No worries: we'll come to that in Module 11. In the meantime, the following illustration shows what the document looks like in Internet Explorer.

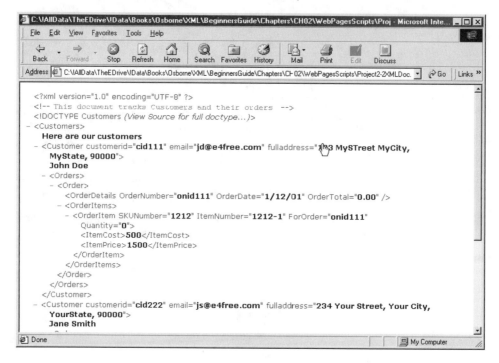

Ask the Expert

Question: Please explain a little more about internal and external DTDs, and how to reference them from an XML document.

Answer: Document Type Definitions (DTDs) are one of the ways the structure and allowed components (elements, attributes, and so forth) of a particular XML document are defined. The other way is with an XML schema.

Internal DTDs are written directly into the XML document as part of the DOCTYPE declaration. External DTDs are written as a separate file, referenced from the XML document in the DOCTYPE declaration.

XML documents can use internal and external DTDs at the same time and can even reference multiple external DTDs if necessary. The components written into the internal DTD take precedence over those referenced in an external DTD, whenever the names are the same.

Referencing an internal DTD is done simply by including it in the DOCTYPE declaration. Referencing an external DTD is done by using the term *SYSTEM* or *PUBLIC* in the DOCTYPE declaration, followed by the reference to the DTD. If SYSTEM is used, it is followed by a URL leading to the DTD. If PUBLIC is used, it is followed by a string with the internally recognized name for the DTD, and that is followed by a URL leading to the DTD. The internally recognized name can be any type of identifier that the computer may understand, even proprietary naming schemes. Of course, if a proprietary naming scheme is used, only machines running under that naming scheme will understand how to find the DTD with that name. That's why the URL is also used—for backup.

Question: Although the syntax for DTDs seems fairly straightforward, I'm a bit confused about when and why I would want to specify child elements and attributes, and how and when they may appear in an XML document. Are there any good guidelines or rules of thumb to follow?

Answer: It's pretty easy to create elements, child elements, and attributes, but how do you know when to create each one? There are no hard-and-fast rules because the elements and attributes you create depend on what you're trying to track and what problems you're trying to solve with your tracking system.

Keep in mind that the purpose of XML is to allow you to create elements and attributes representing real things, such as people, customers, buildings, orders, and so forth. Unlike HTML, in which a table displaying records from a database relies on text labels to indicate the meaning of each field in the record, XML applies meaning to the elements holding the data. Because the meaning of an element (derived from the structure you put into the DTD or schema) is coded into its tags, other machines reading the XML document can make assumptions about data, based on the tags in which it is enclosed.

So, for example, it's pretty obvious what an element named "Customer" refers to. Elements should represent real things that must be tracked, preferably in terms that most everyone will implicitly understand. The next thing to keep in mind is that, just as there might be a Customers table with individual Customer records in a database, in XML you should create container elements (such as the Customers element in our document) to contain multiple individual elements (such as the Customer) for any given thing. Just remember, if there will be more than one of a particular element, create a container element for it.

And think of child elements this way: a customer may have several orders, and an order may have several order items in it. The many side of the relationship is probably a child of the one side. We'll cover the whole process of defining relationships in Modules 3, 9, and 10.

The last area is somewhat more difficult to provide general rules: When is it appropriate to use text data for providing information, versus an attribute or a child element? The problem is that each one can conceivably do the job, so which one is appropriate? For example, in the Customer element, we have chosen to define the name of the customer as text data between the starting and ending Customer tags. At the same time, we have chosen to define the address of the customer as an attribute. And in the OrderItem element, we have chosen to define the ItemCost and ItemPrice as child elements of the OrderItem. Which way is best? Here are some rules that should help.

- An *attribute* is appropriate when only one piece of data is used. If the same piece of data may occur more than once for a single element, it must be written as child elements because the attribute cannot appear more than once for a given element (an element cannot contain two attributes with the same name).

- The data between the starting and ending tags of an element is undefined except for the tags that enclose it. For example, how would you program an application to recognize that the data between the starting and ending Customer tags is a name? If it were enclosed in its own tags (<Name> and </Name>) that would be easy, but if you had to program a rule that said the data between the Customer tags was the customer's name, that would be difficult and would defeat the purpose of using XML in the first place (we did it mainly to provide more examples of how PCDATA fits into the DTD, not because it's a good structure to use in all cases).

☑ *Mastery Check*

1. What is an XML vocabulary?

    A. A markup language

    B. A set of terms applicable to a particular industry

    C. Terms applicable to a particular industry that have been codified as an XML DTD or schema

    D. All of the above

2. What are XML names, how are they defined, and what restrictions are placed upon them?

    A. Names for elements, written from the ASCII character set, no restrictions

    B. Names for XML components, written from the ASCII character set, no restrictions

    C. Names for XML components such as elements and attributes, written from the ASCII character set, may not start with uppercase or lowercase *xml* or digits

    D. None of the above

3. What is a content model?

4. What is the root of an XML document called? Is this the same as the *root element*? What does *root* mean, and what does it mean to be the *root element* of an XML document?

5. What would the DOCTYPE declaration look like for an XML document with an internal DTD defining a root element named "Car" in which any content can appear?

    A. `<!DOCTYPE Car [<!ELEMENT Car ANY>] >`

    B. `<!DOCTYPE [<!ELEMENT Car ANY>] >`

    C. `<!DOCTYPE Car ANY>`

    D. None of the above

    E. Any of the above

✓ Mastery Check

6. What is the purpose of the attribute types ID, IDREF, and IDREFS?

A. ID is suitable for using with an element where the element must be unique across the entire document. IDREF makes a single reference from one element to another with an ID attribute of the same name. IDREFS makes a reference to multiple other elements via ID attribute names in a single element.

B. ID, IDREF, and IDREFS attributes allow linking from one element to another, allowing the formation of relationships from one element to another, when the elements are not in a parent-child relationship.

C. ID, IDREF, and IDREFS are special attribute names that may be used only once in a given document.

D. All of the above.

E. A and B above.

F. None of the above.

7. What elements might you use to build an XML DTD for tracking recipes within a cookbook?

8. What attributes might be appropriate for some of the elements you've created in question 7?

9. What symbol would be used in a DTD to allow a particular element to appear within another element one or more times?

A. No symbol is required; all elements appear one or more times unless otherwise specified.

B. The asterisk (*).

C. The plus sign (+).

D. None of the above.

2

☑ *Mastery Check*

10. What term, when included as part of an ATTLIST attribute declaration, makes it so an attribute is optional?

   A. #IMPLIED

   B. #REQUIRED

   C. #FIXED

   D. None of the above

11. What is a CDATA section?

   A. Any area in an XML document in which character data appears

   B. A special area in a document delimited by CDATA delimiters, in which character data that is not part of the allowed Unicode characters may appear

   C. A special area where scripting content may appear and be passed through without being parsed

   D. None of the above

12. What is meant by the CDATA data type in a DTD, as applied to an attribute?

   A. Character data

   B. Scripting content

   C. Unparsed character data

   D. None of the above

13. What is a notation, and what form does it take?

   A. It's an identifier of the type of content contained in unparsed character data, and it takes the form *data type/specific type*. For example, a set of data that forms a JPEG image would have a notation *image/jpeg*.

   B. It's like a comment but refers to the author's notes about certain elements and attributes.

Mastery Check

C. A named XML document component referring to parsed character data.

D. None of the above

14. What is contained in the prolog of an XML document?

A. Nothing, because the prolog is optional

B. The epilog and the body of the document

C. The DOCTYPE declaration, comments, and processing instructions

D. None of the above

15. What attribute data type might be used to identify an element uniquely across an entire document?

A. The IDREF type

B. The ID type

C. The IDREFS type

D. None of the above

Module 3

XML Schema

The Goals of This Module

- Learn the differences between DTDs and schemas
- Learn about the various languages for creating XML schemas
- Explore data types
- Learn to create simple and complex types
- Learn the structure of XML schemas
- Create an XML schema
- Create an XML document based on an XML schema

As you are now aware, XML documents depend on a formally specified foundation such as a Document Type Definition (DTD). Whether the foundation is part of the document or is contained inside one or more external files or entities, the extensible nature of XML depends on components properly specified in a convenient format. While DTDs have been used extensively for this purpose, DTDs have limitations. The primary liability of DTDs is that they are written in a format called Extended Backus Naur Form (EBNF).

Module 2 covered writing DTDs in EBNF. Although EBNF is not all that easy to read or write, once you are familiar with it, it's not too bad. But by now you are probably thinking "Why not just write the foundation for an XML document in XML?" Good thinking!

XML stands for eXtensible Markup Language, so why can't there be a version of XML devoted to creating elements, attributes, entities, and so forth? There is: XML Schema. A number of languages use the XML format, and these languages are used to write XML schemas, the subject of this module.

The benefits of writing XML schemas over using DTDs written in EBNF are manifold: The processor has to understand only XML. The schema can be navigated and manipulated programmatically, like an XML document. And XML schemas can provide much better support for namespaces, extensibility, data types, and inheritance (these subjects are covered in detail later in this module and in Module 4). All these benefits were desired early on in the creation of XML, and now quite a few languages can be used for writing XML schemas, some of which were noted in Module 1.

XML Schema and Information Processing

The term *schema* refers to the scheme by which information is organized—in this case, in the foundation for your XML documents. You can think of the schema as a written representation of the model followed by your data (the data model). We'll spend more time working with data models in Modules 9 and 10, but for now let's take a look at some of the fundamentals.

Why is it important to design a schema properly? Not only do you want to make sure you have all the elements and attributes you need in place (so you can write XML documents with them), you also want to make sure that the relationships between your elements and attributes are properly defined. For example, think of a single record in a table in a database. If the table is named Customers, you would probably assume that each record in the table corresponds to a single customer, and each field in the record contains a piece of information pertaining directly to that customer.

But wait! Tell me where in the database it is explicitly specified that the FirstName field in the Customers table contains the first name for the customer tracked in that record. As you can see, some of the relationship information contained in a database (and in many other data storage systems) is not explicitly specified but is inherent in the structure of the information storage system.

XML schemas work the same way. Part of the information contained in an XML schema is not explicit; it is inherent in the structure, and you are the author of that structure. You must learn to structure your data so that it makes sense, even when the structure is not defined explicitly.

You should also keep in mind that your XML schemas and documents might be used by both *people* and *machines*. Try to make your schemas and documents understandable to people while at the same time efficient for machines to process. Poor schema design makes it harder on everyone (including machines).

1-Minute Drill

- DTDs are written in what format?
- How is it understood that a table named Employees contains information in each record about a single employee?

One of the most powerful aspects of XML is its ability to model data from many sources, including relational databases (where a great deal of the data that runs the world is stored). Understanding how to structure XML schemas consists partly of learning how to write them and partly of learning basic data modeling, so we've broken it down into several modules. In this module, you'll learn the basics of XML schemas, and in Modules 9 and 10, you'll read about data modeling and XML databases.

- DTDs are written in Extended Backus Naur Form (EBNF).
- This is implicit in the design of databases, rather than explicitly stated.

XML Schema Languages

Before we get started with XML schemas, let's review some of the proposals for the languages that are used to create schemas. Note that the general problem of defining data and content constraints is certainly not a new one, and many coding schemes, both proprietary and open, are in existence today. Next we'll review a few that have been submitted to the World Wide Web Consortium (W3C), some of which are progressing toward final recommendation status:

- **XML-Data**   XML-Data, at the W3C, has the status of Note as of January 5, 1998. It is written in an XML vocabulary so the Document Object Model (DOM) can be used to navigate schemas made with XML-Data, and it supports data types and allowable value constraints.

- **Data Definition Markup Language (DDML)**   DDML, at the W3C, has the status of Note as of January 19, 1999. It is written in XML, provides namespace support, and can be transformed into DTDs as necessary. It is simple and contains no support for data types.

- **Document Content Description (DCD)**   DCD, at the W3C, has the status of Submission as of July 31, 1998. It may be written in XML, and its primary functions are to encode constraints on data types, allow inheritance, and otherwise provide rules concerning structure and content for XML documents in ways DTDs can't.

- **Schema for Object-Oriented XML (SOX)**   SOX, at the W3C, has the status of Note as of July 30, 1999. It is written in XML and supports data types, inheritance, and namespaces.

- **Resource Description Framework (RDF)**   RDF, at the W3C, is composed of a Model and Syntax Recommendation (February 22, 1999) and a Schema Candidate Recommendation (March 27, 2000). The Model and Syntax Recommendation provides for objects and properties, while the Schema Candidate Recommendation expresses relationships between objects. This scheme is complex and can be used to describe and process a wide variety of metadata (data about data), not just database-type metadata.

- **XML Schema**   XML Schema, at the W3C, is a Candidate Recommendation as of October 24, 2000, composed of Part 0, a Primer; Part 1, Structures; and Part 2, Datatypes. It is written in XML, provides support for primitive and complex data types, places constraints on allowable values, and works with namespaces. The remainder of Module 3 covers using XML Schema to build foundations for XML documents.

3

XML Schema

Schemas written using the XML Schema recommendation are technically XML documents connected to an XML application (XML Schema) made from an XML vocabulary particularly suited to the definition of elements, attributes, and so forth. Like DTDs, XML schemas declare and define elements and attributes. However, to accommodate the more advanced structures and relationships, XML schemas also make use of a few other components, which are discussed in the following sections.

Schema Components

The schema is considered a component, and yet it is, in effect, a container for its components, which include elements, attributes, simple and complex data types, attribute group and model group definitions, notation declarations, and annotations. The declaration of the schema component might take this form:

```
<xsd:schema
     xmlns:xsd="http://www.w3.org/2000/10/XMLSchema"
     targetNamespace="http://www.e4free/com/Module3/schema1"
     version="1.0">
The rest of the schema goes here
</xsd:schema>
```

By convention we use the prefix *xsd* to serve as the designator for the namespace of the XML Schema, and the target namespace serves as the designator for the schema we are building. It is necessary to include both, because the schema being built depends on the schema for XML Schema at the W3C Web site. Whenever we use the elements, attributes, data types, and so forth that are built into the XML Schema recommendation, we must make this connection. However, for simplicity, we may not always show the designator in our code examples.

Other schemas may also be used, via the include and import elements, as part of the schema under construction. The include element has an attribute named *schemaLocation* that references the other schema to include (as a URI), and the import element has the attributes *namespace* and *schemaLocation* that reference the namespace and location of the schema to be imported.

Element Declarations

Elements are the main things to be worked with in an XML document, and they are created in an XML schema by declaring them with an element declaration.

In the XML Schema, an element is declared using the <element /> element, as shown here:

```
<element name="Customer" type="string"/>
```

It is interesting to note that not only did we name the element (this name becomes the name of the element in our eventual XML document) in this example, we also gave it a specific data type (string). And we have the ability to create elements composed of several other elements (each with its own data types), thus enabling us to build more complex elements. (Complex elements and data types are discussed in more detail later in this module.)

Attribute Declarations

Elements often must have attributes associated with them, and of course, XML Schema provides a way to do just that. The <attribute /> element creates attributes that can have both a name and a data type, just like elements. Attributes declared like this can also include the cardinality attributes *minOccurs* and *maxOccurs*, specifying whether and how often an attribute must appear in an element, and the *default* and *fixed* attributes, specifying default values and the circumstances in which they apply. XML schema attributes are coded like this:

```
<attribute name="ssn" type="string" minOccurs="1">
```

This code example declares an attribute with a name of "*ssn*", type of "string", that must occur at least once in any element it is associated with. Attributes are associated with elements in a number of ways in XML Schema, such as including them as child elements and referencing them by name.

1-Minute Drill

● What is the function of the type declaration in an element or attribute declaration?

● How does the *minOccurs* attribute of the attribute element affect that attribute in an XML document?

● The type declaration sets an element or attribute to a specific data type.
● The *minOccurs* attribute specifies the minimum number of occurrences for an attribute within an element in an XML document.

3

Type Definitions
Each element and attribute in an XML document may be specified as having a simple or complex data type with XML Schema. For a more detailed discussion of data types, see the section "XML Schema Data Types," later in this module. For now, let's stick with the basics of these two kinds of data types as they relate to the construction of elements and attributes.

Simple Type Definitions   Simple type definitions are based on primitive data types, and they apply to attribute values and element content (for elements with no child elements). They are written using the <simpleType> element (defined in the DTD for schemas in XML Schema Part 2: Datatypes), and they include a reference to their base data type. Primitive data types are discussed later in the section "XML Schema Data Types." The primitive data type "string" is shown in this example for a simple type definition for a part number, in which part numbers are restricted to a total of 12 characters in a string:

```
<simpleType name="PartNumber">
<restriction base="string">
<length value="12" fixed="true"/>
</restriction>
</simpleType>
```

As you can see, the base (or primitive) data type is "string," and this simple type is a restriction of that data type, meaning the values the string data type may take are restricted to a subset of the values for "string" (only strings having 12 characters). Notice that the restriction defines the primitive data type from which the new type is derived, and within the restriction, the properties of the new data type are set with the "length" facet.

Note

While elements may have simple or complex data types, attributes may have only simple data types. The difference between simple and complex data types is that complex data types contain other elements, not just content.

Facets are discussed in more detail in the section "XML Schema Data Types"; for now, think of facets as properties of a data type. In the preceding code, the properties for the new data type are set as a length of 12 characters, and that length is fixed, so that no part numbers can be strings of more or less than 12 characters.

Complex Type Definitions   Complex type definitions use element declarations, attribute declarations, and simple type definitions to assemble complex data types containing content as well as other elements and attributes. For example, if you wish to define a complex type for street address, you might do the following:

```
<complexType name="StreetAddress">
<sequence>
<element name="StreetNumber" type="string" minOccurs="1" maxOccurs="1">
<element name="StreetName" type="string" minOccurs="1" maxOccurs="1">
<element name="Suite" type="string" minOccurs="0" maxOccurs="1">
</sequence>
<attribute name="SideOfStreet">
<simpleType>
<restriction base="string">
<enumeration value="North"/>
<enumeration value="South"/>
<enumeration value="East"/>
<enumeration value="West"/>
</restriction>
</simpleType>
</attribute>
</complexType>
```

In this example, a complex data type is constructed for street addresses, consisting of three elements: street number, street name, and suite, plus an attribute named *SideOfStreet* for specifying the side of the street a particular address is on. Notice in the attribute declaration that a simpleType data type is constructed containing enumeration elements, each of which becomes part of an enumerated list of values that the attribute may assume. The enumeration elements are based upon a restriction of the built-in primitive data type "string", meaning the data for each value is a subset of all strings—namely just the strings "North", "South", "East", and "West".

Another property of a complex type definition is that the elements declared must appear in a specific order (sequence). The sequence element forces any use of this data type to be interpreted as a sequence of street number, street name, and suite, with only one occurrence of street number, one occurrence of street name, and zero to one occurrences of suite. Each element has a data type of "string" (one of the built-in primitive types).

┤Note

Built-in simpleType and complexType types, as well as other types, are defined in the XML Schema for Datatype Definitions in XML Schema Part 2: Datatypes. To use these elements when defining types, you should be sure to use the appropriate namespace designation (more on how namespaces are defined and designated in Module 4).

3

XML Schema Data Types

Module 2 began a discussion of data types (in the section "XML Strings and Character Data"), and here we'll continue and expand upon that discussion, because XML Schema provides elaborate ways to define and extend or restrict data types. Data types are important to applications because an application must know the data type of a given stream of bytes to process it properly. Data types range from quite simple, primitive data types to quite complex data types.

In XML 1.0, a number of simple data types are presented, such as XML names and XML IDs. Although they are strings, they're not the set of all strings; rather they're only a subset of all strings. This concept of using basic data types such as strings and restricting or extending them is central to the way XML schemas enable authors to produce new data types.

The Type Definition Hierarchy

As with most other XML-related applications, XML Schema organizes data types into a tree (hierarchy). A distinguished ur-type definition named anyType is at the top of the Type Definition hierarchy of data types in the XML Schema specification. The *ur-type* is an overall type that may include any types with the least restrictions possible, and it is the default type when no data type is specified. The anyType definition may be of any type or types and is the root of the hierarchy. The ur-type named anySimpleType is at the top of the hierarchy for simple types and is said to be a restriction of the ur-type named anyType.

A *restriction* on a type means that the resulting data type may include only a subset of the possible values of the data type from which the restricted data type is derived. Thus, a data type that includes only a subset of the values allowed in a base data type is said to be a *restriction*. There can also be an *extension* to a data type, which occurs when element or attribute content may be allowed in additional to what is allowed in the data type from which the extended data type is derived. Thus, a data type that includes a superset of the values allowed in a base data type is said to be an *extension*. Figure 3-1 shows the hierarchy of types built into XML Schema Part 2: Datatypes.

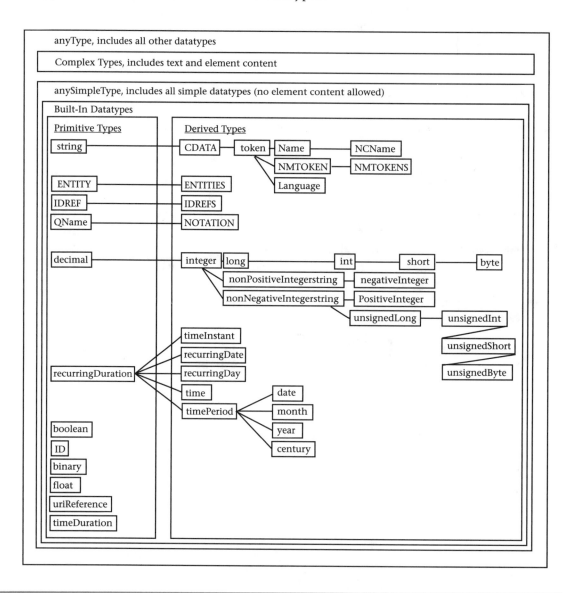

Figure 3-1   The type hierarchy

3

Data Type Components

XML Schema Part 2: Datatypes defines a data type as consisting of three parts: a set of values, a set of *lexical* references to those values, and a set of facets modifying the values or lexical references. For example, the Boolean data type has the *value space* for 0 or 1, on or off, yes or no, true or false values. The *lexical space* for the Boolean data type is simply true and false. The constraining facets are pattern and white space, meaning that the values can be restricted to those that match a particular pattern, and the white space (if any) in the values must be treated a particular way.

Value Spaces

Value spaces for data types are rigorously defined, so that there is no question as to what values are acceptable for a given data type. Lexical representations of these values simply offer a means of specifying a literal value for an actual value. For example, if the actual value for a Boolean is the number 1 (representing yes, on, or true), the only legal literal value is true (according to the specification). And the constraining facets enable authors to modify further the set of values for a data type. For example, the string data type consists of all strings, but setting its length facet to 12 restricts the data type to 12 or less characters.

Value spaces always have the property of *cardinality*, meaning they may be finite (a determinable amount of values) or infinite (an undeterminable amount of values). They also support the notion of *equality*, meaning that there is a way of determining what values in the value space are equivalent to other values in the value space, and they may have an order in which values in them can be sorted.

Data Type Facets

Data types can have two types of facets, fundamental and constraining. *Fundamental* facets are a natural part of a data type and cannot be avoided—such as equality, order, bounds, cardinality, and whether the values are numeric. For example, it can be said that a data type is either numeric or non-numeric, but this is not a restriction that can be omitted. A data type either is or is not numeric.

On the other hand, *constraining* (or nonfundamental) facets can be applied or omitted; if omitted, they place no restriction on the data type. For example, if the length facet is set for a string, the string values must conform to the length setting; however, if there is no length setting, the string values may take any length or none. Among the facets in the specification are these:

- **Length** For strings, length is the number of characters; for lists, the number of items in a list; and for binary values, the number of octets in a sequence of bits.

- **minLength and maxLength** The number of units of length set to a minimum or maximum.

- **Pattern** A pattern matching the construction of a regular expression, like a filter on the allowable values.

- **Enumeration** A set of allowable values that may or may not have an order relationship.

- **whiteSpace** Directs the handling of white space characters (such as tab and space) in the values of a data type. Settings include preserve, replace, and collapse (collapse removes certain white spaces).

- **maxInclusive, minInclusive, maxExclusive, and minExclusive** These facets can be used to set the upper and lower bounds for values of a data type, either inside or outside the bounds.

- **Precision** The number of digits allowed in numbers whose data type is decimal.

- **Scale** The number of digits in the fractional part of a decimal number.

- **Encoding** The type of encoding (hex or Base64) for a binary stream.

- **Duration and period** These two facets both refer to a length of time, either the duration of a specified amount of time or the period between durations (or between particular instants of time).

Categorizing Data Types

The XML Schema recommendation categorizes data types in a number of ways. The first categorization mentioned is the separation of data types into atomic, list, and union data types. the second categorization mentioned is the separation of data types into primitive and derived.

- **Atomic data types** The smallest unit of data type. The term *atomic* means that the type of the data type cannot be subdivided into other

3

data types. For example, a string data type is composed of the type string only—not a combination of string, decimal, Boolean, and so forth.

● **List data type**   A list of string (atomic) data type values. For example, a derived data type called PackageSize may be a simpleType data type with three string values enumerated for it, such as "Small", "Medium", and "Large". The enumerated strings form a restriction of the string data type.

● **Union data type**   Like a list but composed of several different data types, each of which may have their own facets applied. The data types included are called memberTypes, and the order in which they are written must be the order in which the values occur. For example, in a data type named "Weight", the number of units might have a data type of decimal and come first while the unit type (pounds, kilos, and so forth) may have a data type of string and come second.

The second way the XML Schema recommendation categorizes data types is into primitive and derived data types.

● **Primitive data types**   Basic, well-known data types that cannot be defined using other data types. Note that atomic data types can be either primitive or derived; the terms *atomic* and *primitive* are not interchangeable. Essentially, a primitive data type represents every value that a particular data type could assume, while an atomic data type may be equivalent to a primitive data type or may represent just a subset of the values of a primitive data type.

● **Derived data types**   Data Types created from other data types. They may be list or union data types, or atomic data types that have had some restrictions or extensions applied.

Built-in Primitive and Derived Data Types

The specification provides for a broad array of built-in data types, some of which are primitive and some of which are derived. The purpose of building in these data types is to simplify the construction of XML schemas so that every type does not need to be formed from scratch. Of course, users may define any number of new data types from the primitive or derived data types supplied.

XML Schema Part 2: Datatypes lists quite a few built-in data types, which are listed in the following tables based on the fundamental data type from which they are derived. Table 3-1 lists primitive built-in data types, and Table 3-2 lists built-in derived data types.

Primitive Data Types

The first set of built-in primitive data types we'll examine are based on the string data type, as restricted by the definitions that follow them in Table 3-1.

String Data Type	Definition
string	A number of Unicode characters whose length is finite. The constraining facets are length, minLength, maxLength, pattern, enumeration, and whiteSpace. The built-in CDATA data type is derived from string.
uriReference	A string that makes an absolute or relative URI reference, essentially equivalent to a URL. The constraining facets are length, minLength, maxLength, pattern, enumeration, and whiteSpace.
ID	The same as the attribute type ID from XML 1.0. ID values are scoped to the XML document in which they are used, meaning that they must be unique within that document. To be compatible, ID data types should be used only for attributes. The constraining facets are length, minLength, maxLength, pattern, enumeration, whiteSpace, maxInclusive, maxExclusive, minInclusive, and minExclusive.
IDREF	The same as the IDREF attribute type from XML 1.0 and is equivalent to a name, so that it can be used to reference an ID somewhere in a document. To be compatible, IDREF data types should be used only for attributes. The constraining facets are length, minLength, maxLength, pattern, enumeration, whiteSpace, maxInclusive, maxExclusive, minInclusive, and minExclusive. The built-in data type IDREFS is derived from IDREF.
ENTITY	The same as the ENTITY attribute type from XML 1.0. It is a reference (by name) to an unparsed entity, and to be compatible, ENTITY data types should be used only for attributes. The constraining facets are length, minLength, maxLength, pattern, enumeration, whiteSpace, maxInclusive, maxExclusive, minInclusive, and minExclusive. The built-in data type ENTITIES is derived from ENTITY.

Table 3-1　Built-in Primitive Data Types

3

String Data Type	Definition
QName	Stands for qualified name; represents a namespace name and a local name for elements, attributes, and so forth. (Namespaces and qualified names are covered in Module 4.) The constraining facets are length, minLength, maxLength, pattern, enumeration, whiteSpace, maxInclusive, maxExclusive, minInclusive, and minExclusive. The built-in data type NOTATION is derived from QName.
Logical Data Type	
Boolean	The mathematical concept of a 1 or 0, off or on, yes or no value. The constraining facets are pattern and whiteSpace. Its values may be named "true" and "false".
Numeric Data Type	
Float and Double	A single-precision, 32-bit, floating-point number of a given size that allows decimal points. Note that float and double may not be accurate enough for detailed financial calculations. The constraining facets are pattern, enumeration, whiteSpace, maxInclusive, maxExclusive, minInclusive, and minExclusive. Double is a number of 64-bits rather than 32.
Decimal	A decimal number that may contain an arbitrary number of digits (processors must support at least 18). The constraining facets are precision, scale, pattern, whiteSpace, enumeration, maxInclusive, maxExclusive, minInclusive, and minExclusive. The built-in type integer is derived from decimal.
Encoding Data Type	
Binary	The data type used to represent binary data. The constraining facets are encoding, length, minLength, maxLength, pattern, enumeration, and whiteSpace. It must only be used as a derived type, and the character encoding must be specified.

Table 3-1   Built-in Primitive Data Types (*continued*)

Date and Time Data Types

TimeDuration	A coded representation of a time period such as one month. The coded period starts with a *P* and then in sequence numbers and letters representing the amount of years, months, days, hours, minutes, and seconds in the duration. For example, *P2Y8M3D* means a duration of two years, eight months, and three days. The constraining facets are pattern, enumeration, whiteSpace, maxInclusive, maxExclusive, minInclusive, and minExclusive.
RecurringDuration	A duration of time combined with information about how frequently it recurs and the time between occurrences (duration and period), in the form *CCYY-MM-DD-hh.mm.ss.ssss* (for centuries, years, months, days, hours, minutes, seconds, and decimal fractions of seconds). The constraining facets are duration, period, pattern, enumeration, whiteSpace, maxInclusive, maxExclusive, minInclusive, and minExclusive. Duration and period must be specified when this data type is used. This primitive type can be used only as a derived type, not directly in a schema. The built-in data types timeInstant, time, timePeriod, recurringDate, and recurringDay are derived from this type.

Table 3-1   Built-in Primitive Data Types *(continued)*

Built-in Derived Data Types

From built-in primitive data types, XML Schema derives more complex built-in data types, broken down in Table 3-2 by their basic data type. The first set of built-in derived data types are all related to the string primitive data type, or another primitive data type based on strings, such as ENTITY or IDREF.

String Data Type	Definition
CDATA	The base type of CDATA is string, and it consists of characters that have been normalized in terms of white space (white space characters have been removed as appropriate). The constraining facets are length, minLength, maxLength, pattern, enumeration, and whiteSpace. The built-in data type token is derived from CDATA.

Table 3-2   Built-in Derived Data Types

String Data Type	Definition
Token	CDATA strings that do not have leading or trailing spaces, more than one space at a time internally, and no line-feed or tab characters. The constraining facets are length, minLength, maxLength, pattern, enumeration, and whiteSpace. The built-in data types language, NMTOKEN and Name are derived from CDATA.
Language	Consists of all valid language identifiers, such as *en* for English. The constraining facets are length, minLength, maxLength, pattern, enumeration, and whiteSpace.
IDREFS	A list of IDREFs—the same as the attribute type IDREFS from XML 1.0. To be compatible, IDREFS data types should be used only for attributes. The constraining facets are length, minLength, maxLength, enumeration, and whiteSpace.
ENTITIES	A list of ENTITYs—the same as the attribute type ENTITIES from XML 1.0. To be compatible, ENTITIES data types should be used only for attributes. The constraining facets are length, minLength, maxLength, enumeration, and whiteSpace.
NMTOKEN	A tokenized string of characters that constitute a valid XML name—the same as the attribute type NMTOKEN from XML 1.0. To be compatible, NMTOKEN data types should be used only for attributes. The constraining facets are length, minLength, maxLength, enumeration, and whiteSpace. The data type NMTOKENS is derived from NMTOKEN.
NMTOKENS	A list of NMTOKENs—the same as the attribute type NMTOKENS from XML 1.0. To be compatible, NMTOKENS data types should be used only for attributes. The constraining facets are length, minLength, maxLength, enumeration, and whiteSpace. The data type NMTOKENS is derived from NMTOKEN.
Name	The same as the Name attribute type from XML 1.0. It is a string of characters that constitutes a valid XML name. The constraining facets are length, minLength, maxLength, enumeration, and whiteSpace. The data type NCNames is derived from Name.
NCName	The same as a Name but the colon is not allowed. (It is covered in Module 4.) The constraining facets are length, minLength, maxLength, pattern, enumeration, and whiteSpace.

Table 3-2 Built-in Derived Data Types (*continued*)

String Data Type	Definition
NOTATION	The same as the NOTATION attribute type in XML 1.0—a set of all names of notations found in the schema. To be compatible, NOTATION data types should be used only for attributes. The constraining facets are length, minLength, maxLength, pattern, enumeration, whiteSpace, maxInclusive, maxExclusive, minInclusive, and minExclusive.
Numeric Data Types	
integer	Derived from decimal by setting the scale facet to 0—there may be no decimal places. The constraining facets are precision, scale, pattern, whiteSpace, enumeration, maxInclusive, maxExclusive, minInclusive, and minExclusive. The built-in data types nonPositiveInteger, long, and nonNegativeInteger are derived from integer.
nonPositiveInteger	The maxInclusive facet is set to 0—there may be no numbers higher than zero. The constraining facets are the same as for integer. The built-in data type negativeInteger is derived from nonPositiveInteger.
nonNegativeInteger	The constraining facet minInclusive is set to 0.
negativeInteger	A number whose maxInclusive facet is set to –1, meaning there may be no numbers higher than –1. The constraining facets are the same as for integer.
positiveInteger	A number whose minInclusive facet is set to 1, meaning there can be no numbers less than 1.
Long	A number whose maxInclusive facet is set to 9223372036854775807 and whose minInclusive facet is set to minus 9223372036854775808. The constraining facets are the same as for integer. The built-in data type *int* is derived from long.
unsignedLong	A number whose maxInclusive facet is set to 18446744073709551615. The data type unsignedInt is derived from unsignedLong.
Int	A numeric data type whose maxInclusive facet is set to 2147483647 and whose minInclusive facet is set to minus 2147483648. The constraining facets are the same as for integer. The built-in data type int is derived from long.
unsignedInt	A numeric data type whose maxInclusive facet is set to 4294967295. The data type unsignedShort is derived from unsignedInt.
Short	A numeric data type whose maxInclusive facet is set to 32767 and whose minInclusive facet is set to minus 32768. The constraining facets are the same as for integer. The built-in data type byte is derived from short.
unsignedShort	A numeric data type whose maxInclusive facet is set to 65535. The data type unsignedByte is derived from unsignedShort.

Table 3-2 Built-in Derived Data Types (*continued*)

3

Numeric Data Types

Byte	A number whose maxInclusive facet is set to 127 and whose minInclusive facet is set to minus 128. The constraining facets are the same as for integer.
unsignedByte	A number whose maxInclusive facet is set to 255.

Date and Time Data Types

timeInstant	A specific moment in time, made by setting the duration and period facets of a recurringDuration to P0Y, meaning there is no duration and no period between durations. The constraining facets are duration, period, pattern, whiteSpace, enumeration, maxInclusive, maxExclusive, minInclusive, and minExclusive.
time	A specific moment in time that happens every day, such as 12:00 noon. It is made by setting (for a recurringDuration) the duration facet to P0Y and the period facet to P1D, meaning there is no duration and the period between recurrences is one day. The constraining facets are the same as for timeInstant.
timePeriod	A specific amount of time defined by a beginning and an ending time. It is made by setting (for a recurringDuration) the period facet to P0Y and the duration facet to the appropriate duration for the timePeriod, meaning there is only duration and no period (no recurrence). The constraining facets are the same as for timeInstant. The built-in data types date, month, year, and century are derived from timePeriod.
Date	A set of dates made with timePeriods whose duration facet has been set to P1D (one day), beginning at midnight and ending at midnight, following Gregorian calendar dates. The constraining facets are the same as for timeInstant.
Month	A set of months made with timePeriods whose duration facet has been set to P1M (one month), beginning at midnight the first day and ending at midnight of the last day, following Gregorian calendar months. The constraining facets are the same as for timeInstant.
Year	A set of years made with timePeriods whose duration facet has been set to P1Y (one month), beginning at midnight on the first day and ending at midnight on the last day, following Gregorian calendar years. The constraining facets are the same as for timeInstant.
Century	A set of groups of 100 years made with timePeriods whose duration facet has been set to P100Y (100 years), beginning at midnight of the first day and ending at midnight of the last day, following Gregorian calendar centuries. The constraining facets are the same as for timeInstant.

Table 3-2   Built-in Derived Data Types *(continued)*

Date and Time Data Types

recurringDate	A set of dates made with recurringDurations whose duration facet has been set to P1D (one day) and whose period facet has been set to P1Y (one year). The constraining facets are the same as for timeInstant.
recurringDay	A set of dates made with recurringDurations whose duration facet has been set to P1D (one day) and whose period facet has been set to P1M (one month). The constraining facets are the same as for timeInstant.

Table 3-2 Built-in Derived Data Types *(continued)*

Ask the Expert

Question: It seems like there are so many kinds of data types, and so many ways to create them. Can you boil it down a bit, so it makes more sense?

Answer: Sure. In XML 1.0, all data comes in the form of strings, and it is up to the application processing the document to decide what kind of data is represented. When XML Schema is used to create the components of an XML document, one of its most powerful features is its ability to create true data types.

Data types in XML Schema are broken down first into simple and complex types. Simple types contain only data, while complex types may contain data (as simple types) and elements (as complex types themselves).

The Type Definition Hierarchy is a useful way of picturing how data types are related. At the top is the anyType type. From the anyType type, all complex types and all simple types (represented by anySimpleType) are derived.

Twelve primitive data types are built-in to the XML Schema recommendation, including string, decimal, and binary. Primitive data types are simple types that are not derived from any other data type.

3

There are also 32 derived data types built-in to the XML Schema recommendation, including CDATA, integer, time, and ID. All derived data types are derived from either primitive data types or other derived data types.

Question: What is the relationship between data types, value spaces, lexical spaces, and facets?

Answer: A *data type*, when applied to an element or attribute, informs the processor as to the nature of the data referenced. For example, the characters *1999* might be a simple string when they are part of a street address. In that case, the processor would immediately know that the characters are a string and would store them and process them as such.

However, suppose the characters *1999* were a number. If *1999* represented the quantity of items being purchased, the processor would want to store them as a numerical *value* so they could be added to other quantities or multiplied by a price to get a total. That can't be done with strings (at least not without type conversion). And if the characters *1999* were the year part of a date, the processor would have an advantage knowing that up front as well.

The data type tells the processor what kind of data is being used. The *value space* of a data type represents all possible values the data type may have. For example, the value space of decimal is all decimal numbers. If we place some kind of restriction on the possible values of decimal, it is no longer a decimal data type; it is some other derived type. For example, if we restrict the value space to decimal numbers without decimal fractions, we have integers, one of the data types derived from decimal.

So how do we place restrictions on value spaces of data types? By setting the restrictions in what are called *facets*. A facet is a property of a data type. One of the properties of the data type decimal is *scale*, meaning the number of decimal places that are allowed. With no scale setting, there are no restrictions. By setting the scale of a decimal data type to 0, we are saying, in effect, that there may be *no* decimal fractions, and we are left with only integers.

Finally, *lexical values* are the literal values that denote the actual values a data type may assume. In many cases, lexical values are the same as actual values, but this is not always true. For example, what are the actual values of a Boolean data type? Are they yes/no, on/off, 1/0, or what? We know what it means, but a Boolean value needs a lexical value assigned, and the XML Schema recommendation assigns the lexical values true and false.

Proj3-1.zip

Project 3-1: Create an XML Schema

The XML Schema recommendation enables authors to build their own data types from the built-in primitive and derived data types available. In this project, you'll practice building a number of data types that will be used in finished XML documents, called *instance documents*.

The first step in building data types with an XML Schema for use in an XML document is to devise an understanding of the goals of each of your XML documents. Will your XML documents serve as order forms? Will they serve as information-gathering tools? Will they support complex data processing? Answering these types of questions will help you decide what elements and attributes need to be included, as well as what data types are required.

In this project, you are creating a schema for tracking expenses generated by your company's employees. The schema would include representations of the data you need to track employees and expenses. It might be helpful to categorize expenses as well, so they could be grouped logically for tax purposes. So you might end up with sets of data about employees, expense categories, and expense details. For this project, assume that you have appropriate expense categories documented elsewhere, so all you need to do is include an expense categories ID field.

Step-by-Step

1. Determine what information you need to track about employees and expenses, so that you can accurately determine which employees spent how much on what and when. Your goal is to track expenses, but you should track expenses for several specific purposes. Answer questions such as "How much has an employee spent in a given period?", or "Has an employee exceeded the amount originally allocated?", or "Is the employee spending money on items not allowed?"

3

2. Assume you need to know the employee's name, social security number, birth date, contact information (both at home and at the office), and so forth. Make a list of the items you wish to track for a given employee, followed by the data type you think that data item should be, like this (this is an abbreviated list for the example):

- **EmployeeID**   ID
- **FirstName**   string
- **LastName**   string
- **Title**   string
- **PhoneNumber**   string
- **Birthdate**   date
- **EmailAddress**   string
- **DateHired**   date

3. Now assume that you want to track the amounts of the expenses, the date each expenditure was made, a description of each expense, and what expense category each fell into.

Again, you can simply make a list of these data items, followed by their data type, like this:

- **ExpenseID**   ID
- **EmployeeID**   IDREF
- **ExpenseAmount**   decimal
- **DateOfExpense**   date
- **ExpenseCategoryID**   long

4. Now begin building the schema on which your document will depend. Start with the typical XML version and encoding, as with any XML document. Then connect the schema document with the XML Schema for schemas using a namespace designation (by convention *xsd*) and the appropriate URL, as shown here:

```
<?xml version="1.0" encoding="UTF-8"?>
<xsd:schema xmlns:xsd="http://www.w3.org/1999/XMLSchema">
```

5. In the next section, declare an element (as defined by the <element/> element in XML Schema) with the name "Table", and assign it a complex data type made up of elements named "EmployeeRow". Notice that the content model for the "Table" element is "elementOnly".

```
<xsd:element name="Table">
  <xsd:complexType content="elementOnly">
    <xsd:element name="EmployeeRow" type="EmployeeRecordType"/ minOccurs="1">
```

6. In the next section, finish the definition of the complex type for the element "Table" by declaring that it has attributes related to the instance of the document—of type uriReference, string, and string—named "xmlns:xsi", "xsi:noNamespaceSchemaLocation", and "xsi:schemaLocation", respectively. (Namespaces allow you to connect elements of the same name to their respective DTDs or schemas, if you use them in the same document. Namespaces will be explained in Module 4.)

```
    <xsd:attribute name="xmlns:xsi" type="xsd:uriReference" use="default"
value="http://www.w3.org/1999/XMLSchema-instance"/>
    <xsd:attribute name="xsi:noNamespaceSchemaLocation" type="xsd:string"/>
    <xsd:attribute name="xsi:schemaLocation" type="xsd:string"/>
  </xsd:complexType>
</xsd:element>
```

7. In the next section, create another complex type named "RecordType" whose content model is "elementOnly". It consists of a sequence of elements, each of which has a data type set (from among the built-in data types located at the URL referenced by the prefix *xsd*). Notice that these elements each represent a field that you want to track for Employees. After the elements have been declared, place the ending elements for sequence, complexType, and schema to finish the schema.

```
<xsd:complexType name="EmployeeRecordType" content="elementOnly">
  <xsd:sequence>
    <xsd:element name="EmployeeID" type="xsd:ID"/>
    <xsd:element name="SocialSecurityNumber" type="xsd:string"/>
    <xsd:element name="FirstName" type="xsd:string"/>
    <xsd:element name="LastName" type="xsd:string"/>
    <xsd:element name="Title" type="xsd:string"/>
    <xsd:element name="EmailName" type="xsd:string"/>
    <xsd:element name="Extension" type="xsd:byte"/>
    <xsd:element name="Address" type="xsd:string"/>
    <xsd:element name="City" type="xsd:string"/>
    <xsd:element name="StateOrProvince" type="xsd:string"/>
    <xsd:element name="PostalCode" type="xsd:string"/>
    <xsd:element name="Country" type="xsd:string"/>
    <xsd:element name="HomePhone" type="xsd:string"/>
    <xsd:element name="WorkPhone" type="xsd:string"/>
    <xsd:element name="Birthdate" type="xsd:date"/>
    <xsd:element name="DateHired" type="xsd:date"/>
```

```
    <xsd:element name="Notes" type="xsd:string"/>
</xsd:sequence>
 </xsd:complexType>
</xsd:schema>
```

8. For expenses, you could include another element named "ExpenseRow", which has the data type "ExpenseRecordType". This new data type consists of elements such as "ExpenseID", "ExpenseAmount", "ExpenseDate", and "ExpenseCategoryID".

```
<xsd:element name="ExpenseRow" type="ExpenseRecordType"/ minOccurs="0">
<xsd:complexType name="ExpenseRecordType" content="elementOnly">
<xsd:sequence>
   <xsd:element name="ExpenseID" type="xsd:long"/>
   <xsd:element name="EmployeeID" type="xsd:IDREF"/>
   <xsd:element name="ExpenseAmount" type="xsd:decimal"/>
   <xsd:element name="ExpenseDate" type="xsd:date"/>
   <xsd:element name="ExpenseCategoryID" type="xsd:long"/>
<xsd:sequence>
```

9. Together, the element named "Table" may have one or more (but at least one) EmployeeRow elements containing a sequence of elements representing data items you wish to track for employees, and zero or more ExpenseRow elements representing data items you wish to track for expenses.

10. Now that you've completed your schema, you can create XML documents from it. For example, if you want to build an XML document containing one record, you can code something like the following:

```
<Table>
 <EmployeeRow>
  <EmployeeID>1</EmployeeID>
  <SocialSecurityNumber>111223333</SocialSecurityNumber>
  <FirstName>John</FirstName>
  <LastName>Doe</LastName>
  <Title>Dr.</Title>
  <EmailName>jd@e4free.com</EmailName>
  <Extension>123</Extension>
  <Address>111 First Street</Address>
  <City>San Diego</City>
  <StateOrProvince>CA</StateOrProvince>
  <PostalCode>921011212</PostalCode>
  <Country>USA</Country>
  <HomePhone>6195551212</HomePhone>
  <WorkPhone>6195553434</WorkPhone>
  <Birthdate>1970-10-10</Birthdate>
  <DateHired>1990-10-10</DateHired>
  <Notes>Notes</Notes>
 </EmployeeRow>
 <ExpenseRow>
```

3

```
<ExpenseID>1</ExpenseID>
<EmployeeID>1</EmployeeID>
<ExpenseAmount>27.99</ExpenseAmount>
<ExpenseDate>1999-1-10</ExpenseDate>
<ExpenseCategoryID>Notes</ExpenseCategoryID>
</ExpenseRow>
</Table>
```

☑ *Mastery Check*

1. What is one of the major advantages of using an XML schema rather than a DTD to create valid XML documents from?

   A. XML schemas are easier to write.

   B. XML schemas *are* XML documents.

   C. XML schemas offer more powerful type checking.

   D. All of the above.

2. What is a schema?

   A. A representation of data in terms of the types of data and the relationship of data items to other data items contained in an XML document

   B. A formal declaration of elements and attributes for use in an XML document

   C. A set of data types that may be applied to elements and attributes in an XML document

   D. All of the above

3. How are elements declared in an XML schema?

   A. With the <element/> element

   B. With the <element/> element and a name

   C. With the <element/> element, a name, and a type

☑ *Mastery Check*

D. Any of the above

E. B and C only

4. What are primitive data types? Name two.

    A. Primitive data types are data types derived from the anySimpleType type, such as string and number.

    B. Primitive data types are not derived from any other type; they are basic data types built-in to XML Schema, such as string and decimal.

    C. Primitive data types are the basis for complex data types, such as positiveInteger and negativeInteger.

    D. Primitive data types are the basis for all other types in XML Schema, such as Year and Century.

5. The difference between a _____ type and a _____ type is that the _____ type contains no elements as part of its content. To derive a simple type from a primitive data type, you would use either a _____ or an extension.

6. What is the type anyType, and what kind of data type is it?

    A. It is the default data type, and it is always a string.

    B. It is the default data type, and it is always numeric.

    C. It is the default data type, and it may be any data type.

    D. None of the above.

7. What is the value space of a data type?

    A. The set of values that elements, attributes, or content based on the data type may assume

    B. The set of values that only content may assume

    C. The range of values possible

    D. None of the above

3

☑ Mastery Check

8. What are data type facets?

A. Names for values in the data type's value space

B. Properties of data types, such as length

C. Restrictions on the values a data type may assume

D. B and C above

E. None of the above

9. What kind of data type is timeDuration, and how is it coded?

10. From what data type is the data type Integer derived, and how is the derivation accomplished?

A. The integer data type is a primitive data type and is not derived from any other data type.

B. The integer data type is derived from the data type number and is made by setting the precision facet to 128.

C. The integer data type is derived from the data type decimal and is made by setting the scale facet to 0.

D. None of the above.

11. What method can be used to determine the elements, attributes, and data types required for constructing a schema using the XML Schema recommendation?

A. List all the data items to be tracked and the kind of data you think they are.

B. List all of the data items to be tracked and how the data will be stored and processed.

C. List all the data items to be tracked and how they are related to each other.

D. A combination of the methods in A, B, and C.

☑ Mastery Check

12. How is an XML schema different from an ordinary XML document, according to what we've learned so far?

A. The format and structure of an XML schema is the same as for an ordinary XML document.

B. The format and structure of an XML schema is the same as for an ordinary XML document, but an XML schema depends upon the XML DTD for Schemas for the definition of elements, attributes, and data types.

C. The format and structure of an XML schema is the same as for an ordinary XML document, but an XML schema must include a namespace designation.

D. None of the above.

13. What XML Schema element is used to begin the declaration of a new data type with content consisting only of other elements?

A. simpleType

B. complexType

C. derivedType

D. built-inType

E. None of the above

14. What XML Schema elements are used to declare elements, attributes, and their data types?

A. <element/>, <attribute/>, and the *type* attribute

B. <xsd:element/>, <xsd:attribute/>, and the *type* attribute

C. B, if the prefix *xsd* is connected to the URL for the DTD for XML Schema

D. Either A or C

E. None of the above

3

☑ *Mastery Check*

15. What is the purpose of the "sequence" element in XML Schema?

   A. It forces the attributes of an element into a particular sequence.

   B. It forces the elements in a data type into a particular sequence.

   C. It forces the values for an attribute into a particular sequence.

   D. It is for annotation purposes only.

Module 4

XML Namespaces and Advanced Schemas

The Goals of This Module

- Learn what namespaces are and why they're important to XML
- Declare namespaces in XML documents
- Learn about qualified names (QName)
- Learn about namespace scoping
- Apply namespaces to elements and attributes
- Understand namespace defaulting
- Learn how target namespaces relate to XML Schemas
- Create an XML Schema with a target namespace

In mathematical and programming areas, the term *space* often refers to a set of values that may be applied to a given thing. For example, as you learned in Module 3, the value space of a given data type is the set of values that the data of the data type may assume. If the data type is numeric, the set of values consists of some defined set of numbers. If the data type is string, the set of values consists of some defined set of string characters.

An XML *namespace* is a set of names for elements, attributes, and so forth defined within a DTD or XML Schema. This module discusses how namespaces are defined, how they are referenced, to what uses they may be put, and why they're important for XML. This module also uses some of the namespace information as it applies to XML Schemas.

The Importance of XML Namespaces

A recommendation published at the W3C (http://www.w3.org/TR/REC-xml-names/) called "Namespaces in XML" and dated January 14, 1999, gives instructions about how to declare and use namespaces with XML. Because XML is designed for extensibility, namespaces are vital for the contribution they make to that cause.

When you build a Document Type Definition (DTD), you're declaring elements, attributes, and so on for use in valid XML documents. You build the DTD to specify the permissible components and some of their properties in your XML documents. You want to exercise some control over the contents of your XML documents. When you build a DTD or an XML Schema, you must place it in an accessible area, so whatever application reads your XML document can validate the document contents against the DTD or XML Schema. The names for your declared elements, attributes, and other components constitute the *namespace* represented by that DTD or schema. To use this namespace with other DTDs or schemas, you must reference it.

Namespaces in Multiple DTDs and Schemas

Let's say you write an XML Schema to support a group of XML documents. The schema contains elements, attributes, and other components that you'll use for this group of XML documents, and it supports them in accordance with your data tracking, processing, and storage needs for the particular problem you're addressing (customer orders, let's say). And, suppose you write a second XML Schema to support the tracking and processing of employee expenses, similar to what you built in the last module. Also suppose that you need to track employees in relation to customer orders, so you can keep track of which employees are writing or filling individual orders.

Obviously, you could cut-and-paste the employee-related elements, attributes, and other definitions from the second schema into the first schema. However, you would then have to maintain the schemas in two locations—a nightmare situation if they diverged into two sets of employee data that don't match.

In many organizations, different databases, running on different platforms, constructed in different applications all are used to track identical data. For example, I'm aware of one company that has at least eight different databases, each containing tables that track the items the company manufactures. Some of the databases track these items by SKU—some by part number, some by part name, and some by part category—each being maintained and used for various purposes by several departments. Obviously, any communication between departments about these items is a messy affair, and collecting accurate, reliable, and consistent data across departments efficiently is impossible.

Still, this database dilemma is widespread. Among the reasons users often build their own versions of databases are the following:

- They aren't familiar with the other applications in which the data they want to track resides

- They need easy access to the data

- They don't want to modify the data structures or data in the other application

Unfortunately, when users create new databases to house duplicate information in this way, they often use the wrong data structures, the wrong data types, and even the wrong individual data items. For example, users may print a list of manufactured items from a mainframe database application, create a new database in some desktop database application, and then create a table in that application using only the names of the data items they're interested in. Again, this results in two separate sets of data that may or may not be compatible.

If, however, the data stored in the various databases was converted into XML documents based on an XML schema whenever it is to be exchanged, the users could simply create a new schema representing the data items to track (in addition to the ones already being tracked) and construct a new document that uses the existing schema and the new schema together. This way, new XML documents could be created using both schemas. The existing XML documents containing data could be retrieved so that all users are employing the same structures for the same data items. The data in each schema would always come from the same source.

Suppose, in our example of manufactured items, that two different definitions existed for part numbers. One department assigns a special part number representing the item by its ingredients, and another department assigns a part number representing the brand name and category of the item. Each of these departments might create independent schemas (or might import their databases into an XML format), resulting in elements named *PartNumber* in both schemas. But using both schemas to create XML documents with elements named *PartNumber* would be problematic because the validating application (the XML processor) wouldn't know which schema to use to validate the element.

This is where the concept of namespaces enters the picture and saves the day. URLs can be used to refer to namespaces, and then elements in an XML document can be validated against the correct schema by using the appropriate URLs.

1-Minute Drill

● What is a namespace?

● Why are namespaces useful?

Qualified Names

As you know, elements, attributes, and other components of an XML document must be given valid XML names so that they conform to the restrictions listed in Module 2. To conform to the Namespaces in XML recommendation, the names of elements and attributes must be *qualified names*.

● A namespace is a set of names that refer to elements, attributes, and other components included in an XML document, such as a DTD or schema.

● Namespaces allow the reuse of elements, attributes, and other components that are constructed in multiple DTDs and schemas and prevent name collision when two or more elements and/or attributes happen to have the same name.

4

A qualified name (or QName, one of the data types mentioned in Module 3) consists of two parts: the namespace prefix and the local name, separated by a colon (see the next section, "Declaring Namepsaces," for an example). The namespace prefix and the local name are each made from a Non-Colonized Name (NCName, also one of the data types mentioned in Module 3), which is similar to an XML name except that it cannot include a colon. The colon is reserved for separating the namespace prefix from the local name, which is why it may not be used in either of those.

The namespace prefix may be any valid NCName—that is, any valid XML name that doesn't have a colon in it. The local name is constructed in the same way, but the term *local* deserves some attention because it's associated with the scope of the XML document or documents that are created.

The concept of scope is used heavily in programming. *Scope* means the action, effect, and meaning of some objects are limited by the context in which they operate. For example, as a practical matter, a variable found in a VBScript typically is scoped to have meaning and carry its value across the script, but not directly to other scripts, even if they're on the same Web site. In the same way, elements and attributes named in an XML document have local scope, meaning they're valid for that document but not necessarily across other documents.

To broaden the scope of a particular element, the namespace prefix is added. This gives the element universal scope, meaning it can be used in any XML document so long as the namespace from which it originates is properly identified and referenced.

Declaring Namespaces

Namespaces can be declared using the reserved attribute *xmlns* and making it equal to a URL at which the appropriate DTD or schema resides. A namespace declaration for an element might look like this:

```
<PartNumber xmlns:parts1="http://www.nmsp1.com/">
part number content
</PartNumber>
```

This example declares the namespace of the element *PartNumber* to be found at the URL listed, and to be named *parts1*. Notice that the attribute *xmlns* has a colon between it and the namespace prefix *parts1*. The colon serves to *bind* the namespace prefix to the URL specified, so that anywhere in the document (within the scope of the element in which the binding is made), the prefix becomes a kind of shorthand for the URL.

For attributes, namespace declarations work much the same way. In the following code example, a child element named *childelement* within the scope of the *PartNumber* element has an attribute named *att* that is defined in the namespace at the URL specified; that *att* attribute is bound to the namespace prefix using a qualified name.

```
<PartNumber xmlns:parts1="http://www.nmsp1.com/">
 <childelement parts1:att="attvalue"/>
</PartNumber>
```

1-Minute Drill

- What is a qualified name? How is it used?
- What is a Non-Colonized Name?
- How is a namespace prefix connected to a DTD or schema?

Namespace Scope

Namespaces are considered to have scope for elements and their child elements by default. This means that if you write a namespace declaration for the root element in a document, it applies to all elements within that document because they're all child elements of the root element. More than one namespace declaration can be applied to a single element and then used with various child elements, as shown in the following code:

```
<?xml version="1.0"?>
<NMSP1:order xmlns:NMSP1="http://www.nmsp1.com"
             xmlns:NMSP2="http://www.nmsp2.com">
 <NMSP1:partnumber>1L2233G</NMSP1:partnumber>
 <NMSP2:partnumber>Red-G2</NMSP2:partnumber>
</NMSP1:order>
```

- A qualified name is a set consisting of a namespace prefix, a colon, and a local name. A qualified name may be applied to an element type or attribute name.
- A Non-Colonized Name is a name conforming to the rules for creating XML names, with the additional restriction that it cannot include a colon. The colon is reserved for connecting namespace prefixes to local names, each of which must be a Non-Colonized Name.
- The reserved attribute *xmlns* is used to connect a namespace prefix to a URL.

The Default Namespace

XML documents aren't required to be connected to a particular DTD or schema. For example, a well-formed XML document may simply be a succession of elements, attributes, and other components that follow the nesting rules of XML, without any DTD or schema referenced. Of course, such a document cannot be validated. Connecting an XML document to a DTD or schema makes it possible to validate the elements and attributes in that document against that DTD or schema.

In the same way, an XML document isn't required to be connected to a particular namespace. If no namespace declaration is used, but a connection to a DTD or schema is made, all parts of the document may be validated against that DTD or schema. This essentially has the same effect as a namespace declaration, but without the need for using qualified names or namespace prefixes.

If a namespace declaration is made without a namespace prefix, any unprefixed elements, by default, is considered attached to the declared namespace. If a namespace declaration is made, but no namespace prefix or URL is assigned, that element and its child elements aren't considered attached to any namespace—this, in effect, removes the default for those elements. Here's an example of a default namespace with no prefixes applied to the element named order and its child elements:

```
<?xml version="1.0"?>
<order xmlns="http://www.nmsp1.com">
  <partnumber>1L2233G</partnumber>
</order>
```

Here's an example of a default namespace applied, and then removed for a small set of child elements:

```
<?xml version="1.0"?>
<order xmlns="http://www.nmsp1.com">
 <partnumber>1L2233G</partnumber>
 <partname xmlns="">Lag Bolt</partname>
  <brand xmlns="">Steel Works</brand>
</order>
```

Namespaces and Attributes

Attributes may be connected to a particular namespace just like elements, but attributes *do not* take on the default namespace automatically, as elements do. As mentioned in the discussion of attributes in Module 2, no element may have two (or more) attributes with exactly the same name. This is appropriate because attributes represent properties of elements, and it would cause confusion as to which attribute actually specifies a given property for an element if more than one attribute had an identical name.

By the same token, no element may have two or more attributes of the same name that also have namespace prefixes *that are assigned to the same URL*. This rule is spelled out in this way because it *is* possible to have two namespace prefixes with *different* names, but pointing to the *same* URL. Obviously, if two namespace prefixes are pointing to the same URL, for all practical purposes the namespaces are the same and the attributes to which they're connected will be the same, in violation of the rule against multiple attributes of the same name in a single element. Interestingly, there *is* a neat exception to this: it's permissible to have two of the reserved attribute *xmlns* in a single element (but only when they connect different namespace prefixes to URLs).

Let's examine some code examples and see how these rules affect the coding of attributes and namespaces:

```
<?xml version="1.0"?>
<order xmlns="http://www.nmsp1.com">
        xmlns:ns1="http://www.nmsp1.com">
 <partnumber att1="attvalue"
 ns1:att1="attvalue2">1L2233G</partnumber>
 </order>
```

In this code, two namespaces have been assigned to the *order* element, and they both point to the same URL. But, because the default namespace isn't automatically assigned to attributes, the first attribute in the *partnumber* element (named *att1*) isn't assigned to any namespace, while the second attribute is assigned directly to the namespace *ns1* by the namespace prefix attached to it.

Ask the Expert

Question: What's the real difference between a namespace and a DTD or XML schema? They sound very much alike?

Answer: Their functions are similar, and they're referenced in a similar way, but using the *xmlns* attribute with a namespace means you can connect elements and attributes with identical names to different DTDs or XML schemas. This functionality is necessary because there's no practical way in advance to predefine the names for all elements and attributes, such that no two DTD or schema authors use the same names for elements or attributes.

The one thing that *can* be unique is the URL for a particular DTD or schema, and that's why it's used to differentiate between them. No matter what names a DTD or schema author uses, the DTD or schema can always be identified by their location on the Internet.

Question: What if I want to use element and attribute definitions from 20 or 30 DTDs or schemas? Can I do this?

Answer: Yes, but this seems impractical to a degree. In most cases, you should be fine with two or three sources for your documents. However, when automated tools are highly developed, using DTDs or schemas across a wide variety of XML document types might be feasible because computers can more easily keep track of all the namespaces, prefixes, elements, and attributes in use.

Question: What's the practical effect of scope? Why is scope so important to programming XML documents that use namespaces?

Answer: In programming, values are often assigned to variables for processing because it's easier to manipulate values conditionally, based on where the variables come from or what objects they're assigned to.

For example, if you live in the United States, you have been assigned to an object called a *Zip code*. This means that information about you (such as your demographic data) can be manipulated in a group based on Zip code. Outside the United States, the Zip code grouping would be meaningless, because the *scope* of Zip codes is the United States. In the same way, elements and attributes have scope, which allows them to be defined within a single document or to be usable across many documents.

Proj4-1.zip

Project 4-1: Using Namespaces

In this project, you create three different DTDs that define employee data. Then you reference them in a single XML document that uses elements and attributes from all of them.

First, let's define the objective of this project. You want to draw employee data from three different sources and maintain it in the appropriate format for each of the sources, while at the same time using the data to generate a single list of employees with their individual data. Suppose you're coordinating the efforts of a team of employees collaborating on a project that benefits all three of the organizations the team members are drawn from. Organizations do this occasionally—while working on industry standards, for example.

As coordinator, your job is to maintain communications among team members and prepare progress reports, along with summaries of the contributions of (and costs associated with) each team member. Each company from which team members are drawn has its employee data formatted in XML documents (or supplied by databases that export to XML). You want to supply information not only to the lead organization but also back to the member organizations in a format that their systems can understand. You want to manage the information in XML and provide it back to the companies in their native XML formats. Your intention is to create an XML document that uses each organization's DTDs for formatting its employee data. Of course, your XML document might have quite a few other features, but the purpose here is to concentrate on the features required to track employees.

Step-by-Step

1. Create the three DTDs, one for each organization. The top-level (root) element for each of the DTDs is going to be the employee, but one of the organizations calls its employees *associates*, so even though the team members are all employees, the root element of each member isn't going to be named the same thing.

   Let's start with Company 1, whose employees are often short-term contractors who may not necessarily work directly for a particular division. In addition, these contractors frequently work from home and have their own Web sites. Company 1 calls its employees *employees*, and it tracks employee information by the following data items:

   - **Name** A required item containing the full name of the employee
   - **Title** An optional item with the honorific of the employee, such as Dr.
   - **Division** An optional item that specifies the division in which the employee works
   - **Address** An optional item that specifies the home address of the employee
   - **Phone** A required item that lists the home phone number for the employee
   - **Email** An optional item that lists the work e-mail address for the employee
   - **URL** An optional item that specifies the URL of the employee's Web site

We can build a DTD that reflects these requirements as follows:

```
<!Element Employees (Employee)>
<!ELEMENT Employee (Name, Title?, Division?,
 Address?, Phone+, Email*, URL*)>
<!ATTLIST Employee
 position CDATA #IMPLIED
>
<!ELEMENT Name (#PCDATA)>
<!ELEMENT Title (#PCDATA)>
<!ELEMENT Division (#PCDATA)>
<!ELEMENT Address (Street, City, (State | Province),
 Country, PostalCode)>
<!ELEMENT Street (#PCDATA)>
<!ELEMENT City (#PCDATA)>
<!ELEMENT State (#PCDATA)>
<!ELEMENT Province (#PCDATA)>
<!ELEMENT Country (#PCDATA)>
<!ELEMENT PostalCode (#PCDATA)>
<!ELEMENT Phone (PhoneNumber)>
<!ATTLIST Phone
 type (work | home | mobile | fax) #REQUIRED
>
<!ELEMENT PhoneNumber (CountryCode?, AreaCode,
 Number, Extension?)>
<!ELEMENT CountryCode (#PCDATA)>
<!ATTLIST CountryCode
 isoCC CDATA #REQUIRED
>
<!ELEMENT AreaCode (#PCDATA)>
<!ELEMENT Number (#PCDATA)>
<!ELEMENT Extension (#PCDATA)>
<!ELEMENT Email (#PCDATA)>
<!ELEMENT URL (#PCDATA)>
```

As you can see, you begin the DTD with the root element *Employee*. In that element (in a strict sequence indicated by the commas between them), the element *Name* must appear first; the element *Phone* must appear at least once and may appear more (due to the plus sign); the elements *Title*, *Division*, and *Address* are optional (due to the question mark); and the elements *Email* and *URL* may appear zero or more times (due to the asterisk). The only attribute for Employee is *position*, and it's optional (due to the term *#IMPLIED*).

The element *Address* contains the child elements *Street, City, State or Province* (a choice indicated by the pipe symbol), *Country*, and *PostalCode*, in sequence. The element *Phone* contains the child element *PhoneNumber* and the attribute *type*. The attribute *type* is an enumerated list consisting of the choices *work, home, mobile*, and *fax*, and is required (due to the term *#REQUIRED*). The element *PhoneNumber* contains the child elements *CountryCode, AreaCode, Number*, and *Extension*, the first and the last of which are optional, and all of which must appear in sequence. The *CountryCode* element has an attribute named *isoCC*—the appropriate ISO country code—and this attribute is required. The remaining elements are child elements of a root.

To make this DTD accessible, the company has placed it on a protected area of the company Web site that you can access. Let's say this area is accessible at the URL http://www.company1.com/empDTD/.

2. Now you build the other two DTDs. Company 2 calls its employees *associates* and tracks different data items, so some differences will exist between these DTDs and those for Company 1. Here's what you build for Company 2:

```
<!Element Employees (Associate)>
<!ELEMENT Associate (Name, Department?,
 Address+, Phone+, Email*)>
<!ATTLIST Associate
 jobtitle CDATA #REQUIRED
>
<!ELEMENT Name (#PCDATA)>
<!ELEMENT Department (#PCDATA)>
<!ELEMENT Address (Street, City, State, ZipCode)>
<!ATTLIST Address
 location (home | work) #REQUIRED
>
<!ELEMENT Street (#PCDATA)>
<!ELEMENT City (#PCDATA)>
<!ELEMENT State (#PCDATA)>
<!ELEMENT ZipCode (#PCDATA)>
<!ELEMENT Phone (PhoneNumber)>
<!ATTLIST Phone
 type (work | home | mobile | fax) #REQUIRED
>
<!ELEMENT PhoneNumber (AreaOrCityCode, Number, Ext?)>
<!ELEMENT AreaOrCityCode (#PCDATA)>
<!ELEMENT Number (#PCDATA)>
```

```
<!ELEMENT Ext (#PCDATA)>
<!ELEMENT Email (#PCDATA)>
```

The primary differences in these DTDs from those of Company 1 are

● The root element is *Associate* rather than *Employee*

● The *Address* element is required and may occur more than once

● The *Address* element has an attribute named *location* and is required as one of the two choices offered in the enumerated list

● This DTD tracks less data items than the DTD for Company 1

Let's say this company's area is accessible at the URL http://www.company2.com/empDTD/.

3. Now build the final DTD for Company 3. It looks like this:

```
<!Element Employees (Employee)>
<!ELEMENT Employee (FName, MName?, LName,
 SSN+, Department?, Address, Phone+, Email*)>
<!ATTLIST Employee
 position CDATA #REQUIRED
 paygrade CDATA #REQUIRED
>
<!ELEMENT FName (#PCDATA)>
<!ELEMENT MName (#PCDATA)>
<!ELEMENT LName (#PCDATA)>
<!ELEMENT SSN (#PCDATA)>
<!ELEMENT Department (#PCDATA)>
<!ELEMENT Address (Street, City, State, ZipCode)>
<!ELEMENT Street (#PCDATA)>
<!ELEMENT City (#PCDATA)>
<!ELEMENT State (#PCDATA)>
<!ELEMENT Zip (#PCDATA)>
<!ELEMENT Phone (PhoneNumber)>
<!ATTLIST Phone
 type (work | mobile | fax) #REQUIRED
>
<!ELEMENT PhoneNumber (AreaCode, Number, Ext?)>
<!ELEMENT AreaCode (#PCDATA)>
<!ELEMENT Number (#PCDATA)>
<!ELEMENT Ext (#PCDATA)>
<!ELEMENT Email (#PCDATA)>
```

4

The primary differences found in this DTD from the other two are

- The employee name is broken into first, middle, and last names (the *FName*, *MName*, and *LName* elements), of which *Mname* is optional
- The *SSN* element has been included
- The *home* choice doesn't appear in the enumerated list of choices for the attribute named *type* in the Phone element

Let's say this area is accessible at the URL http://www.company3.com/empDTD/.

4. The last step is to produce an XML document that uses the *Employee* element from all three of these DTDs. Assign the prefixes *c1*, *c2*, and *c3* to these DTDs, and use their elements as follows:

```
<xml version="1.0">
<DOCTYPE Employees Public "http://www.company3.com/empDTD/">
<Employees
xmlns:c2=" http://www.company2.com/empDTD/">
xmlns:c3=" http://www.company3.com/empDTD/">
<Employee></Employee>
<c2:Employee></c2:Employee>
<c3:Employee></c3:Employee>
</Employees>
</xml>
```

Advanced XML Schema Development

Now that you have a clear understanding of XML namespaces, it's time to return to XML Schemas and see how you can use their full power, along with namespaces, to create vibrant documents drawn from a number of schemas already available on the Internet.

Elements and Attributes in the XML Schema Recommendation

In Module 3, we discussed and showed examples for a number of elements and attributes built into the XML Schema. Because any schema written following this recommendation depends on these definitions, they're listed here with a short description of what they do and how they work with each other.

XML Schema Elements

First, let's look at some of the elements of XML Schema:

- **Schema**   Declares the root element of a schema, the schema element
- **Import and include**   Adds elements, attributes, and data types from other schemas to an XML schema
- **Element**   Declares elements for use in XML documents
- **Attribute**   Declares attributes for use in XML documents
- **Annotation**   Provides machine- and human-readable information about the schema; contains the *appinfo* and documentation elements (together, these elements are the source of the information they provide via URLs, and for the documentation element, the language of the information)
- **attributeGroup**   Includes in a data type definition all the attribute declarations in an attributeGroup

XML Schema Attributes

Now let's look at some of the attributes in XML Schema:

- **attributeFormDefault and elementFormDefault**   Applicable to the schema element
- **base**   Applicable to the simple and complex type definitions
- **minOccurs and maxOccurs**   Applicable to element declarations; restricts the minimum and maximum occurrences of an element
- **mixed**   Applicable to the complex type definition; specifies the content model for a data type
- **name**   Used for the element declaration, attribute declaration, complex type definition, and simple type definition
- **noNamespaceSchemaLocation and xsi:null**   Applicable to an instance element

4

- **targetNamespace** Used to distinguish between definitions and declaration from different XML vocabularies

Attribute Groups

A requirement often exists to add attributes to a particular XML Schema for a given element. For example, if you're developing an ordering system, you might have an element named *Part*, and it might have attributes for the size and shipping method in its type definition, such as the following code:

```xsd
<xsd:element name="Part" minOccurs="0"
 maxOccurs="1000">
<xsd:complexType>          ← Starts the Complex Type declaration
                              with elements in sequence
<xsd:sequence>
<xsd:element name="partName" type="xsd:string"/>
<xsd:element name="QTY">
<xsd:simpleType>           ← Starts a Simple Type declaration
<xsd:restriction base="xsd:positiveInteger">
<xsd:maxExclusive value="100"/>
</xsd:restriction>
</xsd:simpleType>          ← Ends this Simple Type
</xsd:element>
<xsd:element name="Price" type="xsd:decimal"/>
<xsd:element name="Date" type="xsd:date"
 minOccurs="0"/>
</xsd:sequence>
<xsd:attribute name="sizeHeight" type="xsd:decimal"/>
<xsd:attribute name="sizeWidth" type="xsd:decimal"/>    Adds five attributes
<xsd:attribute name="sizeDepth" type="xsd:decimal"/>
<xsd:attribute name="Weight" type="xsd:decimal"/>
<xsd:attribute name="shipping">
<xsd:simpleType>
<xsd:restriction base="xsd:string">
<xsd:enumeration value="UPS"/>
<xsd:enumeration value="FedEx"/>
<xsd:enumeration value="USPS"/>
</xsd:restriction>
</xsd:simpleType>
</xsd:attribute>
</xsd:complexType>
</xsd:element>
```

Another way to add these attributes, if you think you might have to repeat them several times, is to create an *attribute group*. The group itself can then be added to elements, in effect, declaring all the attributes at once:

```
<xsd:element name="Part" minOccurs="0"
 maxOccurs="1000">
<xsd:complexType>
<xsd:sequence>
<xsd:element name="partName" type="xsd:string"/>
<xsd:element name="QTY">
<xsd:simpleType>
<xsd:restriction base="xsd:positiveInteger">
<xsd:maxExclusive value="100"/>
</xsd:restriction>
</xsd:simpleType>
</xsd:element>
<xsd:element name="Price" type="xsd:decimal"/>
<xsd:element name="Date" type="xsd:date"
 minOccurs="0"/>
</xsd:sequence>
<xsd:attributeGroup ref="PartAtts"/>
</xsd:complexType>
</xsd:element>
<xsd:attributeGroup name="PartsAtts">     ◄─────── Starts the attribute group
<xsd:attribute name="sizeHeight" type="xsd:decimal"/>
<xsd:attribute name="sizeWidth" type="xsd:decimal"/>
<xsd:attribute name="sizeDepth" type="xsd:decimal"/>
<xsd:attribute name="Weight" type="xsd:decimal"/>
<xsd:attribute name="shipping">
<xsd:simpleType>
<xsd:restriction base="xsd:string">
<xsd:enumeration value="UPS"/>
<xsd:enumeration value="FedEx"/>
<xsd:enumeration value="USPS"/>
</xsd:restriction>
</xsd:simpleType>
</xsd:attribute>
</xsd:attributeGroup>
```

Like any kind of grouping mechanism (such as parameter entities in XML 1.0), attribute groups make writing and maintaining schemas easier because the information is grouped in one place, can be written more easily, and needs to be maintained in only one place. Some rules pertaining to the use of attributes and attribute groups exist—the most notable is that they must appear at the end of complex type definitions and that a single attribute group may contain other attribute groups—in effect, nesting them together. The technique of combining groups of data into a single object is known as *abstraction,* which is used time and again in programming and the specifications for markup languages. Abstraction is helpful because it promotes reuse of code and makes the code easy to maintain.

Null Values in XML Schemas

If you've ever written a database, you know one of the types of values that can be entered into a field is the null value (for a more complete discussion of null values and their consequences, see Module 9). In an XML document, adding an element and giving it a value is how you assign values to the equivalent of fields in a database. But how do you explicitly add a null value to an XML document? Good question.

Note

The terms null and nil are equivalent, but the W3C recommendation recently switched from one term to the other. Don't be confused; they both mean the same thing.

To provide an answer, we'll use the XML Schema for instance documents. An *instance document* is an instance of a document based on a schema. The XML Schema for instance documents makes available a number of elements and attributes specifically designed for use in XML Schema document instances, rather than in XML Schemas themselves. One of the attributes you can apply when you're constructing an XML Schema using the XML Schema for schemas is the nillable attribute, as shown in the following code:

```
<xsd:element name="Date" type="xsd:date" nillable="true"/>
```

What this means is the Date element may now have a nil value. If you were reading the XML data from a database and the Date field was empty (and didn't happen to contain a zero-length string), you could set this field to an explicit nil value, as shown here:

```
<Date xsi:nil="true"></Date>
```

Although authors are allowed to use any prefix for the XML Schema namespace for instance documents (at http://www.w3.org/1999/XMLSchema-instance) the prefix *xsi* is used by convention. Only elements may be nil—not attributes—an important consideration when you're deciding how to assign and carry values in your documents. Also, nil elements may still have attributes with values, meaning your documents are actually more flexible than the databases from which they might be derived.

4

☑ *Mastery Check*

1. What is an XML namespace?

A. A set of names applied to specific spaces within an XML document, such as the head and body

B. A set of names representing a specific XML vocabulary

C. A set of names for XML documents pertaining to a particular vocabulary

D. None of the above

2. What is the value of using namespaces with XML documents?

A. Namespaces allow a single XML document to reference the same component names from multiple DTDs or schemas.

B. Namespaces allow XML document authors flexibility in the names applied to elements and attributes.

C. Namespaces compartmentalize XML documents, making them easier to work with.

D. None of the above

3. What method might be used to reference a namespace?

A. Include the *namespace* attribute, set to a URL reflecting the location of the DTD to which the namespace refers.

☑ Mastery Check

B. Include the *xmlns* attribute, set to a URL reflecting the location of the DTD to which the namespace refers.

C. Include the *ref* attribute, set to a URL reflecting the location of the DTD to which the namespace refers.

D. None of the above

4. What is a qualified name?

A. Any name conforming to the XML Names specification

B. A name having a prefix and local name separated by a colon

C. A name applying only to qualified elements and attributes

D. None of the above

5. What is an NCName?

A. A Non-Common Name

B. A Non-Conforming Name

C. A Non-Colonized Name

D. None of the above

6. From what set of names do NCNames derive?

A. Any combination of characters allowable in XML

B. Any names conforming to XML Names, minus the colon

C. Any names for elements and attributes within the DTD to which the namespace refers

D. None of the above

7. What is the purpose of the prefix in a qualified name?

A. Any element or attribute in an XML document to which the prefix is attached is referenced to the DTD for the namespace of the prefix.

☑ *Mastery Check*

    B. It groups all elements and attributes together for parallel processing.

    C. It sets processing parameters for elements and attributes to which it is attached.

    D. None of the above

8. What is the default namespace?

    A. The namespace used by default when no namespace is declared

    B. The namespace used when two or more namespaces are referenced

    C. A namespace that is referenced with the *xmlns* attribute, but without a prefix

    D. None of the above

9. If a namespace is attached to an element by a prefix, what is the effect on nonprefixed child elements?

    A. Nothing

    B. The namespace affects the immediate nonprefixed child elements, but no others.

    C. The namespace affects all child elements of the element to which the namespace is attached, no matter what level.

    D. None of the above

10. If a namespace is attached to an element by a prefix, what is the effect on nonprefixed attributes in its child elements?

    A. Nothing

    B. The namespace affects nonprefixed attributes in its immediate child elements, but no others.

    C. The namespace affects all nonprefixed attributes in any child elements of the element to which the namespace is attached, no matter what level.

    D. None of the above

✓ Mastery Check

11. What are schema, element, and attribute in XML Schema, and what is their purpose?

A. These are XML Schema elements, and they declare the schema and any elements and attributes allowed within XML documents based on it.

B. These are XML Schema attributes, and they are used as references to the appropriate schemas, elements, and attributes in a document based on XML Schema.

C. These are not part of XML Schema per se, but they are often found in XML documents based on XML Schema.

D. None of the above

12. What is the purpose of the *minOccurs* and *maxOccurs* attributes in XML Schema?

A. They specify the minimum and maximum number of times a specific data type may occur in an XML document based on XML Schema.

B. They specify the minimum and maximum number of times an element may occur.

C. They specify the minimum and maximum number of times a particular attribute may occur in the head section of an XML document.

D. None of the above

13. What is the purpose of the *complexType* element in XML Schema?

A. It defines a element having multiple attributes

B. It defines a data type that includes elements and possibly simpleType data types as well

C. It defines an attribute whose data type includes several different primitive data types

D. None of the above

☑ *Mastery Check*

14. What is the rule regarding attributes and the namespaces they may be attached to?

    A. No two attributes may have the same name in a single element, and they also may not have the same prefix applied.

    B. No two attributes may have the same name in a single element, and they also may not have prefixes attached that point to the same namespace reference.

    C. No two attributes may have the same name in a single element, unless their prefixes are different.

    D. None of the above

15. What is the purpose of the *base* attribute in XML Schema?

    A. It sets the base element to which the attribute is attached.

    B. It sets the base data type from which a new data type is derived.

    C. It sets the base document to which the attribute refers.

    D. None of the above

4

Part II

Using XML

Module 5

XML Graphics Basics and SMIL

The Goals of This Module

- Learn the basics of using graphics and image files
- Examine image issues, such as file size and resolution
- Learn about the XHTML IMG DTD
- Review the SMIL 1.0 recommendation
- Check out the RealNetworks SMIL player
- Create a SMIL XML document for RealPlayer

Since the advent of XML, quite a few XML applications (XML languages) have been developed, including languages for graphics and multimedia presentation. Before jumping into these languages, let's review the basic concepts of graphics, image file formats, and multimedia.

In their most basic form, *image files* contain binary data that translates (is rendered) into displayable spots called *pixels,* which is short for *picture* element. Each pixel is rendered as a combination of color and brightness values (assuming you aren't using a monochrome display, of course).

Image files, by convention, are rectangular when rendered. In the typical Web page, image files may be inserted at any point, either by inserting the data directly into the Web page or by referencing the image file via a URL. How the image is rendered depends on the instructions contained in the HTML code of the Web page and how those commands are interpreted by the browser.

The bottom line is this: graphics and multimedia presentation, as rendered on whatever platform is used, is affected by every step in the production and rendering process. Using the right combination of steps, plus the right hardware and software, ensures a finished product that meets the initial objectives. Likewise, using the wrong production process, hardware, or software at any given point may degrade the finished product beyond usability. In this module, you learn all the basics, as well as recent recommendations related to graphics in the XML arena—plus some of the tools available to make the most of the recommendations.

Graphics Basics

We're all used to thinking of graphics in terms of what we see on a Web page or a printed page, but it's important to keep in mind that the graphics you see are just data. When graphics data is incorporated into an XML format, it's possible the graphics might never be seen by people. Instead, perhaps the graphics data will be consumed by a computer performing a pattern matching routine or verifying identity.

You should also remember that graphics—as displayed in a Web page or on some other platform—may not come from an image file at all. For example, the background color for the <BODY> element (the main viewable part of the screen in a Web page) can be set using the *bgcolor* attribute, without using any image files.

So, essentially, graphics are rendered as pixels with color and brightness values. That data might be generated from binary image file data, from markup language commands, or from some combination of those. The rendering software and hardware make their own interpretations along the way.

Color Values and Color Spaces

The HTML and XHTML specifications both recognize color values based on numeric codes, and browsers also recognize specific color names. Therefore, colors can be created using either hexadecimal numeric values (such as #FF0000 for red) or as a color name (because the popular browsers recognize many common color names). In the HTML and XHTML recommendations, the supported color values and names are shown in Table 5-1.

The specification at **www.w3.org/sRGB** refers to the color space made from red, green, and blue (RGB). Browsers support hundreds of color names but unfortunately not always the same colors. A color said to be *Web-safe* or *browser-safe* is supported by both Netscape Navigator and Microsoft Internet Explorer on either Windows or Macintosh systems, when the system is set to 256-color mode.

Color	Value
Black	#000000
Silver	#C0C0C0
Gray	#808080
White	#FFFFFF
Maroon	#800000
Red	#FF000000
Purple	#800080
Fuchsia	#FF00FF
Green	#008000
Lime	#00FF00
Olive	#808000
Yellow	#FFFF00
Navy	#000080
Blue	#0000FF
Teal	#008080
Aqua	#00FFFF

Table 5-1   Recommended Color Values and Names

Displayed colors are, by convention, made from a combination of RGB values. Printed colors are, by convention, made from a combination of cyan, magenta, yellow, and black (CMYK) values.

Color Spaces

Color spaces (or *color models*) describe color values in standard terms and specify colors without reference to any particular rendering device, using the entire range of colors in the space and the color-influencing properties of *reflection, absorption,* and *perception*. The RGB and CMYK color spaces don't overlap completely and, therefore, images might look one way when displayed and slightly different when printed.

Image File Formats

Images can be included within HTML documents with the <IMG> element, which is presented later in this module, to demonstrate the contrast between including images in HTML documents and including image data in XML documents. While any image type can be included, only certain types are currently supported by the major browsers. The supported types are CompuServe Graphics Interchange Format (GIF), Joint Photographic Experts Group (JPEG or JPG), and Portable Network Graphics (PNG). Synchronized Multimedia Integration Language (SMIL) and Super Video Graphics (SVG) require special browsers or player software for rendering.

File Size

No matter what file format is used, the image file types suitable for Internet distribution are usually compressed, which often means the file type has had some data removed so the file takes up less space than the high-resolution original. For GIF and JPEG, the compression is called *lossy* compression, because some data is lost when the image is converted. Unlike most file types (such as executable files), where the loss of bits can render the file unusable, these image file types often appear much the same to the human eye and, therefore, the data loss is acceptable. Smaller file sizes mean faster downloads, an important consideration for Internet distribution.

Unlike text-based XML and HTML files, image files—even when using compressed formats—tend to be large and take a long time to download with ordinary dialup Internet access. Creating image files with scanners and other capture devices, however, provides an advantage by offering some control over the resulting file size. By using various settings, such as color depth, overall file size can be optimized for the type of object scanned. Higher quality scanners are capable of capturing images at a variety of color depths:

- 1-bit, black and white

- 8-bit, grayscale or indexed color mode

- 24-bit, RGB color mode

- 32-bit, CMYK color mode

- 36- to 48-bit, high-bit RGB color mode

The larger the original image and the larger the color depth, the larger the resulting output file. For example, a 24-bit RGB color mode file is roughly 24 times larger than the same image scanned at 1-bit line art mode.

Display Output Sizing   For display output (images to be displayed on computer monitors in Web pages, for instance), if the number of pixels in an image is changed, the size is changed. For instance, if 4-by-4 inch original image is scanned at 100 dpi, it appears 400 by 400 pixels on a video screen. The original size in inches doesn't matter because the image's pixels match up one-for-one with those provided by the screen resolution. The same image scanned at 50 dpi appears half the width and half the height (200 by 200 pixels).

Raster and Vector Images

Raster images are composed of dots (pixels), while *vector* images are made from mathematical calculations. When an image is made with a scanner, the image captured is a raster image and each pixel is assigned an individual value. Vector images can be made with CAD (computer aided drafting) applications, which use equations to calculate appropriate values for each part of an image. When raster images are scaled, they tend to lose clarity, while vector images scale well because the appropriate values for each pixel are recalculated each time the scale is changed.

5

Inserting Images with the HTML/XHTML IMG Element

The final output of an XML document might include images and it might be rendered as an XHTML document, so a bit of the DTD for XHTML documents is included here, along with some of the parameters for IMG elements, the standard HTML/XHTML mechanism for including images in documents.

By default in XHTML, the IMG element inserts an image into a document at the point in the code where the image has been inserted, unless the author uses *x* index, *y* index, and *z* index coordinates to place the image on the page. The use of these coordinates is supported by major manufacturers' browsers in versions 4.0 and above (that is, those that support CSS2).

The IMG element has only a starting tag, and an ending tag is forbidden. This is appropriate because all the information required to insert an image is contained in the attributes of the starting tag, such as the *src* attribute. The XHTML 1.0 DTD of the IMG element starts with the typical "<!ELEMENT" and then names the element IMG. The DTD defines the IMG element as having an empty content model. In addition, the DTD defines a number of supported attributes that are not part of the core attributes, which are discussed in the next section.

Like an XML DTD, the DTD for the IMG element allows the core attributes (*id, class, lang, dir, title, style*) and the intrinsic events, as well as a few other helpful attributes. The *src* attribute value is the URL pointing to the image file and can be an absolute or relative path. One attribute in particular should always be set—the *alt* attribute. The *alt* attribute can contain a text message telling the user the contents of the image. If users have images turned off in their browser preferences (or are unable to display images), the *alt* attribute provides an indication of the contents of an image. The *border* attribute sets the size of a border around the image, in pixels. Here's an example of the code for inserting an image and for setting the *alt* and *border* attributes:

```
<IMG alt="Image of Whatever" Border="0" SRC="whatever.gif">
```

Inserting Images and Graphics in XML Documents

As written, XML documents are pretty useless for the display of graphics and images (or any kind of styles, for that matter) because XML documents are designed for containing data in a flexible way. You can take advantage of this flexibility for rendering data in a number of ways, of course, and you learn about them in detail in Module 11. For now, note that common methods for displaying images and graphics in XML documents include creating a finished HTML document via scripting and the Document Object Model (DOM), as well as transforming XML documents into finished HTML documents (among other types of documents) using eXtensible Style Sheets (XSL) and an eXtensible Style Sheet Transformations (XSLT) processor.

5

Ask the Expert

Question: We've covered a lot of ground for graphics here. What are the most important points from the perspective of using graphics in XML documents?

Answer: When using graphics across the Internet, no matter what format or how rendered, download times are important. One method of viewing image files (the method used with static, HTML Web pages) is to download the image completely and then render it on a Web page. For GIF and JPG images, this isn't ordinarily a problem, as long as the images are relatively small—small being a function of resolution and viewable size.

Another method for viewing multimedia (also included are audio, video, slide presentations, and so forth) across the Internet is called *streaming*, as demonstrated by the popular RealPlayer from RealNetworks. With this method, files are broken up into small chunks and transferred piecemeal. The player software then buffers content until it reaches a size at which viewing can begin, rather than waiting until the entire file is downloaded. Large files or continuous streams of multimedia can, thus, be effectively distributed.

With any multimedia format for the Internet, compression is ordinarily used to speed the transfer process, whether whole files or data streams are used, making the compression technology important. In addition, the capability to query for available rendering applications, system settings (such as screen resolution), and available bandwidth is important for making the highest quality transmission available without forcing the user to select (perhaps) unfamiliar system settings.

Ultimately, decisions regarding file formats, resolution, compression, delivery methods, and supported rendering applications will come down to development effort, quality, and (at least in part) the market share of supportable rendering applications, whether multimedia is being developed for XML documents to be rendered as Web pages in browsers or for use in other applications.

Question: I think I'll make a good XML developer, but I'm not sure how to proceed with the development of multimedia. Should I buy the popular graphics and multimedia applications and produce my own content, or should I rely on subcontractors?

Answer: Unless you already have the training and talent to produce graphics and multimedia—as well as the time and patience required—you might consider farming out multimedia development. Talent (or an artistic eye) is the first requirement and not everyone has it. Even if you were born with all the talent in the world, it still takes years of education and experience to become productive and efficient. The best graphic artists are often fine artists, and the skills acquired while becoming a fine artist are independent of any proficiency with a particular software tool.

That said, the second part of producing excellent multimedia is proficiency with the tools of the trade, and those who are great in traditional multimedia production, especially having had long experience with traditional methodologies, may have a large learning curve to face before becoming excellent at producing multimedia for the Internet. Bottom line: make sure whoever you farm out work to is not only talented and educated but proficient at producing (or converting) their work for the Internet.

The SMIL Recommendation— Multimedia in XML

Two interesting topics related to graphics at the World Wide Web Consortium (W3C) are Synchronized Multimedia Integration Language (SMIL) and Scalable Vector Graphics (SVG), also called Simple Vector Graphics. The SMIL 1.0 specification is a recommendation as of June 15, 1998, while SVG is still in the process of becoming a candidate at press time, so SVG isn't covered in this module. Also, a draft of SMIL 2.0 is in the works at the W3C, but it's beyond the scope of this book. SMIL 2.0 uses many of the same elements as SMIL 1.0, however, so what you learn here is, for the most part, applicable when SMIL 2.0 becomes a recommendation. Following is a discussion of SMIL (as well as a project) as it relates to XML.

5

SMIL 1.0

SMIL (pronounced *smile*) is an upbeat acronym if ever there was one. SMIL documents conform to the XML specification and, therefore, the specification seems likely to become a common multimedia development language. The purpose of SMIL is to enable authors to integrate multiple, independent multimedia objects (such as images, audio, video/movies, presentations, text, and links) into a cohesive whole within the framework of browser-style software. Specifically, SMIL allows

- The control of timing for objects
- The control of display layout of objects
- The connection of hyperlinks to objects

The capability to exercise this kind of control over the display and presentation of multimedia objects offers great potential for rapidly developing rich communications across the Internet, albeit with the added cost of learning a new language or set of software tools. Ideally, the added development cost will be offset by the ease with which the new tools allow development to proceed.

SMIL Elements

SMIL documents are compliant with XML 1.0, so much of what you've learned already is applicable. Not only that, any XML processor/browser combination should be able to read your SMIL documents, and you should be able to integrate SMIL documents into other XML documents relatively easily.

As XML documents, SMIL documents are composed with elements and attributes. Among the elements are these:

- **smil**   The *root* element of a SMIL document

- **head**   For information about the layout, but not timing, of objects in the document as well as meta information

- **layout**   Specific layout data for document objects

- **region**   For the position, size, and scaling of document objects

- **root-layout**   To determine the layout of the *viewport* (window) in which the document is displayed, as opposed to the layout of the other document objects

- **meta**   For information about the general properties of a document, such as expiration date and keywords

- **body**   For the elements affecting the timing and linking of document objects

- **par**   For elements that can overlap in time (are displayed in parallel)

- **seq**   For elements displayed in sequence

- **ref, animation, audio, img, video, text, and textstream**   These are all *media object* elements

- **switch**   For alternative *media object* elements, based on interaction with the platform on which display will occur

- **a**   Similar to the *anchor* element in HTML, for creating hyperlinks from document objects

Each of the elements listed has attributes associated with it, and together these elements and attributes enable authors to build flexible SMIL documents capable of displaying a wide variety of multimedia objects as an integrated presentation on any supported platform, either standalone or as part of other XML documents.

The smil Element   The *smil* element is the root element of a SMIL document, and the only attribute it may have is the *id* attribute, with a value whose data type is an XML ID (all SMIL elements having an *id* attribute have this usage definition). Element content is restricted to the child elements *body* and *head*. The *smil* element is written <smil> and </smil>, and all other content in a SMIL document falls between these two tags.

The head Element   The *head* element is contained in the *smil* element and can have only an *id* attribute. The *head* element's content is restricted to zero or more *meta* elements, and either a *layout* or *switch* element (although these elements may have child elements of their own in the *head* element).

The layout Element   The *layout* element is contained in the *head* element and is responsible for positioning elements within what is referred to as an *abstract rendering surface*. Referring to the method of rendering, this statement reminds us that all objects aren't necessarily rendered visually; some may be rendered as audio or even tactile sensations. If the *layout* element is absent, element positioning is dependent on the implementation of the rendering application. If a *switch* element is used, multiple layout elements may be contained in the *switch* element.

The *layout* element may have the *id* and *type* attributes. The *type* attribute serves as an indicator of the language of the layout, and the default type is *text/smil-basic-layout*. If the rendering application doesn't understand the type given, the *layout* element is ignored. If the *type* attribute is set to the default, the *layout* element may contain as content the *region* and *root-layout* elements. If the *type* attribute is set to something other than the default, the *layout* element contains character data.

The region Element   The *region* element defines a region in which a media object element exists within the body of the SMIL document, in terms of position, size, and scaling. For example, the defined region may be placed a certain number of pixels from the top or left, may be a certain number of pixels in height or width, and may have a *z-index* setting in front of or behind other objects in the body. The *region* element has no content, but it may have the

5

following attributes: *background-color, fit, height, id, left, skip-content, title, top, width,* and *z-index.*

Now that you know enough elements to make a simple document, let's look at an example of code that might be part of a SMIL document:

```
<smil>
<head>
<layout>
<region id="first" top="10" />
</layout>
</head>
<body>
<text region="first" src="mypage.html" dur="20s" />
</body>
</smil>
```

This code starts with a *smil* element, then begins a *head* element, then begins a layout, and then defines a region 10 pixels from the top, with an *id* of "first". In the *body* element, a media object of type "text" is placed, which is associated with the region by its *region* attribute (whose value is set to "first"). The source of the media object is a Web page named mypage.html, and the duration for the media object is 20 seconds. The layout language (similar to CSS2) and timing of media objects are discussed a little later, in the sections "Basic Layout" and "Synchronization and the SMIL Time Model."

The root-layout Element   The *root-layout* element has many of the same functions as the *region* element (and, therefore, many of the same attributes), but it operates specifically for the overall SMIL document, to define the viewport, or window, in which display takes place. Like the *region* element, the *root-layout* element has no content, but it may have the following attributes: *background-color, height, id, skip-content, title,* and *width.*

The meta Element   The *meta* element can be used to define properties of the SMIL document arbitrarily, such as author, expiration date, and keywords. Like the *meta* element in HTML, it has no content (even though it has a *content* attribute), but it may have the following attributes: *content, id, name, skip-content, base, pics-label,* and *title.*

The body element   The *body* element is where the action takes place in a SMIL document. It defines time-based relationships among elements, as well as links. The *body* element may have the *id* attribute, and it implicitly defines a *seq* element and may explicitly contain the following elements: *a, animation, audio, img, par, ref, seq, switch, text, textstream,* and *video.*

The par and seq Elements   The *par* and *seq* elements are synchronization elements, meaning they allow control over the timing of objects in a SMIL document, some parallel and some sequential. The *par* element is allowed to have the same child elements as the *body* element. Child elements of the *par* element may occur simultaneously or simply overlap, and the exact timing has no relationship to the order of appearance in a SMIL document. Rather, timing is defined according to a fairly elaborate set of rules, based on *a clock value,* a relationship established between one element and another, and other parameters (more details can be found in the section "Synchronization and the SMIL Time Model").

A *par* element may have the following attributes:

- **abstract**   For a brief description of the element
- **author**   For the author of the individual element
- **begin**   Contains thes information about when an element begins, explicitly
- **copyright**   A copyright notice for the individual element
- **dur**   The duration of the element, as an explicit value or "indefinite"
- **end**   The explicit end of an element
- **endsync**   A value denoting the end of synchronization
- **id**   The same as other *id* attributes
- **region**   Specifies the region for the element, as defined in the layout
- **repeat**   The number of times an element shall repeat
- **system attributes**   These attributes (explained in more detail in the section "System Attributes") provide a means of testing the capabilities of the system on which the document is to be rendered

5

- **title**   A title for the element, and can be considered mandatory, according to the recommendation

The *seq* element has the same child elements and the same attributes as the *par* element, but its child elements run in sequence, rather than being allowed to run simultaneously or overlapping.

The a and anchor Elements

The hyperlinking elements *a* and *anchor* in a SMIL document have the same capabilities as hyperlinking elements in HTML, meaning they can go in one direction only—with one source and one destination. The difference in SMIL is that to create a hyperlink, the *a* element is used, while to create an anchor (a particular spot, either spatially or time-based, in another document), the *anchor* element is used.

The *a* element must have an *href* attribute, and it may also have the *id, show,* and *title* attributes. The *id* and *title* attributes have the usual functions, while the *href* attribute defines the location of the reference (the URL to the reference), and the *show* attribute controls how the document containing the link behaves when the link is clicked. The *anchor* element may have *id* and *title* attributes, as well as *begin, end, show,* and *skip-content* attributes, and a *cords* attribute. The latter five attributes define the particular spot in the referenced document to which the link leads.

The *a* element may not contain additional child *a* elements, but it may contain all the other elements allowed in the *body* element. The *anchor* element is used inside these child elements (but not within an *a* element) to define individual linking spots or times.

The switch Element

The *switch* element allows document authors to set alternative media elements for rendering, based on which "acceptable" element is found first in the *switch* element. Acceptable elements are those conforming to SMIL 1.0, for which the media type can be processed and all the test attributes (system attributes) return a "true" value. Basically, this means the processor reads through the list of elements in the *switch* element until it finds the first good one. Therefore, the author should place the preferred elements first and default elements last.

The *switch* element can have *id* and *title* attributes, whose functions are the same as for other elements in SMIL 1.0. The *switch* element has content, which may include all the same media elements as the *body* element. In addition, a *switch* element may reside in the *head* element and, if so, may also contain a *layout* element.

Media Object Elements   *Media object* elements represent the actual things that are rendered or played in a SMIL document, such as video, audio, and animations. They are brought into a rendered document by means of URLs. Objects with an inherent duration, such as video and audio, are called *continuous* media, while static objects, such as images and text, are called *discrete* media.

Although the names of *media object* elements in SMIL give a clue as to the kind of media they represent, the exact media type should be defined in the *type* attribute or communicated by the server delivering the document. The *type* attribute takes as values the MIME type of the media object, much the same way as this data is presented in HTML/XHTML.

Media object elements may have the attributes *abstract, alt, longdesc, author, copyright,* and *title* to provide meta information about the element. They may also have the set of system attributes for testing the receiving system prior to rendering. The *src* attribute specifies the location of the object for retrieval and the *begin, clip-begin, clip-end, end, dur, fill,* and *region* attributes to control the appearance of the element. The only child element *media object* elements may have is the *anchor* element.

Basic Layout

The SMIL recommendation has a layout language associated with it that's similar to Cascading Style Sheets 2.0 (CSS2). It may be used to position and define layout properties for *media object* elements. For example, you can set attributes for a *media object* element, which place that element on the screen according to their *x* and *y* coordinates (counted in pixels from the top and left of the screen), and you can define how a *media object* element is rendered relative to other objects on the screen. And, as another example, the *region* element may have the *background-color* attribute set with values identical to those allowed in CSS2, meaning it may take on a color value or be transparent.

System Attributes

System attributes (or test attributes) provide a means for authors to test system capabilities to provide the richest (or most appropriate) rendering of media objects. These attributes are

- **system-bitrate**   Makes a measurement of the bandwidth available and is false if available bandwidth is less than the value specified by the document author

- **system-captions**   Allows the author to specify whether to include closed-captioning, based on whether the user wants to see closed-captioning

- **system-language**   Provides a means of distinguishing the user's language of choice

- **system-overdub-or-caption**   Provides a means of determining user preference for overdubbing or captioning

- **system-required**   Can be set to an extension, meaning (for future versions of SMIL) this would be set to an XML namespace

- **system-screen-size**   Provides data concerning the available screen size, in pixels

- **system-screen-depth**   Provides the color depth available

Synchronization and the SMIL Time Model

As mentioned, the *par* and *seq* elements are concerned with the sequencing of element display on a SMIL document. Each element at some point begins to display itself and at some other point ends the display of itself, with the passing of a duration of time while it displays itself. The recommendation defines the implicit, explicit, desired, or effective points for these characteristics of the *par* and *seq* elements.

If no explicit beginning or ending is defined for an element, it begins or ends implicitly, meaning, for example, when the document is opened, an element without an explicit beginning begins by default. The recommendation sets rules for determining how elements begin and end and what duration they last—both implicitly and explicitly—depending on their relationship to the *par* and *seq* elements of which they are children, and their relationship to other elements in the SMIL document. Altogether, the settings of these attributes and their defined interaction allow SMIL authors great flexibility in creating interesting and unique combinations of *media object* elements rendered spatially and in a time-based manner, within the viewport of a SMIL document.

1-Minute Drill

● Where in a SMIL document are the elements that lay out rendering spaces for media objects?

● Where in a SMIL document is timing of media-object rendering performed?

Proj5-1.zip

Project 5-1: Creating a SMIL Document

Before a multimedia presentation can be constructed, the media objects, such as video, audio, text, and image files, must be created. As mentioned, the construction of media objects is an art in itself, requiring a set of skills that have little to do directly with the building of a multimedia presentation, no matter what software, standard, or protocol is used for rendering. Like making a movie, TV show, commercial, or slideshow, creating a multimedia presentation with SMIL takes talent and skill, not only the ability to program.

That said, once the elements are created, having the right software tools available is of great help in quickly setting up the desired presentation. Although a number of tools are available for construction and editing, we'll limit ourselves to coding by hand and using the RealPlayer client to play back our creations. You can find RealPlayer at **www.realnetworks.com**. You should install this player before continuing with this project.

The SMIL recommendation calls for an optional DTD at the top of the document, just like any XML document, but for our player of choice this isn't necessary.

```
<!DOCTYPE smil PUBLIC "-//W3C//DTD SMIL 1.0//EN"
"http://www.w3.org/TR/REC-smil/SMIL10.dtd">
```

Step-by-Step

In this project, you use text files with HTML tags, images, audio files, and video files as content for your multimedia SMIL document. Because you're using

---

● The elements that lay out rendering spaces for media objects in a SMIL document are in the *head* element.
● The timing of media-object rendering in a SMIL document is performed in the *body* element.

RealPlayer, you'll be using a slight variation of the SMIL recommendation and you'll encode some of your resources (the audio and video files) using the RealSystem Producer Basic application.

1. To tie everything together, create the following SMIL document. This file has the initial layout regions for the screen, and references other files that contain the title screen text, audio, and video:

```
<smil>
<head>
<layout>
<root-layout height="420" width="620"
 background-color="black"/>
<region id="title" left="5" top="150"
 width="400" height="200" z-index="1"/>
<region id="full" left="0"    top="0" height="425"
 width="450" background-color="#206030"/>
<region id="video" left="260" top="240" height="120"
 width="160" z-index="2"/>
<region id="contents" left="450" top="0" height="420"
 width="180"/>
</layout>
</head>
<body>
<par>
<text src="contents.rt" region="contents"/>
<seq>
<text src="titlescreen.rt" type="text/html"
 region="title" dur="10s"/>
<par>
<audio src="shortnarration.rm"/>
<img src="imagemap.rp" region="full" fill="freeze"/>
</par>
<par>
<img src="seqimages.rp" region="full" fill="freeze"/>
<seq>
<video src="niceview.rm" region="video"/>
<audio src="talking.ra"/>
<video src="longnarration.rm"
 region="video"/>
</seq></par></seq>
</body>
</smil>
```

2. Create the titlescreen.rt file. This file contains text content that fades in and out as the presentation progresses:

```
<WINDOW TYPE="generic" bgcolor="#206030"
 WIDTH="400" HEIGHT="200">
<font size="4" color="white">
<CENTER><I>"My favorite view"</I>
</CENTER></FONT>
<font size="3" color="white">
<CENTER>
<time begin="00:05">First, the view
<time begin="00:10"><clear/>
<time begin="00:11"><pos y="50">Then the audio.
</CENTER></FONT>
<time begin="00:13"><FONT size="2" color="white">
<i><P>    Dave Mercer; www.e4free.com</i>
</font>
</CENTER>
</font>
</WINDOW>
```

3. Create the imagemap.rp file to show a series of JPEG images:

```
<imfl>
<head duration="00:47" width="450"
 height="425" bitrate="13500" preroll="00:20"
 aspect="true" timeformat="dd:hh:mm:ss.xyz"/>
<image handle="1" name="view1.jpg"/>
<image handle="2" name="view2.jpg"/>
<image handle="3" name="view3.jpg"/>
<image handle="4" name="view4.jpg"/>
<image handle="5" name="view5.jpg"/
<fadein start="00:01" duration="00:02" target="1"/>
<crossfade start="00:05" duration="00:17" target="2"/>
<viewchange target="2" start="00:30" duration="00:05"
 srcx="290" srcy="139" srcw="98" srch="95"/>
<crossfade start="00:35" duration="00:03" target="3"/>
<wipe target="4" start="00:33" duration="00:08"
 srch="195" dsth="195" type="normal"
 direction="down"/>
<crossfade start="00:43" duration="00:03" target="5"/>
</imfl>
```

Putting several images of the view in

5

4. Finally, create the seqimages.rp file. This file displays a series of nice images one after the other, with a nice cross-fade effect:

```
<imfl>
<head duration="01:41" bitrate="20000" width="450"
 height="425" aspect="true"
 timeformat="dd:hh:mm:ss.xyz" preroll="80" />
<image handle="1" name="niceimage1.jpg"/>
<image handle="2" name="niceimage2.jpg"/>
<image handle="3" name="niceimage3.jpg"/>
<image handle="4" name="niceimage4.jpg"/>
<image handle="5" name="niceimage5.jpg"/>
<image handle="6" name="niceimage6.jpg"/>
<image handle="7" name="niceimage7.jpg"/>
<image handle="8" name="niceimage8.jpg"/>
<image handle="9" name="niceimage9.jpg"/>
<image handle="10" name="niceimage10.jpg"/>
<fill start="0" duration="00:05" color="#602030"/>
<fadein start="00:25" duration="0:04" target="1"/>
<crossfade start="00:30" duration="00:04" target="2"/>
<crossfade start="00:37" duration="00:04" target="3"/>
<crossfade start="00:43" duration="00:04" target="4"/>
<crossfade start="00:51" duration="00:04" target="5"/>
<crossfade start="00:59" duration="00:04" target="6"/>
<crossfade start="01:06" duration="00:04" target="7"/>
<crossfade start="01:13" duration="00:04" target="8"/>
<crossfade start="01:20" duration="00:04" target="9"/>
<crossfade start="01:30" duration="00:04" target="10"/>
<fadeout start="01:40" duration="00:14" target="10"/>
</imfl>
```

Inserting nice images, giving them each a handle, and then cross-fading them by handle

At last, you have your entire production ready and you can play it back in RealPlayer, which is shown when starting in Figure 5-1.

Figure 5-1 The SMIL Document in RealPlayer

5

Mastery Check

1. What is the basic format of image files?

A. Graphics Interchange Format (GIF)

B. Encoded binary data

C. Joint Photographic Experts Group (JPEG)

D. None of the above

2. What image file format supported by most browsers can be animated, interlaced, and can have a transparent background?

A. Portable Network Graphics (PNG)

B. Joint Photographic Experts Group (JPEG)

C. Graphics Interchange Format (GIF)

D. All of the above

3. What is a color space and what color space is currently used by browsers?

A. A range of colors, RGB

B. A range of colors, CMYK

C. An area in the viewport, RGB

D. None of the above

4. What does the term "color depth" refer to?

A. The number of colors supported

B. The number of bits required to encode a range of colors

C. The ability to create color 3-D graphics, thereby producing the illusion of depth

D. None of the above

☑ *Mastery Check*

5. If an image file is scanned from an original that is 2 inches square (at full size) at a resolution of 100 dpi, what size, in inches, would the image appear to be on a screen 12 inches wide with a horizontal resolution of 600 pixels and 8 inches high with a vertical resolution of 400 pixels?

   A. This problem cannot be solved because we don't know how large each pixel is.

   B. The image file would be 200 pixels wide × 200 pixels high, so it would also appear 2 inches square on the screen.

   C. The image would appear 4 inches × 4 inches on the screen.

   D. None of the above

6. What element could be used in an XHTML document to insert images and what attribute provides a text value if the image doesn't appear?

   A. The IMG element, and the *text* attribute

   B. The IMAGE element, and the *text* attribute

   C. The IMG element, and the *alt* attribute

   D. None of the above

7. If you create an XML document that includes an image file, how might you produce finished HTML/XHTML from the XML document?

   A. Write a script to transform the XML elements into viewable HTML.

   B. Use an eXtensible Style Sheet.

   C. Let the application transform and convert the XML document.

   D. All of the above

8. In a SMIL document, in what element does the *region* element appear as a child, and what does the *region* element do?

   A. The *region* element appears in the *layout* element, and it defines a region for one or more media objects.

☑ *Mastery Check*

B. The *region* element appears as a child of the *smil* element, and it defines the region of your screen on which the viewport appears.

C. The *region* element appears as a child of the *par* element, and it defines any parallel regions in the layout.

D. None of the above

9. What code would you write to define a region with a unique identifier of *a1*, appearing 10 pixels from the top of the viewport, and 6 pixels from the left of the viewport?

   A. `<region name="a1" top="10" left="6"/>`

   B. `<region id="a1" top="10" left="6"/>`

   C. `<region name="a1" from_top="10" from_left="6"/>`

   D. None of the above

10. What elements control timing of media objects in the *body* element?

    A. The *time, start,* and *end* elements

    B. The *par* and *seq* elements

    C. The *clip-begin* and *clip-end* elements

    D. None of the above

11. What attribute controls layering of elements in the *region* element?

    A. The *z-index* attribute

    B. The *layer* attribute

    C. The *ref* attribute of the media object

    D. None of the above

12. If no explicit beginning is specified for a media object, when does the media object begin to show itself?

    A. As soon as the entire production begins

☑ *Mastery Check*

B. As soon as any elements of which it is a child element finish playing

C. Never

D. None of the above

13. What is the purpose of the *system* attributes?

   A. They reflect the system on which the SMIL document was created, so users can use the author's system settings to achieve similar results.

   B. They correspond with technical support of the SMIL document processing application online, to resolve any bugs or glitches while playback is occurring.

   C. They allow the SMIL document to query the system on which it's being played back, to select the most appropriate resource to play dependent on the user's system capabilities.

   D. None of the above

14. What is the purpose of the *switch* element, and how does it work?

   A. The *switch* element switches on the appropriate *media* element when the timing is right. It works by detecting the system time on the user's machine.

   B. The *switch* element switches among various regions on the screen, creating an animation effect when using GIF images. It works by detecting system capability to display GIF images.

   C. The *switch* element switches among various *media object* elements, based on which elements are found to be acceptable, and also matching the user's system capabilities.

   D. None of the above

15. What attribute specifies a media object's location for retrieval, and what attribute specifies the region into which the object should be placed?

   A. The *url* attribute specifies the retrieval location for a media object, and the *location* attribute specifies where the object should be placed on the screen.

5

☑ Mastery Check

B. The *location* attribute specifies where the media object may be retrieved from, and the *place* attribute specifies where the media object should be placed.

C. The *src* attribute specifies where the media object should be retrieved from, and the *region* attribute specifies where it should be placed.

D. None of the above

Module 6

XML Applications, XLink, XPath, and XPointer

The Goals of This Module

- Review XML development tools
- Find and Download Microsoft XML tools
- Review the XML Information Items Specification
- Review the XLink Specification
- Learn about XML document fragments
- Review the XPath Specification
- Practice using Microsoft XML tools
- Create an XML document using XLink links
- Create an XML document using XPath

In this module, you examine the software applications available for working with XML documents and W3C XML flavors, such as XLink and XPath. We use Microsoft applications and technologies because they've been on the forefront of development of the standards and tools to work with XML, and much of the functionality required for XML-driven sites has been built-in to Internet Explorer.

Application Development Tools and Languages

Many tools are available for the development of XML applications, such as the Simple API for XML (SAX) parser and the XML development environment you've been using (XML Spy 3.5). At this point, you're going to begin building online applications with XML, so you need to work with operating systems, servers, and browsers that have integrated XML capabilities.

Microsoft XML Tools

Microsoft has a complete tools set available for download at its Web site. Among the tools available are the MSXML 3.0 Software Developer's Kit (SDK), the MSXML 3.0 Parser, a command line validation tool, and some components built into Internet Explorer 5.01 and later. The easiest way to find these tools is to go to the Microsoft Web site (www.microsoft.com) and search for XML, and then choose Downloads for MSXML from the list of links returned.

You go to a page in the online Microsoft Developer's Network (MSDN) Downloads area. You can show or hide the TOC at your discretion. Clicking TOC listings brings up any subheadings for a TOC listing.

One of the first subheadings for XML downloads is Internet Explorer Tools for Validating XML and Viewing XSLT Output. Installing this download gives you two additional options from within Internet Explorer when viewing an XML document, validation, and XSLT viewing, of course. You can also install the MSXML SDK, which contains documentation for programming with XML. You might also want to install the XML Validation Tool.

Under the heading "XSL," you'll find a number of tools available for working with XSL. Some of these come in handy in Module 11. You'll want to download the XSL style sheet for XML Schemas tool and the XSLT Samples Viewer.

Using these tools, plus a good development environment like XML Spy, you can create XML documents quickly, validate them against your DTDs or Schemas, create style sheets, and easily check the output of the style sheets. And with the documentation included in the MSXML SDK, you can find plenty of examples of scripting and programming to make your XML documents an active part of Web sites and other back-end applications.

The XML Information Set

Building XML applications means more than just creating XML vocabularies or XML documents based on them. It means working with XML objects programmatically. The Document Object Model is covered in Module 8, but to lay some groundwork for this, we review the XML Information Set here. The XML Information Set has the status of Working Draft as of February 2, 2001, so it's a fairly recent compilation of particulars about XML and how XML document objects (such as elements, attributes, and so forth) should be viewed from a programming standpoint.

6

Information Items

Information Items are touched on in Module 4 (XML Schema), and are covered in more depth here. XML documents have an Information Set composed of Information Items and they have at least one called the document information item. An XML document needn't be valid to have an information set, but it must be well formed.

Information items are conceptual, an abstract representation of an XML document component, rather than a physically coded thing, like an element. Information items are real, however, and this specification details how applications may derive and work with them. The information set of an XML document contains at least one document element and perhaps several other elements, with each element having a set of properties. To give you an idea what they are, some information items may represent elements, and their properties reveal things such as what namespace they belong to. Their purpose is to provide details about the components making up the XML document, so they can be manipulated by applications.

The XML Information Set specification is meant to be generic, meaning it doesn't necessarily support or require a certain interface or class of interfaces. In the specification, items are formed into a tree structure, but interfaces that work with XML documents using events or queries can also produce data that conforms to the specification.

Information Set Constraints

A number of constraints exist on the way the XML Information Set specification deals with XML documents. For example, if an XML document doesn't conform to the Namespaces specification, it won't have an Information Set. Basically, if a document has element or attribute names with colons in them, it won't have an information set. Another requirement along these lines is that XML documents must have absolute URL references for namespace declarations or an information set won't be defined. Another feature is that entity references are represented in an expanded state, unless the parser doesn't retrieve the expanded entity. And, in an Information Set, items with a Null value are represented as null, rather than simply empty.

Information Item Types

Quite a few types of information item are defined by the specification, again, closely resembling the physically coded elements, attributes, and other document components they represent. The difference is, while physically coded components such as XML elements convey the actual content of the document, an information item conveys interesting properties or qualities of each component to work with them programmatically. The specification lists 17 types of information item, as follows:

- **Document Information Item**   The primary item from which all other items in the set may be accessed. It has properties such as children (a list of child items in document order, processing instruction, and comment items), document entities and elements, notations and entities, base URL (if known), whether the document is a "standalone" document, XML version, and an indicator of whether the entire DTD has been read.

- **Element Information Items**   Each element in the document has an element information item. Element information items contain properties such as namespace name, local name, prefix, an ordered list of child information items, attributes, namespace details, and parent.

- **Attribute Information Items**   Specified and default attributes each have an attribute information item, with properties such as namespace name, local name, prefix, normalized value, whether they were specified (or default), data type (as declared in the DTD), and the owner element for the attribute.

Many more information set items exist, including items for processing instructions, entity references, comments, characters, DTDs, and so on. Each has properties that indicate relevant qualities and they each make dealing with XML documents in a programmatic way easier, no matter what application interface is used.

1-Minute Drill

● What requirements does an XML document have to meet to have a set of information items?

● What are the properties of a comment information item?

XML Linking Language

6

The XML Linking Language version 1.0 is a proposed recommendation as of December 20, 2000. It defines a linking language for creating links internally and externally to XML documents. If you're familiar with how hyperlinks work in HTML documents, that's a good start for understanding XLink but, remember, many more functions could be constructed for links, if you have the tools available.

For example, suppose that, when a link is clicked, a menu appears offering a number of choices, rather than going directly to another document. This is only one example of how the capabilities of links could be expanded with more flexible link-building tools. XLink is designed to provide the basic, HTML-style links, as well as much more complex types of links.

XLink Fundamentals

The specification defines some basic concepts related to links, including six types of XLink element and the nature of resources. You're familiar with resources as anything you can retrieve, no matter how it's stored or created.

● To have a set of information items, an XML document must be well formed and be connected via an absolute URL to a namespace.

● The properties of a comment information item are the following: content, which is a string representing the content of the comment, and parent, which is the document, element, or document type declaration information item of which the comment information item is a child.

The specification calls resources "any addressable unit of information or service," such as files, images, and so forth. Addressing a resource is done by specifying its URL and there's also a means of addressing only a specific portion of a resource. Again, if you're familiar with HTML-style hyperlinks, you know it's possible to have a link that goes not only to a Web page, but to a particular spot on the page. That's an example of linking to a portion of a document. With XLink, however, the sophistication of linking capabilities to portions of resources is increased dramatically.

Resources involved in a link participate in the link and the resources aren't required to be only XML resources; any resource may be part of a link. And even though XLink makes creating ordinary hyperlinks easy, it's also designed for making links used only by computers. For example, a link for a person would probably give some indication of itself visually, while a link for another computer may be identifiable only in code.

In an XLink link, the action of following a link is called *traversal*, and traversal requires the involvement of at least two resources (although creating links with many resources involved is possible). The resource at the beginning of the traversal is called the *starting resource*, while the resource at the destination is called the *ending resource*. Information defining how to traverse resources is called an *arc*, and an arc includes the direction of traversal, and may include application behavior information. If a resource is part of a link because it (or its parent) is a linking element, it's a *local resource*, while any resource (even if coded into the element itself) is considered a *remote resource*. If an arc goes from a local resource to a remote resource, it's *outbound*, while an arc going the other way is *inbound*, and an arc with no local resources is called a *third-party arc*.

1-Minute Drill

- What is an XLink link?
- What is a remote resource?

- An XLink link is an explicit relationship between resources, but not necessarily a hyperlink.
- A remote resource is any resource or resource portion addresses by a URL, even if it's part of the current document.

Coding XLink Markup

If XLink links are to be used in an XML document, the elements and attributes must be connected to the XLink namespace at: http://www.w3.org/1999/xlink. To connect them, use the standard mechanism described in Module 4. For example, an individual element named Customer may be connected in the following fashion:

```
<Customer xmlns:xlink="http://www.w3.org/1999/xlink">
John Doe<Customer>
```

The prefix used (xlink) is used by convention only. Any prefix may be used.

Simple Links with XLink

A *simple link* in XLink creates a hyperlink with the same qualities as an HTML-style link. It may be made using a simpler syntax (because it's expected to be commonly used) and it can be produced using code, such as:

```
<mylink xlink:type="simple" xlink:href="nextdoc.xml">
Click Here</mylink>
```

Notice the type is specified with the XLink type attribute, and the XLink *href* attribute specifies where the link takes the user.

Extended Links with XLink

An *extended link* in XLink creates a hyperlink with all the functionality offered by XLink. Although the syntax is somewhat more complex, it may have any number of participating resources, with elements for remote and local resources, elements for defining arc traversal rules, and elements for making the link human readable.

XML Base

XML Base is a proposed recommendation as of December 20, 2000. The purpose of XML Base is to provide for XLink the same kind of functionality as the HTML BASE element. In HTML (or XHTML, of course), the BASE element gives

6

document authors a way to define the base URL of a document explicitly. If no BASE element is present, browsers assume the URL at which the document was found is the base URL; authors don't always want this to be the case, especially when the document may be copied across many systems while resources connected to the document by way of relative links may stay in their original location. Applying a base URL means no matter where the document travels, any resources specified by relative links will still be found.

XBase uses an XML attribute named xml:base. Obviously, this name is reserved as it begins with the string "xml". It can be used in XML documents to specify a base URL in the same way the HTML BASE element can be used and it provides the capability to specify a base URL for an entire document or for individual XLink elements, as shown in the following code:

```
<?xml version="1.0"?>
<doc xml:base="http://www.e4free.com/"     xmlns:xlink="http://www.w3.org/1999/xlink">
<mylink xlink:type="simple"
xlink:href="nextdoc.xml">Click Here</mylink>
<mydocs xml:base="/docs/"><mylink xlink:type="simple" xlink:href="doc1.xml">Document 1</mylink>
</doc>
```

The first link in this example is http://www.e4free.com. The second link is http://www.e4free.com/docs.

XPath

The XPath Language version 1.0 is a recommendation as of November 16, 1999. The purpose of the XPath Language is to provide a means of selecting individual parts of an XML document. XPath uses the path notation familiar to many people in URLs and DOS, or UNIX style drive, folder, and file navigation. XPath includes functionality for working with strings, numbers, and Boolean values, and also has matching mechanisms for finding particular nodes within an XML document. It works at the level of the information set, rather than the physically coded document. XML documents are viewed as trees of nodes, instead of a collection of elements and other XML document components, although these components are all represented (as discussed in XML Information Items).

XPath Expressions and the Context Node

To use XPath, expressions are constructed. An expression, properly coded, results in an object that is one of four types: a *node-set* (basically an unordered set of nodes with no duplicates), a Boolean value, a number, or a string.

When an expression is evaluated to produce an object, it has context, represented by a context node, context position and size (numerical values), variable bindings, a function library, and namespace declarations. Think of the context node as the current node, so any movement you perform is from the context (or current) node. Also, the context position represents the proximity position of the current node within the node-set in document order, and the context size represents the number of nodes in the current node set.

The XPath Location Path Expression

One of the primary purposes of XPath is to allow the selection of specific nodes from a document. In the same way a path might identify a particular file in a folder on a drive, a location path expression might identify and select particular elements or other document components (nodes) within an XML document.

A location path may be either absolute or relative (like a URL may be absolute or relative). An *absolute location path* points to the document node for context, while a *relative location path* points to some node relative to another node for its context. Each part of a location path expression is called a *step*, because it steps through various levels of nodes in an XML document. A location step contains an axis, a node test, and, optionally, predicates.

XPath Axes

An *axis* tells what relationship is used to identify nodes, such as child, parent, or descendant. A *node test* uses functions to identify the node type/name (such as text() or para, where *para* is the name of the elements being selected). A *predicate* uses additional small expressions to define exactly what node or node-set is being selected.

A number of axes, node test, and functions are available in XPath, and they're set into Table 6-1.

Axis	Description
Child	This axis contains child nodes for the context node.
Descendant	This axis contains all the descendant nodes, including child nodes and child nodes of child nodes, and so on. However, this axis doesn't include attribute or namespace nodes.
Parent	If the context node has a parent, it's contained in this axis.

Table 6-1   XPath Axes Available

Axis	Description
Ancestor	Any parent nodes or parents of parent nodes are contained in this axis. This axis always includes the root node, unless the context node is in the root node.
Following-sibling	This axis contains all the following siblings of the context node, unless the context node is an attribute or namespace node, in which case the following-sibling axis is empty.
Preceding-sibling	This axis contains all the preceding siblings of the context node, unless the context node is an attribute or namespace node, in which case the preceding-sibling axis is empty.
Following	This axis contains all the nodes that come after the context node in document order, except ancestor nodes, attribute nodes, and namespace nodes.
Preceding	This axis contains all the nodes that come before the context node in document order, except ancestor nodes, attribute nodes, and namespace nodes.
Attribute	This axis is used for the attribute nodes of the context node and is empty unless the context node is an element.
Namespace	This axis is used for the namespace nodes of the context node and is empty unless the context node is an element.
Self	This axis contains the context node alone.
Descendant-or-self	This axis contains the context node and its descendants.
Ancestor-or-self	This axis contains the context node and its ancestors.

Table 6-1   XPath Axes Available (*continued*)

XPath includes some functions that must be included in any conforming XPath implementation, called the *core function library*. These functions are broken down into node-set functions, string functions, Boolean functions, and number functions. Their definitions give the return type of the value or values returned, the name of the function, and the arguments the functions may use. Table 6-2 shows the XPath functions.

NodeSet Functions

Last()	The return type is number, the name of the function is *last,* and it has no arguments. The returned number is the context size for the context node found in the expression.

Table 6-2   XPath Functions Available

NodeSet Functions

Position()	The return type is number, the name of the function is *position,* and it has no arguments. The returned number is the context position for the context node found in the expression.
Count(node-set)	The return type is number, the name of the function is *count,* and it has node-set as an argument. The returned number is the number of nodes in the node-set found in the expression.
ID(object)	The return type is node-set, the name of the function is *id,* and it may have the unique ID of a node as an argument, or an expression that gives a list of ID values. The returned node or node-set consists of any nodes matching these ID values.
Local-name(node-set?)	The return type is string, the name of the function is *local-name,* and the argument is a node-set (the question mark means this argument is optional). The returned string is the local name for the node.
Namespace-uri(node-set?)	The return type is string, the name of the function is *namespace-uri,* and the argument is a node-set (the question mark means this argument is optional). The returned string is the URL for the namespace for the node. This function returns nothing, unless the node represents an element or attribute.
Name(node-set?)	The return type is string, the name of the function is *name,* and the argument is a node-set (the question mark means this argument is optional). The returned string is the QName (qualified name) for the node.

String Functions

String(object?)	The return type is string, the name of the function is *string,* and the argument is an object (the question mark means this argument is optional). The returned string may be the string value of the first node (in document order) if the argument represents a node-set, a string value for a number if the argument represents a number, the string "true" or false" for an argument representing a Boolean, and so on.
Concat(string, string)	The return type is string, the name of the function is *concat,* and the argument is a series of strings separated by commas. The returned string is the concatenated strings contained in the argument.

6

Table 6-2   XPath Functions Available (*continued*)

String Functions

Starts-with(string, string)	The return type is boolean, the name of the function is *start-with,* and the argument is a set of two strings separated by a comma. The returned value is "true" if the first string starts with the second string, and "false" if not.
Contains(string, string)	The return type is boolean, the name of the function is *contains,* and the argument is a set of two strings separated by a comma. The returned value is "true" if the first string contains the second string, and "false" if not.
Substring-before(string, string)	The return type is string, the name of the function is *substring-before,* and the argument is a set of two strings separated by a comma. The returned value is the portion of the first argument string that precedes the second argument string, if the second argument string is found inside the first argument string (unless, of course, the second argument string is located at the first position of the first argument string, in which case the returned value is nothing).
Substring-after(string, string)	The return type is string, the name of the function is *substring-after,* and the argument is a set of two strings separated by a comma. The returned value is the portion of the first argument string that comes after the second argument string, if the second argument string is found inside the first argument string (unless, of course, the second argument string is located at the last position of the first argument string, in which case the returned value is nothing).
Substring(string, number, number?)	The return type is string, the name of the function is *substring,* and the argument is a set consisting of a string followed by two numbers, the last number being optional, all separated by commas. The returned value is the portion of the first argument string that starts at the numerical position specified by the first number argument. If a second number argument exists, the string returned is limited to the number of characters specified as the second number argument. The first character position is 1, rather than starting at zero like some scripting and programming languages.

Table 6-2 XPath Functions Available *(continued)*

String Functions

String-length(string?)

The return type is number, the name of the function is *string-length,* and the argument is an optional string. The returned value is the number of characters in the string argument. If no argument is made, the returned value is the same as for the string-value function for the context node found in the expression.

Normalize-space(string?)

The return type is string, the name of the function is *normalize-space,* and the argument is an optional string. The returned value is the normalized (leading and trailing white space removed) string in the argument. If no argument is made, the returned value is the same as for the string-value function for the context node found in the expression.

Translate(string, string, string)

The return type is string, the name of the function is *translate,* and the argument is a set of three strings separated by commas. The returned value is the first argument string, but where characters found in the first argument string, which also appear in the second argument string, are replaced by the same characters of a different case found in the third argument string. This is primarily a case-changing function.

Boolean Functions

Boolean(object?)

The return type is boolean, the name of the function is *boolean,* and the argument is an optional object. The returned value is "true" if the object is a number that isn't positive or negative zero, if the object is a nonempty node-set, or if the object is a string whose length isn't zero.

Not(boolean)

The return type is boolean, the name of the function is *not,* and the argument is a boolean. The returned value is "true" if the boolean is "false", otherwise, the returned value is "false."

True()

The return type is boolean, the name of the function is *true,* and there's no argument. The returned value is "true."

False()

The return type is boolean, the name of the function is *false,* and there's no argument. The returned value is "false."

Table 6-2   XPath Functions Available *(continued)*

Boolean Functions

Lang(string)

The return type is boolean, the name of the function is *lang,* and the argument is a string. The returned value is "true" or false, depending on whether the language in the argument string is the same as the language specified in the *xml:lang* attribute of the context node.

Number Functions

Number(object?)

The return type is number, the name of the function is *number,* and the argument is an optional object. The returned value is "1" if the object is Boolean "true", and "0" is the object is Boolean "false". If the object is a string, the returned value is a number that's been converted from the string argument. Other objects types are also converted to numbers in this fashion.

Sum(node-set)

The return type is number, the name of the function is *sum,* and the argument is a node-set. The returned value is the sum of the values in the node-set.

Floor(number)

The return type is number, the name of the function is *floor,* and the argument is a number. The returned value is the largest integer number that doesn't exceed the argument.

Ceiling(number)

The return type is number, the name of the function is *ceiling,* and the argument is a number. The returned value is the smallest integer number that isn't less than the argument.

Round(number)

The return type is number, the name of the function is *round,* and the argument is a number. The returned value is the closest integer number to the argument.

Table 6-2   XPath Functions Available *(continued)*

The syntax for writing XPath Location Path expressions is available as a verbose syntax and an abbreviated syntax. In the next table, some examples of both are placed side by side to give you an idea how the expressions are constructed. Because you've been using an XML document with Customer elements throughout this book, the element name Customer is used to indicate

Unabbreviated	Abbreviated	Explanation
Child::Customer	Customer	Selects the Customer children of the context node
Child::*	*	Selects all element children of the context node
Child::text()	Text()	Selects all text node children of the context node
Child::node()	Node()	Selects all the child nodes of the context node, regardless of type
Attribute::name	@name	Selects the name attribute of the context node
Attribute::*	@*	Selects all the attributes of the context node
/Descendant::Customer	.//Customer	Selects all Customer elements in the same document as the context node
/	/	Selects the document root (note, both kinds of expression are the same)
Child::Customer[position()=1]	Customer[1]	Selects the first Customer child of the context node

Table 6-3   XPath Unabbreviated and Abbreviated Syntax

6

Customer elements in an XML document. Note that the double-colon separates axis and element names/function names, while the slash and dots are abbreviations for longer axis names. Also, note, retrieval of attributes is simplified with the abbreviation @ for the term "attribute." Table 6-3 shows the XPath unabbreviated and abbreviated syntax.

1-Minute Drill

● What symbol selects all child elements of the context node?
● What symbol selects the parent of the context node?

● The asterisk (*) selects all child elements of the context node.
● Two dots (..) select the parent of the context node.

XML Pointer Language

The XML Pointer Language version 1.0 has the status of working draft as of January 8, 2001. The purpose of the XML Pointer Language is to allow addressing of parts of an XML document based on element types, attribute values, character content, and relative position, a finer degree of addressing control than XPath allows. Addressing is allowed whether or not an explicit ID attribute is available. Parts of a document found with XPointer may be used as link targets or for any other purpose.

Specific extensions to XPath found in XPointer include the ability to address points and ranges in XML documents (rather than just nodes), to find strings via string matching or pattern matching, and to attach XPointer expressions to URL references (like the anchor target can be attached to a URL reference in XHTML).

Proj6-1.zip

Project 6-1: Creating Examples of XLink and XPath

In the following example, because these languages are used with other code to select nodes, you perform a set of exercises designed to improve your skill at generating selection expressions. Each miniproject in the Step-by-Step uses a verbal explanation of the nodes to select, followed by an example of the code required to perform the selection.

Step-by Step

1. The requirement is to select all element nodes in an XML document that have the name Customer. This expression would use the slash to indicate the root node, and the Descendant axis to retrieve all descendant elements of the root node. The element name Customer would then specify that only the element named Customer should be retrieved. The unabbreviated syntax for this selection is this:

```
/Descendant::Customer
```

2. The requirement is to select all element nodes in any Order elements in an XML document that have the name OrderItem. This expression would start with descendant-or-self to indicate the context node or any children of the context node. Next, it would use the node() axis to indicate retrieval of any node. Following that would be a slash, and then the name of the element to retrieve. Finally, it would have another slash, and then the axis Child and the element name OrderItem to indicate retrieval of the child nodes named OrderItems. The abbreviated version would start with the double-slash instead of descendant-or-child to indicate it starts at a level of element other than the root. The element name Orders would indicate the Order element is the correct level to start at, and the Child axis further indicates that only direct Child elements of the Order element should be retrieved. The element name OrderItem specifies the elements to retrieve at this level. The unabbreviated syntax for this selection is

```
descendant-or-self::node()/Order/Child::OrderItem
```

Here is the abbreviated syntax for this selection:

```
//Order/OrderItem
```

3. The requirement is to select the parent elements of any elements in an XML document named Orders. The abbreviated syntax for this selection is this:

```
../Orders
```

4. The requirement is to select all attributes named customerid from Customer elements within an XML document. The abbreviated syntax for this selection would be as follows:

```
//Customer/@customerid
```

5. The requirement is to select the last element named Order from the first Orders element in an XML document. The abbreviated syntax for this selection is shown here:

```
//Orders[1]/Orders[last()]
```

6

☑ *Mastery Check*

1. What XML documents have information sets?

   A. Those that are well formed and valid

   B. Those that are valid

   C. Those that are well formed

   D. All of the above

2. Under what circumstances might a well-formed XML document not have a meaningful information set?

   A. When the document isn't valid

   B. When the document doesn't conform to the specification of the namespaces

   C. When the document is well formed

   D. None of the above

3. What is the purpose of the "All declarations processed" property of the document information item?

   A. It's a Boolean value that indicates whether the complete DTD has been read.

   B. It's part of the infoset that contains null values.

   C. It's part of the infoset that represents the complete DTD.

   D. All of the above

4. How many document information items may be present in an XML document?

   A. Two: one for the root element, and one for the root attribute

   B. One

   C. Zero if no information set is present, otherwise one

   D. None of the above

☑ *Mastery Check*

5. How many element information items occur in the infoset of an XML document possessing an infoset, and what is the purpose of the prefix property for these items?

A. One for the entire document, with properties denoting each additional element within the document

B. One for each element within the document. The prefix property denotes the name prefix in the epilog of the document

C. One for each element in the document. The prefix denotes the namespace prefix, if any, attached to the element

D. None of the above

6. When would an attribute specified in a DTD not appear as an attribute information item in the infoset of an XML document?

A. When the attribute has an unknown value

B. When the attribute isn't found

C. When the attribute has an implied value (#IMPLIED)

D. B or C

E. All of the above

7. Which of the following statements is a good definition of an XLink link?

A. An explicit relationship between resources or portions of resources

B. An explicit relationship between files or portions of files

C. An explicit relationship between elements or portions of elements

D. None of the above

6

✓ Mastery Check

8. In XLink, what is a remote resource and how is it addressed?

A. A remote resource is any resource referenced and it's addressed by a reference, such as a URL.

B. A remote resource is one that's physically separate from the file containing the local resource and it's addressed by reference.

C. A remote resource is one that's part of a linking element and it's addressed by value.

D. None of the above

9. What is a traversal and what terms are used for resources involved in a traversal?

A. A traversal is the act of using or following a link for any purpose. The resources involved are called "involved resources."

B. A traversal is the arc followed when a link is clicked. The resources involved are called "involved resources."

C. A traversal is the act of using or following a link for any purpose. The resources involved are called the starting resource and the ending resource.

D. None of the above

10. What is the purpose of a location path expression, in XPath?

A. A location path expression selects for a set of nodes from the context of the XML document.

B. A location path expression denotes the set of locations for links to click to.

C. A location path expression identifies a series of locations at which the contents of an XML document may be found.

D. All of the above

☑ Mastery Check

11. What is the purpose of the XPointer language?

    A. XPointer allows the creation of pointers to other documents from inside an XML document.

    B. XPointer provides a means of addressing the internal structures of an XML document.

    C. XPointer is used for creating variables in XML documents that point to specific locations in memory.

    D. None of the above

12. What extended capabilities does XPointer bring to XPath?

    A. The ability to locate data via string matching

    B. The ability to identify certain points in XML documents

    C. The use of addressing expressions in URL fragments

    D. All of the above

13. What XML development tools might make up a good set of applications for creating, modifying, and maintaining XML vocabularies and documents?

    A. A validating XML parser, development environment, and XSL processor

    B. Programming development environment

    C. SAX

    D. None of the above

14. From what XML language is XPointer built on?

    A. XLink

    B. XPath

    C. XQuery

    D. All of the above

6

✓ Mastery Check

15. What is one of the primary uses for XPath and XPointer?

A. To assist in the transformation process performed by XSLT

B. To help make links valid between XML documents

C. To assist in the production of Web queries

D. None of the above

Module 7

XML and the Web

The Goals of This Module

- Learn how the Web works
- Learn about browsers and Web servers
- Create a structure for an XML-based Web site
- Perform common XML functions with XHTML documents
- Learn about XML Signatures
- Learn about P3P
- Create an XML document integrating XForms

XML documents, without being transformed into a suitable format for display in a browser, appear as XML code, which is not an appropriate format when people are browsing your site. Module 11 covers XML document translation using style sheets, including XSL and CSS2. In this module, you'll learn how to build a Web site based on XML: the structure, navigation, and other elements that might go into a finished Web site. In addition, you learn about XML Signature, Platform for Privacy Preferences (P3P), XForms, and a variety of technologies that can be used to make your Web site dynamic.

The Nature of the Web

Whether being accessed by a browser manipulated by a person or directly from another server, a Web site, by definition, is made available on the Internet via software called a Web server. Within the Web site may be files and references to other files, references to stored data, and programming capable of generating content. Altogether, the data referenced is referred to as *resources,* reminding us that not all data comes as files.

How data is arranged and referenced within a Web site is the subject of the first half of this module. How data is retrieved from a Web site depends on the capabilities of the browser or other application performing the retrieval, and the server software, data storage methods, and programming constructed by the Web site author. Let's talk about the simplest case first.

Plain HTML Web Sites

The simplest Web sites are made from plain text files containing HTML tags and character content, stored in a special folder tied to a Web server. Using a protocol called *HTTP* (HyperText Transfer Protocol), browser and server communicate quite a bit of information during the retrieval of copies of the text files. The browser interprets the HTML tags to arrange the character content in the fashion intended by the author, no matter which operating system the browser runs on. HTML is called a *platform-independent language* for this reason. However, the constant evolution of HTML as a markup language and competitive pressures on browser makers subvert this independence. Browsers often incorporate "extensions" to the HTML standard that aren't supported in competing browsers, and earlier versions of browsers don't support the most recent upgrades to the HTML standard.

The general problem is how to render content, no matter what the intended platform. In Module 11, you'll learn about eXtensible Stylesheet Language (XSL), which offers a means of transforming XML elements and content into a format suitable for rendering on any platform (at least, all the known platforms at the time). But how should resources be arrayed on the server side, when should processing be done on the client side, and how should the client-side user-interface be constructed?

In a plain (or static) HTML Web site, navigation is performed via hypertext links from one location to another, both inside the Web site and to other Web locations. Because the earliest HTML is understood by virtually all browsers (early browsers ignore HTML tags they don't understand, such as incompatible extensions or new standard tags), using relatively early versions of HTML to get the broadest support is common. Creative use of tables and graphics make the construction of nicely done page layouts possible, while the Cascading Style Sheet language has features useful in the later browsers for gaining exact control over the placement and appearance of elements.

Web-Building Tools

Notepad, the plain text editor that's provided as part of the Windows operating system, can be used to build plain HTML Web pages manually. Quite a few more advanced tools, such as Microsoft FrontPage and Macromedia Dreamweaver, make the page development process easier and more efficient. And, because graphics play such an important role in Web sites, many graphics tools have been developed specifically to assist in the construction or conversion of graphics for the Web.

All in all, many technologies are available for properly rendering Web pages in browsers, but these still fall short of total flexibility in rendering. And navigation is still mainly done via simple hypertext links. For simpler sites, the construction of five or six pages seems enough to serve immediate purposes. A typical Web site might be laid out as shown in Figure 7-1.

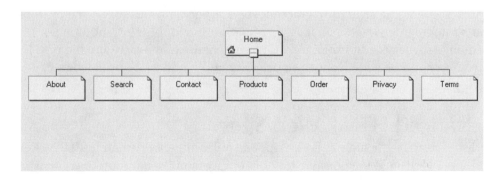

Figure 7-1   A simple Web site layout

Coding a Simple Web Site

Writing the code for a simple Web site is no longer much of a chore, especially if an HTML-editing program, such as FrontPage or Dreamweaver, is used. The hardest part is figuring out what content should be included and how it should be arranged. For example, FrontPage has built-in templates for starting Web sites. The following code example for an index page was constructed in about five seconds (but remember that using such a Web page under most circumstances wouldn't be appropriate without extensive customization):

```
<html><head>
<meta http-equiv="Content-Type" content="text/html; charset=windows-1252">
<meta http-equiv="Content-Language" content="en-us">
<title>Home</title>
</head>
<body>
<hr align="center">
<p>   </p>
<h2>Company Profile</h2>
<p>   </p>
<hr align="center">
<p>   </p>
<h2>Contact Information</h2>
<dl>
<dt><strong>Telephone</strong> </dt>
<dt><strong>FAX</strong> </dt>
<dt><strong>Postal address</strong> </dt>
<dt><strong>Electronic mail</strong> </dt>
</dl>
<p> </p>
</body>
</html>
```

Today, basic Web pages like the one in this example are supplemented by graphics, including structural graphics such as backgrounds, bars, and buttons and photographic images, such as people, places, and things. In addition, scripting languages add programmatic functionality and nearly any file type or resource can be added, such as streaming audio and video or Adobe's PDF format for documents.

Advanced HTML Web Sites

Scripting languages, such as JavaScript and VBScript, can run on both the client and server side, making possible much more dynamic generation of content and rendering. Detecting the capabilities of the browser making requests for Web pages makes providing pages formatted specifically for the requesting browser possible. By combining scripting with HTML forms, you can produce fully interactive Web sites, with two-way communication in real time. In fact, some Web sites now resemble typical desktop applications both in terms of the user interface and their functionality.

On the server side (often called the *back end*), the bulk of the content of a Web site may be stored in a database or other formatted information structure. Scripting languages can connect to databases, retrieve content, and format the retrieved content into Web pages for rendering. Many more programmatic functions can be accomplished through the activation of component programs written in traditional programming languages, such as the C language. Web sites allowing access to a variety of back-end databases and processing functions are called *multitier* or *n-tier* applications.

More and more, the Web site is evolving into a user interface that allows access to unlimited resources. The general problem, then, becomes the integration of all these back-end resources. Because XML is a standard that uses data that describes itself, XML is the preferred means of formatting data for use across multiple platforms and applications.

XML Web Sites

The end product, or rendered resource, on an XML Web site being viewed by a user will most likely include Web pages constructed with XHTML and style-sheet commands in some fashion. In many cases, a database (or some form of database access) is also included. The database application used to store content will probably be capable of storing XML data in a format that takes advantage of the Document Object Model (the DOM, discussed in Module 8) so the structure complements the XML, rather than simply storing the data as text files in fields. Note that some databases already do this, and the majority of database application products are expected to have this capability soon.

Proj7-1.zip

Project 7-1: Outlining an Architecture

For this project, you're going to create a Web site based on XML documents for distributing and managing documents. First, you define an overall structure, and then you define how each page should look and what its content should be.

Step-by-Step

1. Decide what pages should be present. For example, a home page (typically named index.html) must be available to greet users when they first access the site. Most Web sites also include About, Contact, Search, Order (if ordering is allowed), Privacy, and Terms.

2. Web site design usually includes the top-level pages in the root folder of the site, so you load your pages into the root folder. The purpose of the site is to allow documents to be managed and distributed, however, so you make a folder to keep the documents in and reference them from the Search page.

3. Because management of documents implies that only designated users (working for the Web site owners) can have access to management pages, you must also create a Management folder, in which document management pages are present. This folder should be secured (using SSL, for example), and pages in this folder should be password protected.

4. Now decide what the general layout and design for the site should be. Use a professional graphic artist to get a professional look. Although this is quite common, many Web sites find it practical to have the company logo/banner at the top of the page, menu choices down the left-hand side, and the primary content of the pages in the remaining area. Drop-down style menus across the top under the logo are also quite common, and copyright and other information of that nature can appear at the bottom with a set of text links.

5. The first page in the site, named index.html, is simply coded with XHTML, as follows:

```
<?xml version="1.0" encoding="UTF-8"?>
<!DOCTYPE html PUBLIC "-//W3C//DTD XHTML 1.0 Strict//EN"
 "DTD/xhtml1-strict.dtd">
<html><head><title>Untitled Document</title>
<meta http-equiv="Content-Type" content="text/html; charset=iso-8859-1">
</head>
<body bgcolor="#FFFFFF"><center>
<table width="416" border="0" cellspacing="0" cellpadding="0">
<tr>
<td><img src="baby.gif" width="116" height="150"></td>
<td><img src="text.gif" width="427" height="100"></td>
</tr>
<tr>
<td colspan="2">
<div align="center">
<div align="center">
<table border="0" width="400" cellpadding="0" cellspacing="0" height="515">
<tr>
<td width="100%" background="mission.gif"><a href="events.asp">
<marquee style="font-family: Arial; font-size: 10pt; color: #0000FF;
font-weight: bold">
Conference Coming Up!! Click Here For More Information</marquee></a>
</td></tr></table></div>
<p> </p></div>
</td></tr><tr>
<td colspan="2"><!-- #include file = "footer.inc" --></td>
</tr></table></center>
</body></html>
```

And here's how the Web page looks:

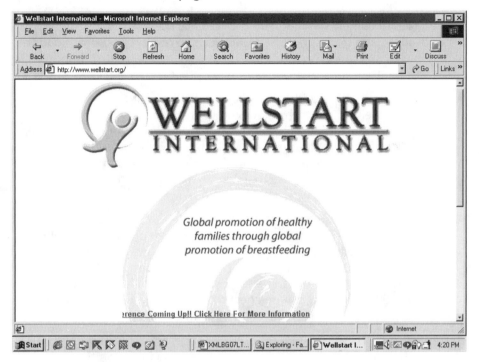

6. Notice this HTML file has a line near the bottom for an "include" file. This mechanism allows the author to insert identical information at the bottom of every page, making maintenance a much easier task. Include files are supported by all the major Web servers; the only requirements are that the filename extension for the pages into which the content is inserted must be .shtm, .shtml, or some other special extension that indicates extra processing is required (.asp and JSP files automatically support include files). Here's the code for the include file:

```
<center><font size="2" face="Arial, Helvetica, sans-serif">
<a href="donations.asp">[Donations]</a>
<a href="publications.asp">[Publications]</a>
<a href="contact.asp">[Contact Us]</a>
<a href="about.asp">[About Wellstart]</a>
<a href="privacy.asp">[Privacy]</a>
<a href="events.asp">[Events]</a>
</font>
<hr>
<b><font color="#999999" face="Arial, Helvetica, sans-serif"
size="-2">Wellstart International - A Non-Profit Corporation <p>
All trademarks and registered trademarks are of their respective companies.<br>
© Copyright 2000, 2001 Wellstart International, Inc., all rights reserved
©</p></font></b></center>
```

7. Now you begin the construction of the design of the database and the flow of processing and screens within the Web site so users can search, browse, and order documents in hard copy. Of course, users with high-speed connections and good printers might prefer to retrieve and download the documents and print them themselves. But users who require hundreds of copies of a given document, this ordering process may be more efficient.

8. The database must hold identifying information about the documents available as well as links to those documents and, perhaps, the number in stock, the prices, shipping charges, shipping times, author and publisher information, and other information. In Modules 9 and 10, the design of databases such as these is covered in depth; for now, assume all you need is a simple, one-table database that can be searched to find the desired documents.

9. Now you must create a search form so documents can be searched by category, and an ordering form so users can enter contact and shipping information as well as pertinent information about the quantity of each document they want to receive. These pages and forms must be connected to the database, so orders can be entered. You must also include an administrative page that can be checked on a regular basis for orders (you could also build in e-mail notification of orders).

10. The database, because it's so simple and usage isn't expected to be heavy, can be built with Microsoft Access and placed in a folder on the Web site. An easy way to connect to the database is via a Data Source Name (DSN). The DSN holds information about the filename of the database, the given name for the DSN (this is what is placed in the code to make the connection), and the Open Database Connectivity (ODBC) driver that allows the code to perform actions on the database. Actions on the database are written in Standard Query Language (SQL), programming is done in Visual Basic Scripting Edition (VBScript), and the built-in (to the Windows NT operating system) Web technologies Active Server Pages (ASP) and Active Data Objects (ADO) provide added functionality to make the job easier.

1-Minute Drill

● What are the components of Web sites?

● Where are these components located?

● The components of Web sites are files, data in information structures such as databases, and processing instructions resulting in content.
● These components are located anywhere on the Internet, often in a Web site.

XML Signatures

XML-Signature Syntax and Processing has the status of Candidate Recommendation as of October 31, 2000, and, thus, is on its way to becoming stable and usable as a specification. Its purpose is to provide standard rules for creating and presenting digital signatures. As you may be aware, laws passed recently make digital signatures as valid as hand-written signatures, but they don't specify what technology must be used to accomplish digital signatures. This proposed standard is one of several that may end up in wide use.

The recommendation states that an XML Signature can be applied to any data object, and specifies an XML signature element and an XML signature application. An example of the code that might be included in an XML signature is shown here, based on an example in the recommendation:

```
<Signature Id="MySignature"
 xmlns="http://www.w3.org/2000/09/xmldsig#">
<SignedInfo>
<CanonicalizationMethod
 Algorithm="http://www.e4free.com/canonalgorithm>
<SignatureMethod
 Algorithm="http://www.e4free.com/sigmethod"/>
<Reference URI="http://www.e4free.com/
XMLBeginnersGuide/Module07/XMLSig/example.htm">
```

7

The SignedInfo element contains a CanonicalizationMethod element and a SignatureMethod element. The former specifies the algorithm used to canonicalize the SignedInfo element before it's digested, and the latter is used to convert the product of the former operation into the SignatureValue.

```
<Transforms>
<Transform
 Algorithm="http://www.e4free.com/tranalgorithm"/>
</Transforms>
<DigestMethod
 Algorithm="http://www.e4free.com/digmethod"/>
<DigestValue>ste5gu7kj4w4y66766fc</DigestValue>
</Reference>
</SignedInfo>
<SignatureValue>ertawewewertrtt43566r4rer…
</SignatureValue>
<KeyInfo>
<KeyValue>
<DSAKeyValue>
```

```
key value elements and content
</DSAKeyValue>
</KeyValue>
</KeyInfo>
</Signature>
```

This example includes the signature element (connected to the namespace for XML Signature), the signedinfo element containing the canonicalization method and signature method algorithms, the reference element identifying the location of the data to be signed, the transform and digest method algorithms, and the DSAkeyvalue element.

The Signature Element

The Signature element is the root element of an XML Signature and all other elements in the signature document are child elements of it. In the recommendation, both a Schema and a DTD are present. Looking at the Schema provides more information about the nature and purpose of the Signature element:

```
<element name="Signature">
<complexType>
<sequence>
<element ref="ds:SignedInfo"/>
<element ref="ds:SignatureValue"/>
<element ref="ds:KeyInfo" minOccurs="0"/>
<element ref="ds:Object" minOccurs="0"
 maxOccurs="unbounded"/>
</sequence>
<attribute name="Id" type="ID" use="optional"/>
</complexType>
</element>
```

As you can see from the Schema code for the Signature element, its content consists of a sequence of elements (SignedInfo, SignatureValue, KeyInfo, and Object) all coming from (via the *ds* prefix) the namespace for the XML Signature recommendation (**www.w3.org/2000/09/xmldsig**), as well as an attribute named Id of type ID.

The SignatureValue Element

The SignatureValue element contains the value of the digital signature, which is simply an element named SignatureValue with a data type of CryptoBinary, as defined in the recommendation, based on the data types found in XML Schema. The data type is defined as a simpleType, as follows:

```
<simpleType name="CryptoBinary">
<restriction base="binary">
<encoding value="base64"/>
</restriction>
</simpleType>
```

This shows the type is a restriction of the binary base type, encoded in base64.

The SignedInfo Element

The SignedInfo element includes a sequence of elements (the Canonicalization Method element, the Signature Method element, and one or more Reference elements) as well as an attribute named Id of type ID. The SignedInfo element is required and represents the information that's actually signed.

1-Minute Drill

- What is the purpose of XML Signature?
- What are the limitations of XML Signature?

7

Platform for Privacy Preferences

The Platform for Privacy Preferences (P3P) 1.0 specification has the status of Candidate Recommendation as of December 15, 2000. The purpose of this recommendation is to provide Web sites with a standard way to express their privacy policies to make these policies easily downloadable and read by user agents (browsers, for example). Then, users may quickly sift through Web sites to find those in which the privacy policies match their own needs or expectations. P3P doesn't transfer or secure data, however, and it doesn't enforce privacy policies at any particular Web site. P3P is a notification mechanism only.

- The purpose of XML Signature is to provide a standard, XML-based means of applying digital signatures to data objects, either as a part of the object or externally.
- XML Signature doesn't authenticate the actual association of a given key to a given person or organization.

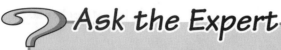

Ask the Expert

Question: Why the focus on traditional HTML/XHTML Web sites?

Answer: Much of the XML work you'll do ends up as a Web site in someone's browser. Of course, the same XML may also be read by other applications, but the first step in understanding transformation of XML documents from one format to another is a good idea of the target format—in this case, a standard Web site. Before you get into building complete online XML-based Internet applications, you need to know what's currently found on Web sites, so you understand exactly what you're aiming for when you begin performing transformations in Module 11 and building applications in Module 12.

Question: So, what might be in an online XML-based application, besides XML?

Answer: All resources that aren't XML documents (such as image, video, and audio files) are present, although they don't necessarily have to be located at the same URL. Structured data sources, such as databases, spreadsheets, and the like should also be accessible, but not necessarily at the same URL. Style sheets coding transformations of XML documents should be available, as well as any DTDs or schemas. XML documents present may include any of the XML formats discussed and any new ones required for supporting the functionality of the application.

According to the specification, P3P "provides a way for a Web site to encode its data-collection and data-use practices in a machine-readable XML format known as a *P3P policy*." To support the policy, a policy reference file is used, which details references to the policy itself, locations of the pages covered by the policy, cookies, and access methods covered by the policy, and the period of time for which the policy is valid. Policies may be referenced and defined using code such as that in the following example:

```
<META xmlns="http://www.w3.org/2000/12/P3Pv1">
<POLICY-REFERENCES>
<EXPIRY max-age="144800"/>
```

```
<POLICY-REF about="/P3P/Policy1.xml">
<INCLUDE>/*</INCLUDE>
<EXCLUDE>/oldproducts/*</EXCLUDE>
<EXCLUDE>/images/*</EXCLUDE>
</POLICY-REF>
<POLICY-REF about="/P3P/Policy2.xml">
<INCLUDE>/oldproducts/*</INCLUDE>
</POLICY-REF>
<POLICY-REF about="/P3P/Policy3.xml">
<INCLUDE>/newproducts/*</INCLUDE>
</POLICY-REF>
</POLICY-REFERENCES>
</META>
```

In this example, policy references have been defined using the meta element, in code that's considered well-formed XML. Policy elements define sections of the structure of a Web site as being included or excluded within a policy referenced in a subdirectory (the P3P subdirectory) of the Web site, and named Policy1.xml, Policy2.xml, and Policy43.xml. Obviously, each of these three policies treats privacy in a different way.

The actual XML documents' coding policies are somewhat more complex and must be considered carefully in terms of what the actual privacy policies of the Web site in question are or should be. For example, the following code examples (based on examples given in the recommendation) form a fairly commercial privacy policy for a Web site engaged in product sales:

```
<POLICY xmlns=http://www.w3.org/2000/12/P3Pv1
ns1=http://www.e4free.com/XMLBeginnersGuide/
Module07/P3P/Policy1.xml
ns2="http://www.e4free.com/P3P.html">
<ENTITY>
<DATA-GROUP>
<DATA ref="#business.name">
CustomerExample</DATA>
<DATA ref="#postal.street">2000 Washington Ave.</DATA>
<DATA ref="#postal.city">San Diego</DATA>
<DATA ref="#stateprov">CA</DATA>
<DATA ref="#postalcode">92101</DATA>
<DATA ref="#country">USA</DATA>
<DATA ref="#email">customer@e4free.com</DATA>
<DATA ref="#telephone.intcode">1</DATA>
<DATA ref="#telephone.loccode">619</DATA>
<DATA ref="#telephone.number">222-5151</DATA>
```

7

```
</DATA-GROUP>
</ENTITY>
<ACCESS><contact-and-other/></ACCESS>
<DISPUTES-GROUP>
<DISPUTES resolution-type="independent"
 service=http://www.e4free.com
short-description="www.e4free.com">
<IMG src="http://www.e4free.com/Logo.gif"
 alt="e4free's logo"/>
<REMEDIES><correct/></REMEDIES>
</DISPUTES>
</DISPUTES-GROUP>
<STATEMENT>
<CONSEQUENCE>
This site records information to
 serve customers and to secure and
 improve Web site performance.
</CONSEQUENCE>
<PURPOSE><admin/><develop/></PURPOSE>
<RECIPIENT><ours/></RECIPIENT>
<RETENTION><stated-purpose/></RETENTION>
<DATA-GROUP>
<DATA ref="#clickstream.server"/>
<DATA ref="#http.useragent"/>
</DATA-GROUP>
</STATEMENT>
<STATEMENT>
<CONSEQUENCE>
This information is used when a purchase is made.
</CONSEQUENCE>
<PURPOSE><current/></PURPOSE>
<RECIPIENT><ours/></RECIPIENT>
<RETENTION><stated-purpose/></RETENTION>
<DATA-GROUP>
<DATA ref="#name"/>
<DATA ref="#postal"/>
<DATA ref="#telephone"/>
<DATA ref="#business.postal"/>
<DATA ref="#business.telephone"/>
<DATA ref="#email"/>
<CATEGORIES><purchase/></CATEGORIES>
</DATA>
</DATA-GROUP>
</STATEMENT>
```

```
<STATEMENT>
<CONSEQUENCE>
Marketing materials
will be sent.
</CONSEQUENCE>
<PURPOSE>
<contact required="opt-in"/>
<customization required="opt-in"/>
<tailoring required="opt-in"/>
</PURPOSE>
<RECIPIENT required="opt-in">
<ours/><same/></RECIPIENT>
<RETENTION><stated-purpose/>
</RETENTION>
<DATA-GROUP>
<DATA ref="#name" optional="yes"/>
<DATA ref="#postal" optional="yes"/>
<DATA ref="#telephone" optional="yes"/>
<DATA ref="#business.postal" optional="yes"/>
<DATA ref="#business.telephone" optional="yes"/>
<DATA ref="# email" optional="yes"/>
</DATA-GROUP>
</STATEMENT>
<STATEMENT>
<CONSEQUENCE>
A password will allow you
access to your own information.
</CONSEQUENCE>
<PURPOSE><customization required="opt-in"/>
</PURPOSE>
<RECIPIENT><ours/></RECIPIENT>
<RETENTION><stated-purpose/>
</RETENTION>
<DATA-GROUP>
<DATA ref="#dynamic.miscdata">
<CATEGORIES><uniqueid/></CATEGORIES>
</DATA>
</DATA-GROUP>
</STATEMENT>
<STATEMENT>
<CONSEQUENCE>
This site will be tailored to
highlight products related to your interests.
</CONSEQUENCE>
```

7

```
<PURPOSE>
<customization required="opt-in"/>
<tailoring required="opt-in"/>
</PURPOSE>
<RECIPIENT><ours/></RECIPIENT>
<RETENTION><stated-purpose/></RETENTION>
<DATA-GROUP>
<DATA ref="#user.bdate.ymd.year" optional="yes"/>
<DATA ref="#user.gender" optional="yes"/>
</DATA-GROUP>
</STATEMENT>
<STATEMENT>
<CONSEQUENCE>
We tailor our site based on your past visits.
</CONSEQUENCE>
<PURPOSE><tailoring/><develop/></PURPOSE>
<RECIPIENT><ours/></RECIPIENT>
<RETENTION><stated-purpose/></RETENTION>
<DATA-GROUP>
<DATA ref="#dynamic.cookies">
<CATEGORIES><state/></CATEGORIES>
</DATA>
<DATA ref="#dynamic.miscdata">
<CATEGORIES><preference/></CATEGORIES>
</DATA>
</DATA-GROUP>
</STATEMENT>
</POLICY>
```

XForms

XForms is currently a working draft at the W3C (**www.w3.org/TR/xforms**). This means XForms shouldn't be used as a standard yet and may be changed or made obsolete at any time. However, because some type of specialized XML vocabulary for forms will most likely be commonly used with XML documents, particularly when rendered for human use, XForms are reviewed here.

Simple HTML/XHTML forms offer a simple set of controls and functions for Web-based interaction. The controls in HTML include fill-in fields, radio and check boxes, a drop-down menu, and buttons. A few variations on these exist, but the number of choices is limited compared to the extensive set of controls available in the user interface of most modern applications. Also, only two functions are available—submit and reset—either submitting the contents of the form to the Web server (or whatever action was prescribed by the author) or setting the contents of the form back to its initial state.

Like many other implementations of XML, XForms strives to separate the functionality and purpose of an XForms document from the rendering or presentation of the document. The purpose of the document is defined in the *XForms model,* which is written as an XML form definition. The XForms model may be worked with via the XForms user interface, an XHMTL document, a Wireless Markup Language (WML) document, or even proprietary user interfaces. Each of these latter methods for working with the XForms model is a user interface to the controls in the model. The application processing the form is called an *XForms Processor.* Data is submitted to the XForms Processor via the *XForms Submit Protocol,* which defines operations between an XForms document and the back-end processing.

The XForms Model

The XForms model defines model items, the structure of data in the form (called *XML instance data*), data types for the model items, limits and restrictions on the model types as the form is being filled, and relationships and dependencies between model items. Model items are individual pieces of data collected in a form; the XForms model is essentially a data model. In the draft, the XForms model is broken into two parts: Data Structures and XForms Extensions.

Data Structures includes the structure of the data and the data types applied to individual pieces of data. *XForms Extensions* is used to apply constraints, dependencies, expressions, and calculations to the data collected. Although XForms retains the features of XML Schema (such as data types and constraints), it also allows extensions to these capabilities, such as the ability to make certain fields read-only or to make certain fields active based on the condition of other fields. And XForms is designed to work with data using decimal numbers for accuracy and to allow forms to be prefilled with data (such as choices in a drop-down menu).

The XForms Submit Protocol

The *XForms Submit Protocol* is in the process of being defined, but it has as its goals "to allow rich, internationalized, hierarchical XML instance data, transferred over the XForms Submit Protocol." In addition, the protocol allows remote serialization of instance data, meaning a form half filled-in could be stopped and resumed at a later time.

XForms Data Types

All *XForms data types* are extensions or restrictions of XML Schema data types, so it's fortunate these were already reviewed. String, Boolean, Number, Duration, and other data types are all nearly identical, even to the definition of lexical and canonical terms and the applicability of facets such as precision and scale. The primary difference is that facets defined in XML Schema (which can be used when the appropriate namespace is applied) are static and unchanging, while facets defined in XForms (which may have the same name, but a different namespace) are dynamic and can be changed on the fly when the form is rendered or during use. What this means is the following code example would be valid:

```
<weight name="finalWeight" min="beginningWeight" />
<date name="beginningWeight" max="finalWeight" />
```

In this example, the data type finalWeight has a minimum equal to the beginningWeight, which, in turn, has a maximum equal to the finalWeight, thereby binding the two data types to each other and making them fully dynamic and dependent on the values each take on when the form is filled out.

Model Item Properties

Model items are like containers for data in an XForms document. Through the use of *Model Item Properties,* properties can be attached to individual model items such that the behavior of these items changes when rendered. For example, applying the read-only property to a model item means that item may be read but not modified. Model Item Properties include name, read only, required, relevant, calculate, priority, and validate. They can be applied and changed dynamically.

Dynamic Constraint Language

Part of the XForms working draft is a definition of what is called the Dynamic Constraint Language (DCL), the purpose of which is to provide an easy way to express constraints that apply across several fields rather than to a single field. For example, if one field on a form is supposed to contain the sum of a column of fields, the DCL can address a single or multiple elements, attributes, or content within an XForms (or XML) document; perform conditional operations on those nodes using ordinary conditional operators such as if…then…else; and even have a function library capable of getting sums, computing averages, and concatenating strings. It appears that many of the abilities of current scripting languages will be built into XForms.

XForms Form Controls

The working draft specifies abstract, core, and custom form controls (loosely based on those found in HTML) with the addition of new capabilities, but it also says that a much larger variety of controls will be considered for inclusion in any eventual standard. To be considered for inclusion are the following:

- Group boxes used to group form controls, so the controls functions will be bound to each other
- Explanatory text and graphics, such as captions for fields and buttons
- Output form controls used for computed values, the fields whose values are calculated
- Single-line and multiple-line text entry form controls, such as text boxes and text area controls (comments boxes)
- Check boxes for yes/no questions
- Radio buttons and drop-down menus (the SELECT element) for multiple-choice questions
- Lists allowing multiple selections (like the SELECT element)
- Buttons for navigation or instance data submission
- Image maps functioning as one or more buttons
- Tree controls with the ability to open and close nodes
- Sliders or rotary controls for picking from a range
- Spin controls for incrementing or decrementing a value
- Custom pickers (for example, for dates or colors)

7

- Additional (pop-up) help

- Mechanisms for navigation through form controls

- Keyboard shortcuts for moving to particular form controls

- The ability to disable particular form controls, thereby removing them from the navigation order and from the submitted data

- The ability to prevent users from changing the values of particular form controls (read only)

- The ability for form controls to indicate an error

- The ability to hide or reveal groups of form controls selectively

- The ability to present XForms as a sequence of cards (for WAP, discussed in Module 12)

When XForms form controls are used, they may be arranged and their appearance modified using CSS2 commands, and they may be bound to underlying data sources using binding expressions. An attribute in XForms named *ref* is used to reference (bind to) a specific model item from a form control.

1-Minute Drill

- What is the difference between the XForms Model and the XForms User Interface?

- What is the purpose of the Dynamic Constraints Language (DCL)?

- The XForms Model is the structural model for XForms Model Items, while the XForms User Interface establishes the connection between individual form controls and the underlying data in the XForms Model.
- The DCL allows constraints to be placed on one or multiple form controls dynamically.

Project 7-2: Using XForms in an XML Document

In this project, you'll begin to create documents with some of what you learned—specifically XForms. You make a form for placing an order, using the Web site you began developing in Project 7-1. The purpose of the form you're going to create is to allow users to search for documents.

Step-by-Step

1. Write out the code for the DOCTYPE declaration, as shown here:

```
<!DOCTYPE html PUBLIC "-//W3C//DTD
XHTML 1.0 Transitional//EN"
"http://www.w3.org/TR/xhtml1/DTD/
xhtml1-transitional.dtd">
<html xmlns=http://www.w3.org/1999/xhtml
xmlns:xsd=http://www.w3.org/2000/10/XMLSchema
xmlns:xform="http://www.w3.org/2001/02/xforms">
```

2. Start the head of the document, with a title element and the submitInfo element.

```
<head>
<title>Search Form</title>
<xform xmlns=http://www.w3.org/2001/02/xforms
id="criteria">
<submitInfo target="http://www.e4free.com/
XMLBeginnersGuide/searchform" />
<bind id="Search" ref="/search/searchcriteria"/>
```

3. Place a model element in the head element, and create a search element as well as an attribute named *searchcriteria*, using the XML Schema elements and namespace.

```
<model>
<schema xmlns="http://www.w3.org/
2000/10/XMLSchema">
<element name="search">
```

```
<complexType>
<attribute name="searchcriteria"
type="string" />
</complexType>
<element>
<schema>
</model>
```

4. Create an instance and set the query element's *searchcriteria* attribute to **Search for criteria**.

```
<instance model="search"
xmlns="http://www.e4free.com/">
<query searchcriteria="Search
for criteria" />
</instance>
</xform>
</head>
```

5. That ends the head element of this document. Now create the actual body element, captions, and text boxes using XForms controls.

```
<body>
<xform:textbox ref="id('Search')">
<xform:caption>Search for Documents<xform:caption>
<xform:help>Enter your search
criteria here:</xform:help>
</xform:textbox>
<xform:submit xform="search">
<xform:caption>Search</xform:caption>
</xform:submit>
</body>
</html>
```

☑ *Mastery Check*

1. What XHTML structures are used to arrange objects on Web pages for browsers that don't understand CSS2?

   A. Frames

   B. Tables

   C. Special graphics

   D. All of the above

2. What are some of the common page types found in most Web sites?

   A. About, Search, Select, Sign-on, Sample, and Send

   B. About, Contact, Connect, Configure, Collaborate, and Cancel

   C. About, Contact, Order, Search, Privacy, and Terms

   D. None of the above

3. Why might a Web site author place all Web pages in the same folder on a Web site?

   A. The pages shouldn't be in the same folder because they are harder to manage in the same folder

   B. To simplify the management of hyperlink and image references

   C. Because there is no other practical way

   D. None of the above

4. The XML Signature Syntax and Processing specification provides what capabilities?

   A. The encryption of digital signatures

   B. The application of digital signatures to digital objects

   C. The authentication of digital signatures against a third party

   D. None of the above

7

☑ Mastery Check

5. What is the root element of an XML Signature document?

   A. The Dsig element

   B. The signedInfo element

   C. The Signature element

   D. None of the above

6. What elements make up the content of the Signature element and how many times may they occur? Place them in the correct order.

   A. The SignedInfo element (once), the SignatureValue element (once), the KeyInfo element (zero or more times), and the Object element (zero to an unbounded number of times)

   B. The SignatureValue element (once), the KeyInfo element (zero or more times), the Object element (zero to an unbounded number of times), and the SignedInfo element (once)

   C. The KeyInfo element (zero or more times), the Object element (zero to an unbounded number of times), the SignedInfo element (once), and the SignatureValue element (once)

   D. None of the above

7. If a Web site has several security policies in force, with different policies applying to different areas on the Web site, how might these policies be represented to users?

   A. A Privacy Policy Page should be linked from every page.

   B. A Privacy policy should be published as a P3P XML Document.

   C. Privacy statements should be attached to every form collecting personal information on the site.

   D. None of the above

☑ *Mastery Check*

8. What are the components of forms in documents, and what is the purpose of XForms?

A. Forms usually contain labels identifying the information to be supplied and fields for entering the information. XForms supplies the information automatically from a central database maintained by the government containing everyone's personal information.

B. Forms usually contain labels identifying the information to be supplied and fields for entering the information. XForms separates the structure of the form from the presentation of the form.

C. Forms usually contain labels identifying the information to be supplied and fields for entering the information. XForms retrieves the information and sends it into a central database automatically.

D. None of the above.

9. What are some of the abilities of XForms extensions?

A. The ability to make some fields read-only

B. The ability to make some fields dynamically dependent on other fields

C. The ability to make the data in some fields the result of a calculation on other fields

D. All of the above

10. What are some of the abilities of the XForms Submit Protocol?

A. The ability to submit the contents of a form to the server

B. The ability to allow a form to be half-filled out, suspended, and then resumed later

C. The validation of fields in a form

D. A and B above

11. What is the difference between static and dynamic Web site content?

A. Static content never changes, while dynamic content might change daily.

7

☑ Mastery Check

    B. Dynamic content refers to Web site content that is generated on the fly, often by scripts from data in databases.

    C. Dynamic content refers to data generated using Dynamic HTML, while static content is generated from fixed data that has been entered into databases.

    D. None of the above

12. What would be a good description of how public key encryption works?

    A. Public key encryption involves a public key and a private key. A user who wants to send an encrypted message to a recipient uses the recipient's public key to encrypt the message, with the assurance that only the recipient can decrypt the message with their private key.

    B. Public key encryption is sponsored by the government, so all transmissions are safe from other citizens but can be easily decrypted by the government using the public key.

    C. Public key encryption uses both a public and private key, where the user uses the private key of an individual to encrypt a message for the individual and the individual uses the user's public key to decrypt it.

    D. None of the above.

13. What properties are available for model items in XForms?

    A. Name, status, calculate, priority, and validate

    B. Name, status, calculate, relevant, validate, and id

    C. Name, read-only, required, relevant, calculate, priority, and validate

    D. None of the above

14. How would the use of P3P help people manage access to Web sites?

    A. Adult sites would automatically be blocked if the user is under age 18.

    B. Sales material and advertisements would be blocked at the user's discretion.

☑ *Mastery Check*

    C. Sites could be queried automatically and, if they don't provide P3P data or don't meet the user's preset restrictions based on P3P, the site would be blocked.

    D. None of the above

15. Why would a Web site author bother with XML, if all data is stored initially in a database format?

    A. Data in databases cannot be browsed without XML.

    B. Transforming data into XML makes the data more accessible to other servers.

    C. Everyone else is doing it, and, eventually all Web sites will either be XML or will no longer be available on the Web.

    D. None of the above

7

Part III

Extending XML

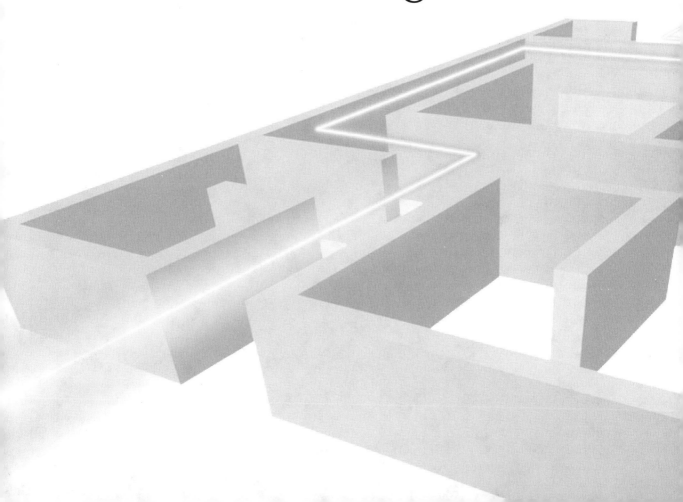

Module 8

The Document Object Model

The Goals of This Module

- Review the DOM specifications
- Learn how the DOM relates to XML
- Understand the structure of XML documents in the DOM
- Learn about the DOM supported in major browsers
- Learn about DOM APIs
- Work with the DOM on the client side
- Work with the DOM on the server side

It's one thing to create an XML document and quite another to access the information in it efficiently. To render XML documents, you translate them (discussed in Module 11). To set up a Web site architecture, the structure on the server was created (in Module 7). But to access and manipulate the data and elements efficiently in an XML document, you need to understand the Document Object Model (DOM), which is the focus of this module.

The official standards for the DOM are maintained at the W3C's site (**www.w3.org/DOM**). They currently consist of three levels of specifications. Level 1 and Level 2 are recommendations, while Level 3 is still a working draft. The Level 1 recommendation has a first and second edition. Level 2 has as its parts the core, view, style, events, and traversal-range specifications. Level 3 has as its parts the core, events, content model, and load and save, as well as views and formatting specifications.

Not all these levels and specifications are supported by all the major browsers. In fact, Microsoft Internet Explorer 5.0 and later versions seem to do the best job of any of the browsers in XML support. Of course, many fine Java and C++ parsers and XML tools are also available. Although other browsers often support *some* DOM, it isn't always the same as the one specified in the recommendations at the W3C.

The DOM Recommendation

The DOM has its roots in attempts by browsers and other software manufacturers to turn Web pages into sets of objects that can be manipulated. Plain HTML and XHTML documents were created and, once these documents were written, that was it. The content was static and unchanging. Naturally, you'd like to find ways to modify content, structure, and style of documents based on conditions either at the server, at the client, or both.

If you've ever done any JavaScript development, you know the browser windows, the page, the body, and the individual elements on a Web page are all capable of being treated like objects with properties, methods, and events, and can be manipulated or changed conditionally. So what are properties, methods, and events?

The BODY element on a Web page is an example of an *object,* as supported in the major browsers. Rather than simply being static HTML, the BODY element can be treated as an object with its own properties (attributes) and events (called *intrinsic events* in the HTML specification). For example, if the background color of the BODY element is set to the hexadecimal value FF0000, you know it'll be red. Setting this value is accomplished using the *bgcolor* attribute of the HTML/XHTML BODY element. This attribute's value is considered a *property* of the element (and the element itself is considered an object in the hierarchy of objects on the Web page).

The hierarchy of objects on a Web page is the structure the DOM brings to the document. All elements in an HTML document may be treated as objects in a hierarchy produced by the DOM, and they may be found (addressed), navigated (up and down through the hierarchy), modified in terms of content and attributes (properties), and worked on programmatically with the methods provided by the scripting language or program interacting with them.

A *method* is a programmatic action that can be applied to an object. The elements available in HTML/XHTML don't have methods directly associated with them, but JavaScript commands can call methods, which then operate on the properties of HTML/XHTML elements in a Web page. And these methods may be activated in response to events that occur during a user session with the Web page. Events are directly supported by HTML/XHTML elements in a Web page, such as the onMouseover event that may occur for the IMG element.

DOM 1.0, 2.0, and 3.0

Several specifications are associated with the DOM. Most of this module looks at the DOM Level 2 and 3 specifications, but we'll also look at the Level 1 specification and see how it forms a foundation for later specifications. Because the Microsoft implementations seem to be the most advanced, we'll use them when it's time to produce real-world examples.

The DOM Level 1 Specification

The DOM Level 1 specification has the status of Recommendation as of October 1, 1998, and its goal is to define a programmatic interface for HTML and XML documents. The DOM Level 1 specification is "a language and platform-neutral interface that allows programs and scripts to dynamically access and update the content, structure, and style of documents." It has a set of core and extended interfaces that can represent any structured document and a set of higher level interfaces specifically for HTML documents. XML documents can be represented with only the core and extended interfaces.

8

When documents are interpreted by the DOM, they're arranged as objects in a hierarchy, as the following code example and illustration show:

```
<TABLE border="1"><TR>
<TD>Cell 1</TD><TD>Cell 2</TD>
</TR><TR>
<TD>Cell 3</TD><TD>Cell 4</TD>
</TR></TABLE>
```

This code makes a table in HTML. In the DOM, this code would be represented as the objects shown in Figure 8-1.

1-Minute Drill

● What might be a node in the DOM of an XML document?

● What can be done to a node in the DOM?

The DOM Level 2 Specification

The DOM Level 2 specification includes those specs mentioned previously (core, views, style, and so on). The purpose is essentially the same as for the DOM Level 1, with some added definitions and functionality. The DOM Level 2 Core Specification version 1.0 has the status of Recommendation as of November 13, 2000, and closely follows the content of the Level 1 core interfaces specification.

Level 2 Core Specification   The core contains interfaces to create, modify, and manipulate the content, structure, and style of documents, and specialized interfaces for XML documents. It includes a DOM Structure Model that creates a set of node objects in a hierarchy. For XML and HTML (or XHTML), the node types are

● **Document**   May have a single Element node, Processing Instruction (PI) nodes, Comment nodes, and a single DocumentType node

● **DocumentFragment**   May have Element, PI, Comment, Text, CDATA, and EntityReference nodes

---

● The parts of an XML document, such as elements, text content, comments, processing instructions, and so forth, may be represented as nodes in the DOM.

● A node may be addressed, modified, or deleted, and new nodes may be added using the DOM.

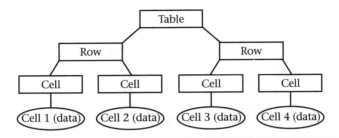

Figure 8-1   Nodes (objects) in the DOM

- **DocumentType**   May have no child nodes
- **EntityReference**   May have Element, PI, Comment, Text, CDATA, and EntityReference nodes
- **Element**   May have Element, PI, Comment, Text, CDATA, and EntityReference nodes
- **Attr (attribute)**   May have Text and EntityReference nodes
- **Comment**   May have no child nodes
- **Text**   May have no child nodes
- **CDATA**   May have no child nodes
- **Entity**   May have Element, PI, Comment, Text, CDATA, and EntityReference nodes
- **Notation**   May have no child nodes

Level 2 XML Namespaces   The DOM Level 2 supports XML namespaces to allow creation and manipulation of elements and attributes associated with a particular namespace. The special attributes for declaring namespaces are present in the DOM, just like any other element or attribute nodes, but are permanently bound to their namespaces, so any elements or attributes created from them are still defined by the namespace from which they came. Note that DOM Level 1 interfaces are not sensitive to namespaces (this is one of the advances in DOM Level 2).

Level 2 Interfaces   The DOM Level 2 Core lists a number of fundamental and extended interfaces for dealing with XML and XHTML documents. Fundamental interfaces include DOMException, ExceptionCode, DOMImplementation, DocumentFragment, Document, Node, NodeList, NamedNodeMap, CharacterData, Attr, Element, Text, and Comment. Extended interfaces include CDATASection, DocumentType, Notation, Entity, EntityReference, and ProcessingInstruction.

For each interface, the name of the interface is listed as well as its purpose, its attributes, its methods, and the allowable parts of its methods. For example, the Element interface is described as follows:

● **Description**   The Element interface represents an element in HTML or XML. The Element interface inherits from the Node interface, and the Attribute interface may be used to retrieve the attributes of an element.

● **Attributes**   This interface has only one attribute: *tagName*. The *tagName* attribute is a read-only attribute of type DOMString (it has a data type based on the string data type). A DOMString is a sequence of 16-bit units encoded in UTF-16. The attribute value for the *tagName* for an element is the element's XML name.

● **Methods**   This interface has several methods that can operate on it. For example, the getAttribute method gets an attribute value by searching for an attribute with the name specified. It returns the value of the attribute named (if found) as a DOMString or as an empty string of no attribute of that name is found.

The DOM Level 2 Views Specification

The DOM Level 2 Views specification is rather short as specifications go. It defines an abstract view and a document view. The purpose of these definitions is to make distinctions between views based on a source document. For example, the specification defines a view as "some alternate representation of, or a presentation of, and associated with, a source document." Essentially, a view could be any transformation of an XML document into a viewable format (and not necessarily renderable in a browser, but possibly renderable in some other medium, such as spoken word).

Views may be found in a browser window, on a WAP phone screen, and so forth, and may also be *static* (unchanging once rendered) or *dynamic* (changeable depending on conditions at the browser over time). The *abstract view* interface is the base view from which all other views must be derived. The document view may be implemented by a document and may have a default view attribute representing the connection between a view and its target (rendered) document.

The DOM Level 2 Style Specification

The purpose of style sheet languages is to enable authors to provide style directions without mixing them in with the elements in an XML document. Once again, separating form from function makes sense because the basic data remains intact, while the resulting format may be separately maintained and supplied conditionally, depending on the platform on which rendering will take place. Style sheets are discussed in detail in Module 11, as they are critical to many transformations. The DOM is often used with style sheets to modify style properties dynamically, so let's discuss style sheets a bit here for reference.

The DOM Level 2 Style specification is broken into two parts: DOM StyleSheets and DOM CSS (Cascading Style Sheets). The DOM StyleSheets portion defines the base interface that can be used to represent any style sheet language, and the DOM CSS portion defines interfaces specific to CSS. CSS2 and the DOM CSS specification are covered in Module 11.

In DOM StyleSheets, the StyleSheet interface represents a single style sheet connected to any structured document (such as XHTML or XML). In an XHTML document, a variety of ways exist for associating a style sheet or style instruction with the document: inline in an element, as a set of instructions in a CDATA section, or as a separate document. In an XML document, style sheets may be associated with the document via the xml-stylesheet processing instruction. Here's an example that shows how to connect style sheets and XML documents:

```
<?xml-stylesheet alternate="yes" title="smallfonts"
href="SS2.css" type="text/css"?>
```

The StyleSheet interface includes a number of attributes for specifying characteristics of the style sheet to be used, such as the following:

- **Type**   The style sheet language

- **Href**   The URL of the external style sheet

- **Media**   The medium on which the style sheet is intended to render the document

8

The DOM also specifies several other interfaces for building lists of style sheets (more than one may be associated with a document), lists of the media for which style sheets are intended, and provides other pertinent information.

The DOM Level 2 Event Model

Events are an interesting part of programming in general and come in handy when dealing with rendered documents. When a document is rendered, it's placed onto a screen (or, in the case of acoustically rendered documents, played) in a particular format. The elements in your document become objects on the screen (according to the DOM) and their properties may be modified dynamically. But what triggers this dynamic modification? Events.

In XHTML, elements have events associated with them, and these events follow a particular pattern of action. For example, when you place the mouse over an onscreen image, the onMouseover event occurs. The occurrence of this event can be detected, and programmatic functions can take place in response to the occurrence of the event.

Moreover, an event occurring for a particular object travels the hierarchy of objects in the DOM, from the lowest level object to the highest (the root object) and back again. Events can be detected (captured), stopped, initiated, and so forth to provice a rich ability to perform programmatic actions in response to user interaction and other forms of interaction with the environment in which the document is rendered.

Event Flow   The application implementing the DOM (such as a browser) initiates events. For example, if the mouse is placed over an object in the browser screen, the browser initiates the onMouseover event and sends notice that it has occurred to the DOM.

Using the DOM with MSXML 3.0

Now that you have an understanding of the purpose and functions of the DOM as specified by the W3C, you can begin to examine how the DOM is implemented in Microsoft's version of XML MSXML 3.0. In Module 6, you were set up with Microsoft's XML Tools (such as the XML Software Developer's Kit 3.0); here, you'll use those tools as you work with the DOM.

The Microsoft implementation of the DOM conforms to the DOM Level 1 specification but adds features that make its capabilities similar to the DOM

Level 2 specification. It runs in the MSXML Parser and allows documents to be loaded and created, errors to be gathered, information and structures in the document to be accessed and manipulated, and the results to be saved back out to an XML document.

What the MSXML Parser Does

When an XML document is read by the MSXML Parser, it creates an object tree managed by the parser. The document is read from start to finish, and the object tree is loaded entirely into memory, thereby making it easy to access or manipulate any part of the document. The document is considered a *node,* and it contains all other nodes, including the root node that contains all elements, attributes, and so forth. For example, an XML document, as shown in the following code, has an element named Customers as its root element:

```
<?xml version="1.0" encoding="UTF-8"?>
<!--This document tracks Customers and their orders-->
<!DOCTYPE Customers PUBLIC "Project2-2DTD.dtd"
http://www.e4free.com/XMLBeginnersGuide/Module02/Project2-2DTD/
Project2-2DTD.dtd">
<Customers>Here are our customers
<Customer customerid="cid111" email="jd@e4free.com" fulladdress=
"123 MySTreet MyCity, MyState, 90000">John Doe
<Orders>
<Order>
<OrderDetails OrderNumber="onid111" OrderDate="1/12/01" OrderTotal="0.00"/>
<OrderItems>
<OrderItem SKUNumber="1212" ItemNumber="1212-1" ForOrder="onid111">
<ItemCost>500</ItemCost>
<ItemPrice>1500</ItemPrice>
</OrderItem>
</OrderItems>
</Order>
</Orders>
</Customer>
</Customers>
```

This XML document would produce a DOM structure like the following (indented to indicate the root, tree, branches, and leaf nodes):

```
Document (DOMDocument)
    XML Declaration (XMLDOMProcessingInstruction)
    DOCTYPE Declaration (XMLDOMDocumentType)
    Customers (XMLDOMELement)
```

8

```
Customer (XMLDOMElement)
    Attributes (XMLDOMNamedNodeMap)
        customerID (XMLDOMAttribute)
            Cid111 (XMLDOMText)
        email (XMLDOMAttribute)
            jd@e4free.com (XMLDOMText)
```

The DOM structure would continue until all element, attribute, and text nodes were represented in memory.

The Microsoft DOM

The DOM Level 1 and 2 specified by the W3C and the Microsoft DOM implementation match quite closely, with a few extensions provided by Microsoft for convenience. Like an XML document, the DOM has interfaces to the document, element, attributes, text, character data, processing instructions, entity references, and other entities. Each of these interfaces may be created as objects, and each then may be manipulated via its properties with the methods and events associated with it.

For example, an element in an XML document is represented in the DOM as an IXMLDOMElement object. It may contain other IXMLDOMElements, IXMLDOMText objects (these store the text content of the element), IXMLDOMComment objects, and so forth, just like the XML element in the document from which it came. Attributes aren't stored as child objects of the IXMLDOMElement object but can be found via an IXMLDOMNamedNodeMap object derived from the IXMLDOMElement object with the attributes property.

The properties of the IXMLDOMElement object include the following:

- **attributes**   Read only; consists of a list of attributes for this node (element)

- **firstChild**   Read only; contains the first child node of this node

- **nodeName**   Read only; contains the qualified name of this element

Quite a few other properties exist for this object type, and they provide information useful to programmers for determining the properties of an element within an XML document. This object also provides methods for modifying the element and its properties, as well as creating and deleting other objects connected with this object, including these:

- **setAttributeNode**   Adds or changes an attribute for this node

- **appendChild**   Adds a new child node to this node

- **cloneNode**   Creates a new node that's an exact duplicate of this node

Many other methods are associated with this object, and all the objects found in an XML document have their corresponding objects implemented in the DOM. As you can see from the examples here, not only are the objects represented in the DOM, but the DOM implementation provides properties, methods, and events that allow easy programmatic manipulation in any suitable programming or scripting language. Of course, the language you're using is Visual Basic Scripting Edition (VBScript) along with ASP objects, as though you're using a Web interface for manipulating your XML document. Although you're using Microsoft products and technologies, Java-, C++-, Perl-, and Python-based implementations of the DOM also exist, so don't be afraid to experiment with other methods to perform the same functions.

Important Microsoft DOM Interface Objects

As mentioned, the DOM as implemented by Microsoft makes available a number of objects/interfaces for script and program developers. A few of the most important are listed here:

- DOMDocument

- IXMLDOMNode

- IXMLDOMNodeList

- IXMLDOMNamedNodeMap

- IXMLDOMParseError

The DOMDocument Interface   The DOMDocument interface represents the top-level node in the XML source document and includes members for retrieving or creating all other XML objects. In a Visual Basic script, the object would be created using code like this:

```
Dim myDOMobjDoc
Set myDOMobjDoc = Server.CreateObject("msxml2.DOMDocument")
```

In this code, the name of the document variable for the DOMDocument interface is myDOMobjDoc. The object's type is set to msxml2.DOMDocument.

Another object that may be created with Microsoft's implementation of the DOM is IXMLDOMNode, representing an individual node (such as an element, attribute, character data, and so forth) in an XML source document. To create one, you might use code such as this:

```
Dim myDOMobjDoc
Dim myNode
Set myDOMobjDoc = Server.CreateObject("msxml2.DOMDocument")
Set myNode = Server.CreateObject("msxml2.IXMLDOMNode")
myDOMobjDoc.Load ("mysource.xml")
Set myNode = myDOMobjDoc.documentElement.childNodes.Item(1)
```

This code creates the overall document object, creates a node object, loads the source document into memory, and sets the variable myNode to a node in the document using the index number associated with the first node (1). From that point, the node can be manipulated programmatically.

Naturally, having an object designed for navigating through nodes would be helpful, and that's what the IXMLDOMNodeList object is for. This is a *collection,* meaning properties such as the number of nodes can be retrieved, and all objects in the collection can be iterated through without necessarily knowing their names, using the For...Each programming construct. This object is *live,* meaning that adding or deleting nodes affects the contents of the collection in real time.

The following code shows an example of retrieving all the nodes named Customer from the source XML document using the getElementsByTagName method, and then determining the number of elements retrieved by reading the length property:

```
Dim myDOMobjDoc
Dim myNodeList
Set myDOMobjDoc =
Server.CreateObject("msxml2.DOMDocument")
Set myNodeList =
Server.CreateObject("IXMLDOMNodeList")
myDOMobjDoc.Load ("mysource.xml")
Set myNodeList =
myDOMobjDoc.getElementsByTagName("Customer")
Response.Write myNodeList.length
```

Like the IXMLDOMNodeList object, the IXMLDOMNamedNodeMap object is a live collection, but in this case the collection consists (typically) of attributes within the source document. Code for retrieving a node map might look like this:

```
Dim myDOMobjDoc ────────┐    ┌──────────────────────────┐
Dim myNode              ├────┤ Dimensions the variables │
Dim myNodeMap ──────────┘    └──────────────────────────┘
Set myDOMobjDoc =
Server.CreateObject("msxml2.DOMDocument")
Set myNode =
Server.CreateObject("IXMLDOMNode") ────┐  ┌────────────────────────┐
Set myNodeList =                       ├──┤ Creates the Document,   │
Server.CreateObject("IXMLDOMNodeList") ┘  │ Node, and NodeList objects │
myDOMobjDoc.setProperty                   └────────────────────────┘
"SelectionLanguage", "XPath"
myDOMobjDoc.Load "mysource.xml"
Set myNode =
myDOMobjDoc.selectSingleNode("//Customer")
Set myNodeMap =
myNode.Attributes
Response.Write                 ┌──────────────────────────────────────────────────┐
myNodeMap.length ◄─────────────┤ Responds to the browser with the length of the Node Map │
                               └──────────────────────────────────────────────────┘
```

This code creates document, node, and node map objects; sets the SelectionLanguage property of the document object to XPath (so a particular node may be found using the XPath language); sets the node object to the node desired; sets the node map object to the attributes of the node object; and then provides the number of attributes found at that node.

When XML documents are read into memory, there's always a chance that an error might occur. Capturing errors and dealing with them gracefully is a standard part of programming. Microsoft's implementation of the DOM has objects, properties, and methods built-in specifically for this function, and the IXMLDOMParseError object is the main interface. This object provides data about the most recent parse error, such as the error code, the line number and character position where the error occurred, and a description of the error. The following example shows how errors might be captured:

```
Dim myDOMobjDoc
Set myDOMobjDoc =
Server.CreateObject("msxml2.DOMDocument")
```

8

```
myDOMobjDoc.Load ("mysource.xml")
If myDOMobjDoc.parseError.errorCode <> 0 Then
  Response.Write "Parse Error."
Else
  Response.Write myDOMobjDoc.documentElement.xml
End If
```

This code creates and loads a document object. If an error occurs, it's captured by checking for a particular error code value (anything but zero) and either an error message is returned or the XML code of the document element is returned.

Proj8-1.zip

Project 8-1: Creating an XML DOM Document Object

In this project, you make a set of Web pages and scripts that examine an XML document, find and manipulate parts of the document, and save the resulting document back to a new XML document. The purpose isn't to create a full-blown XML-based Web application, but to become comfortable with using XML documents as part of Web applications and VBScript and ASP for working with XML documents. For a good grounding in ASP 3.0 and its related technologies, as well as VBScript, please see *ASP 3.0: A Beginner's Guide,* by Dave Mercer (Osborne/McGraw-Hill).

Step-by-Step

1. The first step in working with XML via Web pages, ASP 3.0, and VBScript is to get set up with a Web server running Windows 2000 Advanced Server or some other compatible operating system. Make sure Internet Information Server 5.0 and ASP 3.0 are installed, as well as the Microsoft Parser (either download the parser from the Microsoft site or make sure Internet Explorer 5.0 or above is installed). If you don't happen to have this environment available, don't worry. Just follow along with the code examples and test them when you have the chance.

2. Decide what your code will do and how you'll interact with it. You'll use an existing XML document from Module 2—the file Project2-2XMLDoc.xml. You'll load it, read from it, add new elements and attributes to it, and save it with a new name, so you need a Web page that can initiate these functions, tied to an ASP script that actually performs the functions.

3. Make a Web page named index.asp and load it on your server. Give it some buttons to initiate your ASP actions. You can use code like the following to start the page:

```
<html><head><title>Untitled Document</title>
<meta http-equiv="Content-Type"
 content="text/html; charset=iso-8859-1">
</head>
<body bgcolor="#CCFFCC">
<form method="post" action="index.asp">
```

Notice that the contents of the form will be submitted back to the Web page from which it came. This is because your ASP functions will be built into the page and, when any submissions occur on the page, they will be captured and conditionally responded to by the scripting in the page.

4. Now code a table structure in the HTML, and place descriptions of the functions available next to text boxes for input and buttons for submission. Each button will have a distinct value so you can use a Select...Case function to respond conditionally to the submissions, depending on which button is clicked.

```
<table width="100%" border="0"><tr><td colspan="2">
<b><font size="5">XML 1.0 Beginner's Guide DOM Example
</font></b>
</td></tr><tr><td colspan="2"> </td></tr><tr>
<td colspan="2">
This page allows users to examine an XML document,
 add elements, add attributes, add content, and save
 the result to a new XML document
named according to their wishes.
</td></tr><tr><td colspan="2"> 
</td></tr><tr><td width="49%">
<div align="right"><b>Examine the XML
 Document named </b></div>
</td><td width="51%">
<input type="text" name="examine" size="40">
<input type="submit" name="cmdButton"
 value="Examine XML Document">
</td></tr><tr><td width="49%">
<div align="right"><b></b></div>
</td><td width="51%"> </td></tr>
<tr><td width="49%">
<div align="right"><b>Add an Element
```

```
 named </b></div>
</td><td width="51%">
<input type="text" name="addelement"
 size="40">
<input type="submit" name="cmdButton"
 value="Add Element">
</td></tr><tr><td width="49%">
<div align="right"><b>Add content to
 the new element </b></div>
</td><td width="51%"><input type="text"
 name="addcontent" size="40">
<input type="submit" name="cmdButton"
 value="Add Content">
</td></tr><tr><td width="49%">
<div align="right"><b>Add an Attribute
 named </b></div>
</td><td width="51%">
<input type="text" name="addattribute" size="40">
<input type="submit" name="cmdButton"
 value="Add Attribute">
</td></tr><tr><td width="49%">
<div align="right"><b></b></div>
</td><td width="51%"> </td></tr>
<tr><td width="49%">
<div align="right"><b>Save the new XML
 document as </b></div>
</td><td width="51%">
<input type="text" name="savexml" size="40">
<input type="submit" name="cmdButton"
 value="Save XML Document">
</td></tr></table>
</form>
</body></html>
```

Now that you have a Web page that provides a user interface, you can build the ASP functions to work with your XML document. Let's start with the functions for examining the XML document.

1. Add some lines to the top of your Web page to set VBScript as the language for the ASP engine and to make the declaration of variables mandatory. Notice the ASP code is separated from the HTML code using the <% and %> delimiters. They go like this:

```
<%@Language = VBScript
Option Explicit
%>
```

2. Next, *dimension* some variables, the VBScript term for declaring variables. In VBScript, all variables are dimensioned as Variant data types, so there's no need to worry about what kind they are.

```
<%
Dim myDOMobjDoc
Dim myNode
Dim myE
Dim myA
Dim myC
Dim myNodeList
Dim myNodeMap
Dim myElement
Dim myAttribute
Dim myContent
Dim myFileNameSave
Dim myFileNameRetrieve
Dim btnClicked
%>
```

3. To make the functions work, you need to capture the value, if any, of the incoming submissions from the form. You can look for a value of the button named cmdButton and, if you find one, use the Select...Case construct to designate the appropriate action:

```
<%
If Not LEN(Request.Form("cmdButton")) = 0 Then
%>
```

The code now checks to see whether any value is attached to the button named cmdButton. If not, no submission was made, so the ordinary Web page can be displayed. Therefore, the HTML code for your page would appear here, after the ending %> delimiter, and would be displayed to the user whenever the page appears without having had a form submission made. However, if a form submission was made, then the button would have a value, and the Else statement would apply.

4. At this point, you want to pick up the values entered for any of the text fields on the screen as well as the value of the button, as follows:

```
<%
Else
bntClicked = Request.Form("cmdButton")
myFileNameRetrieve = Request.Form("examine")
myElement = Request.Forms("addelement")
myAttribute = Request.Forms("addattribute")
```

```
myContent = Request.Forms("addcontent")
myFileNameSave = Request.Forms("savexml")
Select Case btnClicked
Case "Examine XML Document"
```

5. Now it's time to perform the actions that examine the source document and return some of the information you can find out about it. Create a DOMDocument object and look at some of its properties.

```
Set myDOMobjDoc =
Server.CreateObject("msxml2.DOMDocument")
myDOMobjDoc.load(myFileNameRetrieve)
Set myNode =
ServerCreateObject("msxml2.IXMLDOMNode")
myNode =
myDOMobjDoc.DocumentElement.ChildNodes.Item(0)
Response.Write "The type of node is "
 & myNode.nodeType
Response.Write "The name of the node is "
 & myNode.nodeName
Response.Write "The DTD or Schema for
 this document is " & myNode.definition
```

6. Now do the same for the other cases in your ASP script:

```
Case "Add Element"
Set myDOMobjDoc =
Server.CreateObject("MSXML2.DOMDocument")
Set myDOMobjDoc.load(myFileNameRetrieve)
Set myNode =
ServerCreateObject("MSXML2.IXMLDOMNode")
Set myE =
Server.CreateObject("MSXML2.IXMLDOMElement")
Set myE = myDOMobjDoc.documentElement
Set myNode =
xmlDoc.createNode(NODE_ELEMENT, myElement, "")
myE.appendChild myNode
Response.Write "Element named "
 & myElement & " appended."
Case "Add Content"
Set myDOMobjDoc =
Server.CreateObject("MSXML2.DOMDocument")
Set myDOMobjDoc.load(myFileNameRetrieve)
Set myNode = ServerCreateObject("MSXML2.IXMLDOMNode")
```

```
Set myE = Server.CreateObject("IXMLDOMElement")
Set myC = Server.CreateObject("MSXML2.IXMLDOMText")
Set myE = myDOMobjDoc.documentElement
Set myC = myDOMobjDoc.createTextNode(myContent)
Set MyNode =
root.insertBefore(myC, root.childNodes.Item(1))
Response.Write "Text " & myContent & " appended."
Case "Add Attribute"
Set myDOMobjDoc =
Server.CreateObject("MSXML2.DOMDocument")
Set myDOMobjDoc.load(myFileNameRetrieve)
Set myNode = ServerCreateObject("MSXML2.IXMLDOMNode")
Set myNodeMap =
Server.CreatObject("MSXML2.IXMLDOMNamedNodeMap")
Set myE = Server.CreateObject("IXMLDOMElement")
Set myA =
Server.CreateObject("MSXML2.IXMLDOMAttribute")
Set myNodeMap = myE.Attributes
Set myE = myDOMobjDoc.documentElement
Set myA = myDOMobjDoc.createAttribute(myAttribute)
myNodeMap.setNamedItem myA
For i = 0 To (myNodeMap.length - 1)
Response.Write myNodeMap.Item(i).xml
Next
Case "Save XML Document"
Set myDOMobjDoc =
Server.CreateObject("MSXML2.DOMDocument")
myDOMobjDoc.load(myFileNameRetrieve)
myDOMobjDoc.save(Server.MapPath(myFileNameSave))
End Case
End If
%>
```

1-Minute Drill

● What is the purpose of the IXMLDOMNode object?

● What is the purpose of the IXMLDIMNodeMap object?

● The IXMLDOM Node object represents a node in the DOM of an XML document, such as an element or text content.

● The IXMLDOMNode Map object represents a map of all nodes in the current node from which it is derived.

Ask the Expert

Question: Once I've learned how to write XML documents, will I need to use the DOM very much? We seem to be getting back to scripting and programming languages, and I thought XML was a new way to create Web-related documents that avoided most of that.

Answer: As you may know, Web pages and their associated applications are complex creatures that tend to absorb any new technology, and it's the same with the DOM and XML. XML is simply a nice way to structure your data—no matter what the intended use—because it's becoming a universal language. Therefore, you'll probably find yourself storing data in databases, retrieving it in XML format, but then interacting with it using a number of programming languages, such as ASP and VBScript, JavaScript, and hard-core programming languages such as Java, C, and C++.

Question: Does this mean I should also learn ASP and VBScript? Or should I learn JavaScript? Do they all function the same way for the DOM?

Answer: This depends on what you think you'll be doing, but, from a Web standpoint, if you're going to work with lots of Web functions, you'll probably want to know XHTML, ASP, VBScript, JavaScript, and also SQL (you learn more about this in Modules 9 and 10). However, if most of your programming is going to be on the back end, programming languages like Java, C, and C++, and scripting languages like Perl and (for the Web) Php are going to be helpful.

☑ *Mastery Check*

1. Why is the DOM compared to a tree?

   A. Diagrams of objects in the DOM look like a tree.

   B. A single object is the parent of all other objects, and the objects may have one or more child objects, with some having no child objects. When drawn out as a diagram, the objects and their relationships often resemble a tree.

   C. The top object in the hierarchy is the root object, its child objects (if they have child objects of their own) are called branch objects, and objects without any child objects are called leaf objects, so it's only natural to compare the DOM to a tree.

   D. None of the above.

2. Why is working with the DOM easier than working with an XML document as is?

   A. XML documents are plain text and there's no easy way to address or navigate individual elements. Objects in the DOM expose properties and methods, making it easy to find and manipulate them programmatically.

   B. The DOM is more compact than XML documents and uses less memory.

   C. The DOM is a more recent innovation and programmers like it better than XML.

   D. None of the above.

8

✓ Mastery Check

3. What are some of the interfaces listed in the DOM Level 2 Core and how are they described?

A. Element, Attr, and CharacterData. They are described in terms of what function they perform, what attributes are available, and what methods may be used to work with them.

B. DOMAttr, DOMElement, and DOMCharacterData. They are described in terms of what function they perform, what attributes are available, and what methods may be used to work with them.

C. ElementInterface, AttrInterface, and CharacterDataInterface. They are described in terms of what function they perform, what attributes are available, and what methods may be used to work with them.

D. None of the above.

4. Style sheet languages allow document authors to add styles to XHTML, XML, and other structured documents. What style sheet languages may be used with the DOM Level 1?

A. Cascading Style Sheets 2.0 (CSS2)

B. JavaScript and Visual Basic Scripting Edition

C. All style sheet languages

D. None of the above

5. Why must the DOM be aware of style sheets?

A. The DOM may be used to address a particular element or set of elements and change the values of some of their attributes, including style attributes.

B. The DOM is programmable and style sheets are not.

C. The DOM must know what style sheets are doing behind the scenes.

D. None of the above.

✓ Mastery Check

6. Give an example of the kind of action that might be directed toward a component of an XHTML document via a style sheet.

    A. Calculations could be performed on form elements, such as the totaling of costs.

    B. Media elements might be transformed from one media type to another.

    C. The background color of a table cell might be set to light blue.

    D. None of the above.

7. What are events, and what are they used for in XHTML Web pages?

    A. Events are things that might happen to an object on a Web page, such as the *onclick* event happening to a button object within a form on a page.

    B. Events are specialized Web pages that show current events for the author of the Web site.

    C. Events are programmatic functions that occur when unauthorized users load pages.

    D. None of the above.

8. What is the relationship between events and the DOM in DOM Level 2?

    A. There is no relationship.

    B. DOM Level 1 events communicate directly with DOM Level 2 events.

    C. Events travel through the DOM hierarchy of objects, so an event occurring to a button on a form in a page would travel from the page, to the form, to the button, and back up again.

    D. None of the above.

8

✓ *Mastery Check*

9. In the Microsoft DOM, what object is used to represent elements in an XML document?

A. The MSDOMElement object

B. The IXMLDOMElement object

C. The DOML2Element object

D. None of the above

10. What property contains attributes for Microsoft DOM elements and how might this property be changed?

A. The IXMLDOMAttrs property contains attributes of elements in the Microsoft DOM, and the changeProperty method is used to change this property.

B. Attributes of elements in the Microsoft DOM are represented as attributes, not properties, and can be changed using the setAttribute method.

C. The attributes property contains attributes of elements in the Microsoft DOM, and the setAttributeNode method is used to change this property.

D. None of the above.

11. What property of a DOMDocument object (in the Microsoft DOM) could be set to specify the language to be used for selecting nodes within an XML document represented in the DOM?

A. The SelectionLanguage property

B. The QueryLanguage property

C. All NodeSelector property

D. None of the above

☑️Mastery Check

12. When an object is a collection, what benefits does that structure offer?

   A. Collections are read only, so properties cannot be changed by mistake.

   B. Collections may have more than one item in them and can, therefore, be iterated through using a For…Next loop, without necessarily knowing the names of each item in the collections.

   C. Collections are compact and, therefore, take up less memory.

   D. None of the above.

13. What collection of the IXMLDOMNode object contains attributes, and what property of this collection tells how many exist?

   A. Attributes and length

   B. Attributes and count

   C. Nodes and length

   D. None of the above

14. When a DOMDocument object is created, what method could be used to bring an XML document into the DOMDocument object in memory?

   A. The store method

   B. The memory method

   C. The load method

   D. None of the above

15. What properties of the IXMLDOMNode object tell its type and name?

   A. The Type and Name properties

   B. The nodeType and nodeName properties

   C. Type and name aren't properties of this object

   D. None of the above

8

Module 9

Designing Data
Models for XML

The Goals of This Module

- Learn about data modeling
- Examine various models for data
- Understand the relationships between data
- Learn about popular database formats, including relational databases
- Learn the basics of Structured Query Language (SQL)
- Build simple data models

Before you can use data effectively, it must be arranged in some understandable fashion. Not only should your data be organized in a meaningful way, but the relationship of the data to the structures within which it's held must be clear. Data modeling helps with the development of logical structures for holding data in a meaningful way.

For example, consider records in a table in a database. If the table is named Customers, you might assume that each record pertains to one customer. Furthermore, you might also assume that each record represents a unique customer. And it would be natural to assume each field in the table holds a piece of data pertaining to the customer identified in the record. No one has to tell you the data in the "HomePhone" field represents the home phone number of the customer identified in the record.

Databases may contain many tables—with many records and many fields— and the types of relationships defined by their structure (data model) are often defined by the way the tables are connected to each other. But data isn't found only in a database. Unstructured and semistructured data is found in many other sources of data, such as e-mails, Word documents, spreadsheets, and XML documents. Modeling the appropriate structure and preserving that structure through various transformations and conversion, are the subjects that occupy this module and Module 10.

Databases, XML, and Data Models

Some data never changes, some data changes infrequently, and some data changes all the time. Raw data may simply be a series of numbers or samples, which by themselves are meaningless, but when examined in a series as a trend might be useful. So, then, *data* has a variety of states and values, sometimes dependent on other data. In database terms, a database that contains no data is said to be *empty*, but it still has a structure defined. When a database is populated, it's in its *initial* state; after a change has been made to the data, it has been *updated*. If the changes result in erroneous data, the database is said to be in an *invalid* state, but, if the data is error-free, the database continues to be in a *valid* state. Building an appropriate data model and including the proper constraints help ensure that your database always remains valid.

The value of a particular piece of data is dependent on who is viewing the data and how relevant it is to the problem that person trying to solve. Data itself, technically, is just data. Without context or data model, data is meaningless.

It's like asking what is the value of the number 2? By itself, nothing. But if the number 2 is one of a sequence of numbers (2, 8, 15, 35, 36, and 47), these numbers are identified as the winning lottery numbers, and you happen to have the winning ticket, the number 2 turns out to be quite valuable to you.

Information can be said to be data with context and structure. But information alone isn't necessarily the answer either. If you know you have the winning numbers on your lottery ticket, but you don't know how to cash it in (and, for some reason, you're unable to figure it out), the value is lost. Knowledge of what to do with the information you have is also important. An application that tells you information and also provides a means of using it to your advantage is more valuable than an application that gives only the information. The application is then supplying knowledge.

But suppose you have knowledge of some information and how to use it, but you don't recognize that if you use this knowledge, the outcome can actually hurt you. That's where wisdom comes into play. Unfortunately, applications cannot yet supply wisdom; it's up to you to use the knowledge you get from your applications wisely.

The Entity-Relationship Data Model

Structure in data is derived from organizing data according to what the data pertains to. An address is pretty meaningless until you associate it with a particular customer, for example. XML elements serve this purpose quite well, by enabling you to associate data with a particular element, which then tells you what "thing" the data pertains to. Elements can represent an unlimited variety of *things*—real *things* as well as virtual *things*. For example, elements can represent customers (a real, physical thing) and elements can also represent orders (an abstract idea that embodies a commitment on the part of a customer to make a purchase of specific items or services).

Entities and Attributes

In data modeling terms, these *things* are sometimes called *entities* (not to be confused with entities or entity references in XML) and the relationships between them are called *relationships*. Data models structured as entities and the relationships between them are called Entity-Relationship (ER) models.

Entities usually have attributes (again, not a direct reference to the XML attribute, although the meaning is related). For example, a person has a name, address, and phone number, all considered attributes for this type of data model.

9

Attribute values can change, depending on the status of the entity. For example, while a person's date of birth would never change, his or her address might change many times.

Attributes can be classed as *simple* or *composite*. A person's age attribute is a single number that cannot be meaningfully broken into smaller pieces, but a phone number with an area code is considered composite. This is because the area code alone has meaning in certain circumstances (such as when a search is done for all customers residing in a given area code).

Attributes may also be classed as *stored* or *derived*. A person's age may be stored as a number or it may be calculated whenever a view of her record is presented, based on the number of years since the value in her date of birth field. Obviously, stored values that change frequently are more labor intensive to maintain, while derived values that are viewed often might be processor intensive to calculate each time.

Attributes and Null Values   Attributes that don't currently have any value are said to have a *null* value. This is different from a value of zero or a zero-length string, and might occur when a user simply doesn't enter data in a field, rather than entering "none" or "not applicable." If an attribute has a null value, it may mean

- **Not applicable**   This attribute isn't applicable to the entity being tracked, although in many other cases it will be applicable

- **Unknown, missing**   The value exists, but you don't know it

- **Unknown, nonexistent**   The value doesn't exist

Relationships

Entities have a direct, one-to-one relationship with their attributes—that is to say, the *relationship* between entities and their attributes is defined by their nature and no other relationship is possible, except as noted in the section on null values. However, entities may also have relationships with other entities, which may take on a number of types. For example, a person may work for a company and the company may also be said to employ the person. The person not only has a relationship with the company, but the company has a relationship with the person. They are two *different* relationships, though—a *works for* relationship and an *employs* relationship. The former is a relationship of employee-to-employer, while the latter is a relationship of employer-to-employee. Each relationship implies a different set of commitments and obligations. In the *works for* relationship, the person has an obligation to come to work, perform assigned tasks, and so forth; in the *employs* relationship, the company has an obligation to provide a place to work, issue paychecks in a timely way, and so on. In data modeling terms, these relationships may be thought of as a single relationship that has two different *roles,* depending on which side you're on.

Relationships involving two entities (such as person-company) are said to be *binary,* and relationships with three entities are said to be *ternary.* Descriptions that refer to the number of entities involved are said to describe the *degree* of the relationship. All the relationships used in this module are *binary* degree relationships.

Here are the types of relationships covered in this module:

- **One-to-one**   A direct correspondence exists between one entity and another—for example, a person's credit record contact information and Social Security record contact information. Both relate to the same person and only one of each should exist.

- **One-to-many**   A single record exists for one entity with a direct connection to multiple records for the related entity. For example, a single person may have multiple orders at a given company. Each order record is directly related to the person's record maintained by the company.

- **Many-to-many**   Any of multiple records for an entity has a relationship with any of multiple records for another entity. For example, a given company may have many employee records and many customer records, and each employee may have taken orders from many customers, while each customer may have had their orders taken by many employees. The employees and customers are said to have a many-to-many relationship.

Relationships between entities are quite varied. If two entities participate in a relationship without any intervening relationships or other entities, they are said to be in a *direct* relationship. For example, if you own your own home (or several homes), you have a direct relationship with your home or homes. If, however, you rent your home, you have a relationship with the owner (or manager) of your home; the relationship between you and your home can be said to be *indirect.*

9

One measure of the relationships between entities is the *cardinality ratio.* A strict, one-to-one, one-to-many, or many-to-many relationship is said to have a cardinality ratio of 1:1, 1:N, or M:N, respectively. Note that a direction is implied by the cardinality ratio notation. That is because the direction of a relationship affects what is called the *participation constraint.* For example, if you're creating a data model for customers and their orders, you may want to disallow orders for which no customer exists. In the direction from orders to customers is *total participation,* meaning no orders can be generated without a customer. In the direction of customers to orders, you can certainly have customers entered in your system who don't currently have an order (perhaps they placed and then cancelled an order, or they expressed interest in making a purchase). In this case, customers have a *partial participation* in the relationship— that is to say, they aren't dependent on orders for their existence as a record in your database.

In database terms, relationships may be thought of as attributes. For example, the relationship between customers and orders can be seen as an attribute of either the customer or the order. When developing data models for XML documents, expressing relationships as attributes can be handy because it's easy to create attributes in XML.

Key Attributes

To establish a relationship between the records in one table and the records in another table, some piece of data must appear in both tables that connects them. *Key attributes* are values that are unique for every record in a table, such as a customer ID or number. This piece of data is the same in every table. *Key values* may be represented in XML using the ID data type. In relational databases, these values are often constrained to be unique, meaning the database itself won't allow a nonunique value to be entered in this field. Also, no null values are allowed, although at least one record may have an empty key value (with a zero-length string). Database applications often have the ability to generate sequential ID values automatically whenever a new record is started. In Microsoft Access, this can be accomplished by setting the data type to AutoNumber. In Microsoft SQL Server, this can be accomplished by setting the attribute to Identity.

Key values that are unique in a table are called *primary keys.* To connect a table by its primary key to another table (for example, in a one-to-many relationship), the other table must have an attribute that contains the primary key of the first table. In the other table, this attribute is called a *foreign key.*

For each record in the first table, only one unique key value exists for the primary key, but that value may be repeated many times in the other table in the foreign-key attribute.

If a primary key is composed of two or more attributes, it's called *a composite key*. Using composite keys can come in handy. For example, if you make a credit card purchase, the primary key for each transaction may be a combination of your account number and the store number where you made the purchase, as well as the date and time. This would have the effect of capturing this information and also making sure no two purchases can be recorded with a simultaneous data and time, which would result in duplicate primary keys in the transactions table.

In Module 3, you learned about data types and the restrictions that can be placed on the values data may assume, using XML Schema data type construction methods. Formally, these restrictions limit the value set or domain that makes up the values possible for a given data type. For example, passwords are often restricted to eight characters, but within that restriction, the value set is nearly unlimited. On the other hand, the value set of an attribute named Gender may be restricted to two characters, *M* and *F*.

In some cases, providing an attribute for a piece of data may be unnecessary. Suppose you build a table meant to contain only records of folks born in the year 1988 and you name it "People Born in 1988." If data entry or data import isn't flawed, there's no need for an attribute for year of birth, unless you need to do some calculations on that value. You must be careful when you construct this kind of table, however, because we all know what happened in the year 2000 when so many records and programs had to be examined for the missing century value of 19.

As you build your data model, you set data types, value ranges, cardinality, ratios, participation constraints, relationship and entity types, and so forth. These are the logical, operational rules of the *miniworld,* our miniature model of the real world. However, good data modeling sometimes means breaking the rules (perhaps a better term would be *optimizing*), so a particular function is less complex, less processor intensive, and so on. Knowing the difference between what rules can and can't be broken, and being able to design for practicality rather than strict adherence to every logical rule modeled, is what makes data modeling an art rather than a science. Use your best judgment, and be prepared to modify your design as you learn more about the problem you're trying to solve with your data model.

9

1-Minute Drill

● What is the meaning of a null value?

● What is a foreign key?

Relational Algebra

Relational algebra is the term used to describe the methods you use to create queries. *Queries* are selection operations on sets of data, such as records in the tables of a database or nodes (elements and attributes) in an XML document. They're called *selection operations* because they often select subsets of data from all available records or nodes. Of course, what's done with the records or nodes varies. Some queries simply retrieve the records, while others delete selected records, update selected records, or perform other tasks. In working with XML documents, you may want to transform selected XML nodes. Specialized XML-based query languages are springing up to assist you in this process. The particulars are discussed in more detail in Modules 10 and 11.

For now, let's look at how queries are formed for databases. Two general types of operations exist: set theoretic operations (from mathematical set theory) and operations designed specifically for databases. Set theoretic operations include the following:

● **Union**   Two sets of records are combined and duplicate records are eliminated

● **Intersection**   Only records in both original sets of records are produced

● **Difference**   Only records *not* in both original sets of records are produced

Relational operations include these:

● **Select**   A subset of records is selected, based on selection criteria. For example, if you want to retrieve all records for which the attribute "lastname" equals the value "Smith", the value you seek would be the

---

● A null value might mean the attribute and value aren't applicable, the value is applicable but simply missing, or the value doesn't exist at all.

● A foreign key is a field representing a value from another table that links the records in the other table to the table in which the foreign key resides.

selection criterion, and only those records in which the attribute "lastname" matches the value "Smith" would be retrieved. In database applications and in XML query languages, selection criteria may also be expressed as *wildcard* values, meaning special characters can be substituted for specific characters, and all records matching the parameters implied by those special characters are then retrieved.

- **Project**   All records are selected, but only a subset of the available attributes is included. In a database, this means only certain fields are included in the resulting set.

- **Joins**   Multiple operations may take place. For example, two sets of records may be combined in a union, selected, and then projected, so the result is a subset of the records from the union and the select, further modified to limit the attributes produced by the project operation. In relational databases, joins are often used to gather records based on the combination of one table with another when a relationship is present.

- **Aggregate Functions**   Not only are records selected, but they may be grouped by a particular value and then a sum or average (or some other type of aggregated value) may be produced across all the records in the group.

Selection Clauses   When selecting records based on criteria, wanting to select records with criteria for multiple attributes isn't uncommon. For example, you may want to select all records with a value of "Smith" in the "lastname" field and a value of "John" in the "firstname" field. Performing select operations for single or multiple criteria requires the use of Boolean operators and expressions to make selection clauses. These expressions and operators include equals, less than, greater than, AND, OR, and NOT. Ordered values (such as dates and numbers) can use comparison operators, while unordered values (such as passwords) can only be compared for equality. The Boolean operators AND, OR, and NOT may specify multiple criteria for one or more attributes. A select operation may be performed on one attribute to retrieve all records with a value of A OR B, while another select operation may retrieve all record with the value *A* in one attribute AND the value *B* in another attribute.

9

1-Minute Drill

● What does a select operation do?

● What does a union operation do?

The Hierarchical Parent-Child Relationship

As you learned in the construction of XML documents, elements have a specific type of relationship that continues throughout XML-based languages. Elements form a hierarchy, with one element at the top and the rest as child elements and subchild elements of that top element. This structure continues into the Document Object Model (DOM), the definition for programmatic interfaces reviewed in Module 8 (although the specification makes clear that a tree-node or parent-child structure isn't the only way elements and attributes may be represented in conformance with the DOM).

The parent-child relationship (PCR) structure implies that a record, a node, or an element has a relationship with either its parent or its children, although the nature of that relationship (one-to-one, one-to-many, and so forth) is further definable. The PCR data model defines relationships in a hierarchical way similar to that used for XML elements:

● The root of the data model isn't a child record or an element of any other record or element.

● Every other record or element may be a parent record or element but is also a child record or element in one parent record or element.

● Parent records or elements can have zero or more child records or elements.

● If a record or element has no child records or elements, it's called a *leaf*.

As you already know, the XML and XML Schema specifications provide means to further define elements, attributes, and so forth, so some elements may have child elements, while others may not. Because attributes, text content, and the like may not have child nodes, they are called *leaf nodes*.

● A select operation retrieves a subset of records from a table based on the criteria in one or more fields.

● A union operation combines records from two tables into another table, eliminating any duplicate records.

Data Model Design Goals

The difference between a good data model design and a poor design can be determined in terms of the following criteria. Although it's outside the scope of this book, you may want to review Unified Modeling Language (UML). This language is expressly designed for elaborate data modeling. In any case, these criteria (good and poor design) require the use of some judgment, but remembering them as guidelines can be helpful:

- **An easily understood structure**   Separate sets of attributes into well-defined groups based on the thing they refer to. For example, don't put all data relating to customers in the same element as attributes. Separate the attributes according to their type, and then relate them to an element with ID attributes.

- **Low-storage space requirements**   Don't make it impossible to create a new element without creating lots of attributes along with it. Make sure you design your content models to contain the minimum data required. Otherwise, you'll have lots of wasted space in your documents (or in the database from which they're generated).

- **Not prone to errors**   Design your elements and attributes with well-defined value spaces and constraints, so it'll be hard for erroneous data to creep in.

9

Structured Query Language

Structured Query Language (SQL) is the standard language used to create, access, and manipulate database objects and the data within them for the bulk of the database applications in common use. In this module and the next, you use SQL statements in conjunction with scripting language commands to produce and control your database interactions. As you'll see in Module 10, both Microsoft Access and Microsoft SQL Server use SQL extensively.

The next section in this module covers important SQL commands and syntax. SQL is case insensitive, but some DBMSs aren't, so be careful to check your documentation when writing SQL statements. The objective here is to build a foundation for the SQL statements you'll use in the next module. Because SQL statements are fairly similar to statements in English, the language is, to a degree, intuitive and easy to understand. For example, to select a subset of records from a table with certain criteria applied to a given attribute (field), the command might be coded like this:

```
SELECT * FROM table WHERE attribute = criteria
```

This code example selects all fields (the * means all) from the table named *table* in which all records must contain the value *criteria* in the attribute field.

Writing SQL Statements

Writing SQL commands in uppercase is conventional, as was just demonstrated in the code example, in which SELECT, FROM, and WHERE all appear in uppercase. The WHERE portion of a SQL statement is called a *clause*. If your intent is to insert or append records to a table, you use INSERT instead of SELECT. If you want to delete records, you use DELETE. These statements would still select the records for the action desired, as this code example illustrates:

```
DELETE FROM table WHERE attribute = criteria
```

Notice it's unnecessary to include an asterisk (*) to signify the fields to be removed. All fields are removed when records are deleted from a table.

A number of other SQL commands, such as these, can be used for structural operations:

- **CREATE TABLE**   Creates a table and can have fields specified, as well as a table name

- **ALTER TABLE**   Makes changes to the structure of a table, such as adding or removing fields

- **DROP TABLE**   Deletes a table from the database

Ask the Expert

Question: What kind of data model should I use? How do I start the process of deciding how I should model the data to be contained in my XML document or databases?

Answer: No hard and fast answer fits every situation, but several general methods can get you started and help you find acceptable, if not perfect, solutions.

You might start out with what you know and build up from there, or start out with the end result you want and work backward. Either way, you'll be getting started, which is often the best way to see a project through. Don't be surprised if you need to redo part of a data model you built, to take into account things you hadn't anticipated or make practical compromises that are required.

For example, let's say you want to build a data model for tracking customers and orders. Starting with what you know and building up, you assume you need records in your table or elements in your XML documents representing customers. In a database, you build a table named Customers, wherein each record would represent a single customer. In XML, you create an element named Customers that can have many individual Customer elements. Essentially the XML element Customers is equivalent to the database table Customers, and each record in the Customers table is equivalent to a child element (Customer) of the Customers element.

And now that you have individual records for customers, you might take another look at the other problem of tracking customers and decide that part of tracking them (and fulfilling their orders) depends on your ability to contact them. Therefore, you need to capture contact information such as name, address, phone numbers, e-mail addresses, and so forth. In your database, you'd add fields for each of these attributes, and in your XML definition, you might add some of these as attributes and some of these as child elements, according to the distinctions you made in previous modules. To reiterate, if an attribute may occur more than once, it should be a child element. In the same way, if a field occurs more than once, you might want to make it into its own table. An example of this would be address information. If your

9

problem requires that you store 10 different addresses for each company (mailing address, shipping address, billing address, contact address, headquarters address, and so forth), a better idea might be to give all these addresses their own table and connect them to the main Customers table via a foreign-key field.

And, of course, once you decide what data you need for tracking purposes, you'll decide what kind of data goes in each field (text, numbers, dates, and so on) and what are the appropriate value ranges and other information for the data.

Starting from what you want to accomplish is another method for arriving at the same structures, but this involves working backward from what you want the database or XML definition to accomplish. In the scenario just described, you might work backward from the specific goal of being able to manage orders for customers. From managing customer orders, you might conclude that you must be able to contact customers. From that conclusion, you might recognize the need to store customer contact information. And from that conclusion, you might recognize that you need records or elements for individual customers. Of course, if you already have an XML document to begin with, tools are available that can convert from document to schema with little work.

Question: Do I need to be a database designer to build good XML definitions and schemas? What if I'm working with relatively unstructured data such as e-mails, or building presentations with SMIL, or making Web pages?

Answer: XML documents aren't required to be connected to a DTD or schema to be well formed, but they must be if they're intended to be validated. A valid XML document connected to a schema may be similar in structure to a relational database, but may also be just as useful for storing unstructured or semistructured data, depending on the definitions and data types found in it.

The beauty of XML is that it lends itself to data storage and structures that are varied and flexible, and as a standard format it's becoming universally used. Much of the data already in existence, however, is found in databases, and it's likely that you'll need to know how relational databases are structured to make compatible XML applications.

Project 9-1: Designing a Data Model

In this module, you read lots of the technical details about designing a data model. Now it's time to build a few examples. With this project, you cover several situations in which the data models produced reflect unique requirements that may not appear on the general run of databases or XML definitions. Exposure to unusual situations can, hopefully, illustrate the circumstances under which various data model solutions are appropriate.

Step-by-Step

Before you start building a data model, you need to delineate the *problem domain,* or the problem you're trying to solve. Clearly defining the initial problem to be solved is important, even at the expense of leaving some things out, so there's the possibility of producing something usable in a reasonable time. As data models are created to model real-world problems, if you think about it, you can generate data models that begin to encompass the entire real world—but, of course, you'll never reach your goal. Focusing on a small but significant area of the problem and starting there is much wiser. Usually you can add on, rebuild, or remove some portion of the model without too much trouble as you become more familiar with the problem domain.

1. Your first problem domain is the management of customers and orders (because this is what we've been using for examples throughout this book). Start with some assumptions about what you need to fulfill the requirements (solve the problem) and reverse engineer the data model from those requirements.

   To manage customers and orders, you need to store information about customers, orders, the line items in those orders, and so forth. This implies you can track customers, orders, and order items as individual things, and this offers a good clue as to the tables or higher-level elements that must be designed from the data model.

   From a management standpoint, you need to retrieve records or elements reflecting a single customer, order, or line item from an order, as well as views of all customers, orders, and line items in an order. You might also want to retrieve records or elements based on some criteria, such as the date a customer first entered your system, number of orders, total dollar value of orders in a given time period, backlogged orders, unpaid orders, or returned orders. These are all typical examples of order management—data that might be required on a daily basis or information that assists managers in making better long-term decisions.

9

2. Now that you have a small list of some of the things you need to achieve with your data model, you should write it out as a starting point for your data model. The list might look like this:

Customer/Order Management Data Model

Management Capability Objectives

- Store information about customers
- Store information about orders
- Store information about order items
- Retrieve individual customers, orders, and order items
- Retrieve all order items for an order
- Retrieve all orders for a customer
- Retrieve subsets of records for order items or complete orders based on criteria, such as order date, customer name, geographic location, and order items
- Aggregate data for management reports based on date ranges, answering questions such as total dollar value, paid or unpaid, collection status, and so forth

3. From this beginning, you can determine that you need to track three categories: customers, orders, and order items. Now you shall determine the relationships of these three categories. This is a logical exercise that can be done by simply talking out properties you intuitively know about customers, orders, and order items. The following statements illustrate how this method works:

- You may have zero or more customers. When a business starts, it may have no customers, although it surely hopes to have some customers eventually.

- A customer may have zero or more orders. You intend to allow customer records even before a customer has made an order, and each customer may have zero or more orders. Therefore, you decide that customers have a one-to-many relationship to orders.

- An order must have at least one line item. Some companies allow only one line item per order and, therefore, the identifying information about the line item ordered may be part of the order itself. Far more common, however, is to allow multiple items to be ordered as part of a single order. Intuitively, you know an order without any line items doesn't make sense because how could it be an order if the customer isn't ordering anything?

Each order, therefore, must have at least one and possibly more than one line item ordered. So, you can say orders have a one-to-many relationship to order items.

4. In a relational database, you would build a separate table each for customers, orders, and order items. In an XML DTD or schema, you would build elements named Customers, Orders, and OrderItems to contain individual Customer, Order, and OrderItem elements (these would be equivalent to individual records in the relational database). In the database, you would establish relationships between the tables, based on primary- and foreign-key attributes. In an XML DTD or schema, you would relate elements by using an ID attribute value as the primary key and the IDREF attribute value as a foreign key. Another useful piece of information that's surfaced using this method is this: some of the elements may be allowed zero or more times, while others must appear one or more times, and both of these states can be represented in XML DTDs or schemas.

5. After you've decided what needs to be tracked and set up data relationships, you need to look at the properties or attributes that must be included to serve your overall customer/order management objectives. Some of these attributes are easy to conjure up, while others take a bit more thought. A workable method is to start with the easy ones and work through the list of objectives to determine the more difficult ones, like this:

- **Primary Key** For the majority of cases, tables should have a primary key and, in the case of customers, you know they need a primary key. Include that attribute right off the bat and name it **CustomerID**. An easy way to make primary keys is to use a sequence of numbers, starting with the number 1, and adding to it for each new record or Customer element. Microsoft Access uses a datatype of *Long* (meaning an integer with a large range of possible values) and adds a special feature in the program to increment the value automatically and insert it each time a new record is started. In XML, you can set up the attribute as an ID (constraining it to be unique across a document), but you must program the incrementing function yourself. In the future, this could change if you use XLink or XPointer.

- **Name** All your customers should have a name. If your customers are businesses or a mixture of businesses and individuals, you might need to include the business name as well as the name of your contact. And it would be sensible to divide names up by first, last, and middle initial. As you may recall, separating out values that might be searched on later—such as last name, or area code, and so forth—is wise. You might

9

have as attributes BusinessName, ContactFirstName, ContactMI, and ContactLastName. The data type for these attributes may be text (perhaps 50 to 100 characters) for the database and text for an XML DTD (or, perhaps, a set of attributes for the three names for each contact). For an XML schema, you might create a complex data type consisting of the three names as a sequence of elements, each with a data type of *string*, and call it ContactName.

- **Addresses**   Depending on the type of business you're in, you may need or want an e-mail address for communications and product/service delivery (if you're selling online newsletter subscriptions, for example) or you might want a number of physical addresses, such as mailing, shipping, and so forth. Let's assume you're selling something that requires communications and physical delivery in the United States, so you'll have MailingAddress1, MailingAddress2, ShippingAddress1, and ShippingAddress2 and, for both of these, City, State, and Zip code. And, in some cases, billing address or other addresses may be required. For databases, when multiple examples of a similar type of data are required to be associated with a single record, it's an indication that you might need to establish another table and relate it to the primary table by key values. In XML DTDs and schema, you can create a child element (of the Customer element) named *address* and give it an attribute of *type* (meant to stand for "home," "business," "billing," "shipping," and so forth), and then add as many addresses to the record as you like. All the address data should be typed as text or as a string, even street numbers, because it's unlikely that arithmetical calculations will ever take place on these values.

- **Phone Numbers**   Because you might, at some point, want to segregate customer records by area code, this should be its own attribute; otherwise, the only additional attribute might be *type*, so you can tell a fax number from a cell phone number. In fact, you could even make separate elements for each type of number. Again, the data type should be text/string.

- **Billing Information**   Depending on who you're dealing with and how you bill, you might want to include elements/fields for CreditCardNumber, NameOnCard, ExpirationDate, PurchaseOrderNumber, and the like. Everything should be a text/string data type, except the expiration date.

6. Now you can create properties and attributes for each Order. Start with the easy ones and work your way down:

- **Primary Key**   The same type of attribute as for Customer, named OrderID.

- **Foreign Key**   A field or attribute with a data type that's the same as the data type you chose for each Customer. Of course, to make understanding the intended value for the field or attribute easier, you should give it a similar name, such as CustomerID. This field/attribute is required to relate customers to orders. For a database (such as Microsoft Access), this field/attribute would have a data type of Long, while for XML, it would use IDREF data type.

- **Date**   Each order is initiated on a particular date, so you want an OrderDate field, with a data type of Date. In some situations, you might also want to include the time—if so, you'd make another field or attribute or include the value together with the date. Not only can the date tell you when the order was placed, but it can also help you in retrieving subsets of records based on a date range.

- **Order specific data**   You might want to record the employee who took the order, in which case you want to include EmployeeID (assuming you also have a set of records for your employees, and each of them has an ID). Including an OrderTotal field or attribute might also be appropriate. This data can be derived as the sum of the quantities times the costs for each order item that is part of the order. Keeping it as a calculated total is also advisable in many circumstances, however. Any other data about the order by itself should also be kept with the Order record or element. Of course, order total should be kept as a numeric data type.

7. For each order item, you'll most likely pull data about the product or service from another table containing your inventory or available items. Because inventory quantities can change, and prices for each item might also change, it's important to separate inventory data and order item data. Much of the information will be duplicated in both tables, but once item data becomes part of an order, it shouldn't change unless an order change is submitted and approved. For each order item, you'll probably need the following:

- **Item number**   The Stock Keeping Unit (SKU) number or another code that identifies the item specifically.

- **Quantity**   A numeric data type that reflects the number of the particular item that was ordered.

- **Configuration parameters**   Size, weight, color, and so forth that don't affect the price of the item. They may be text/string data type or numeric values with units (such as length, size, or weight). In a database, if a fixed number of values can be assigned (six colors only, for example),

9

these values can be kept in a small table to choose from. In XML DTDs and schemas, these values can be an enumerated list.

- **Product name and description**   Text/string values that help to identify the product but don't define the product with the precision of the SKU or ProductID.

You've now created a fairly complete picture of the data you need to track, the data's relationships, and the attributes that must be tracked to serve the management objectives you originally defined. This data model also happens to fit well with the DTDs and schemas defined in Modules 2, 3, and 4. Using these methods and a little common sense, nearly any problem can be defined and modeled usefully, if not perfectly.

Ask the Expert

Question: How can I tell when to use a particular data type, attribute, element, or structure? If I make the wrong choices or find I need to make changes downstream, will this be impossible or cost-prohibitive? What can I do to maximize my chances of developing a good data model and structure from the start?

Answer: Spend some time defining how and under what circumstances the data is going to be used. Meetings or conversations with users and managers can tell you a lot about how data should be organized. If it's important for each customer to be reachable at the workplace, for example, you might require a workplace phone number for each customer. On the other hand, if no materials are faxed to customers, having a fax number field or element might be superfluous.

Often, you'll find a data model already in place, in the form of a relational database (or maybe even just a bunch of paper forms filled out and stored in a filing cabinet). Don't assume that just because a database already exists that it's a good way for the data to be modeled, however. The world is full of poorly modeled databases with inappropriate data types. On top of that, design flaws often mean the data in these databases is polluted, inconsistent, and missing. Your new design should, by the structure you give it, correct many of these flaws and work to prevent the entry of incorrect data.

As you build your data model, enter some test data to see how it works in your model. You should be able to tell if you need to make changes by testing it with queries and in various views. Making changes is much easier and more cost-effective while the design is still in work rather than after the fact, with thousands or millions of records already entered. Although you can make changes at any time, the amount of work that goes into those changes depends on how much has been done, how complex the overall system has become, and how much data has already been entered.

Elements, attributes, and data types used depend on what needs to be tracked and what needs to happen to the data as it's gathered, used, and summarized. For example, it's a good idea to classify data as static or dynamic, and to build in ways to track what happens to it during its lifetime. An order, once created, should be a static record of that order at that moment in time. Any changes to the order should be reflected in an addition to the order history—so someone looking at the order sees the current order but can also trace any changes along the way (as well as who made the changes and why).

Question: Making a data model to track and manage customers and orders seems fairly straightforward, but what about when a complex process is involved—for example, when an application for life insurance is processed? How are these things modeled?

Answer: You're talking about business process engineering, which is closely related to data modeling, because a data model should support both static and dynamic information. At the top level, business processes are often defined in terms of the overall mission of a company. Then a hierarchy is built from each level of processes required to support the mission. For example, a company may want to have the best quality and the best customer support in the industry. This would be the company's overall mission. Major goals might then be to hire and train excellent support personnel and material buyers, and build high-quality manufacturing processes. These major goals directly support the mission.

From there, processes are further broken down until they get to the daily operational tasks required to support higher level processes. At

9

that point, information to be gathered, used, and summarized goes back up the hierarchy as more concise and less-detailed reporting about how well the company is achieving its goals.

Data modeling to meet these requirements means, at the lowest level, all the data required to support the highest level requirements (and all the levels in between) must be collected and appropriately transformed across processes (between the people using it) and between process levels. Sometimes, this is a matter of approvals (signing off throughout the work hierarchy) and sometimes actual changes are made to the data, summarizing or evaluating data in relation to other data. Your data model should support not only the raw data requirements, but also the summarization and transformation requirements.

✓ Mastery Check

1. What are two methods of approaching the development of a data model?

    A. Starting with what you know and building up from there

    B. Starting with the requirements and working backward

    C. Both A and B

    D. None of the above

2. Can a database or XML document be empty and still have structure?

    A. A database may be empty, but an XML document cannot be empty. Therefore, the answer is no.

    B. Both a database and an XML document may be empty, but they may still have structure.

    C. Both A and B.

    D. None of the above.

☑ *Mastery Check*

3. What kinds of things can be modeled with a data model?

   A. Physical things, such as cars, people, buildings, and so forth

   B. Virtual things, such as orders, messages, calculations, and so forth

   C. Both A and B

   D. None of the above

4. In the ER type of data model, what is an attribute?

   A. An attribute is the same thing as an XML element

   B. An attribute is the same thing as an XML attribute

   C. An attribute is a property of an entity

   D. None of the above

5. What values can the null value represent?

   A. Zero, missing, or a blank space

   B. Missing, not applicable, or a zero-length string

   C. Not applicable, unknown but existent, and unknown-nonexistent

   D. None of the above

6. What relationships may exist between entities?

   A. An entity may have a one-to-one, one-to-many, or many-to-many relationship with another entity.

   B. An entity may have an unlimited number of relationships with other entities, depending on how they are described—such as works for, rides, lives in, walks on, buys from, and so forth.

   C. An entity has a direct participation relationship or a partial participation relationship with other entities.

   D. None of the above.

9

☑ *Mastery Check*

7. In the ER type of data model, what characteristics may an attribute have?

A. An attribute's value may be stored or derived.

B. An attribute's value may be composed of one or more individual pieces of data (simple or composite).

C. An attribute's value may change over time.

D. All of the above.

E. None of the above.

8. What are key attributes and how do they work?

A. Key attributes are unique values within a set of records in a table or elements in an XML document. Their uniqueness makes them ideal for identifying individual records.

B. Key attributes are used to provide security for databases and XML documents. Public and private encryption keys are stored in them.

C. Key attributes unlock database tables when join queries are made.

D. None of the above.

9. How are key values used to form relationships between records in a relational database?

A. If the key value is 1N, a one-to-many relationship exists; if the key value is NN, a many-to-many relationship exists.

B. Each primary key in one table may be directly connected to a primary key in another table, forming a linked relationship between the tables.

C. The primary-key values for one set of records may be included as the foreign-key values for another set of records. Thereafter, any record with a foreign-key value (in the second table) is connected by that value to the record in the first table with a matching primary-key value.

D. None of the above.

☑ Mastery Check

10. What value may not be allowed in a primary key field?

    A. A duplicate value

    B. An null value

    C. A Boolean value, where more than three records exist

    D. All of the above

11. What is the purpose of the reserved word WHERE in SQL?

    A. It provides the location of the table from which to select records.

    B. It provides the location of the field from which to select records.

    C. It provides criteria by which to select records.

    D. None of the above.

12. What reserved word in SQL is used to delete tables from a database?

    A. DELETE

    B. DROP

    C. ERASE

    D. None of the above

13. Modeling the relationships between children and their toys, which of the following might be a good data model?

    A. Children and toys might be entities, and the children and toys might have a one-to-many (one child to many toys) or many-to-many relationship (where the children share toys).

    B. Children might be entities, and toys would be attributes of those entities, with a one-to-one relationship between each child and each of their toys.

    C. Children and toys might be entities, and the relationship between children and their toys would always be many-to-many.

    D. None of the above.

9

✓ *Mastery Check*

14. What do the SELECT, DELETE, and INSERT SQL reserved words share in common, and how do they differ?

A. These words perform different functions and don't share characteristics in common, other than all being part of SQL.

B. These words all form queries, but SELECT selects certain records, DELETE deletes certain records, and INSERT inserts new records.

C. These words are used for working with tables; SELECT selects certain tables, DELETE deletes certain tables, and INSERT inserts new tables.

D. None of the above.

15. What symbol is used to return all fields in a SELECT query in SQL, and what is used to return only a selected set of fields in a SELECT query in SQL?

A. The word ALL is used to select all fields, and the word SOME is used to select some fields.

B. All fields are always returned for every query.

C. The asterisk is used to return all fields, and individual field names separated by a comma are used only if selected fields are desired.

D. None of the above.

Module 10

Databases and XML

The Goals of This Module

- Learn to create databases with Microsoft Access 2000
- Learn to create databases with Microsoft SQL Server
- Review the XML Query specification
- Examine XML Data and Internet Explorer
- Build XML Data Islands for use with MSXML 3.0
- Retrieve database data with ASP and create XML Data Islands

To demonstrate how to use databases with XML documents, you need a few database applications. Many fine products are available. In this book, we use Microsoft Access and SQL Server, both of which are in common use and familiar to many users.

In this module, you'll also learn about a query language called XML Query, which is under development at the W3C. A number of other methods and languages for querying XML documents are available. One set of tools you can use is Microsoft XML (MSXML) 3.0.

Using Databases and XML in Scripted Applications

If you've ever used a search engine, you probably realize that much of the data available is stored in databases. Web sites that provide services (such as search functions) are called *Web site applications*. The term *application* is used to relate the Web site applications to desktop application programs because, like a desktop application, the Web versions provide a user interface and perform processing based on user input. Web site applications also have the advantage of having other sources of current information available online while processing the user's input. Much of the data used during processing is stored in databases internal to the site and recently methods for retrieving data from databases external to the site are becoming more common.

Data is retrieved via internal or external database connections. In the case of internal databases, you can use Microsoft's Active Server Pages (ASP) and ActiveX Data Objects (ADO) to work with data from a variety of data sources, including Microsoft Access and Microsoft SQL Server. Because large amounts of data are already stored in these relational database management systems (RDBMSs), you might not have to build or populate databases to create a usable Web site application. And if you need to communicate with other servers or external data sources, XML provides a standard exchange mechanism. Using tools such as MSXML 3.0 for the conversion to and from an XML format, therefore, makes your life a little easier.

In the next section, you quickly review the physical design of a simple database to provide a foundation for the projects you build and to demonstrate the relationship between database design and interactions with your XML documents. Microsoft Access 2000 is used as a construction tool.

Designing Databases

In Module 9, you learned what you need to know when designing data structures, such as databases, XML DTDs, and schemas. In this module, the focus is on the basics of database design using common database application programs.

The Objects That Comprise a Database

The purpose of a database is to store and present data, so it often consists of several standard objects—perhaps with a few more, depending on specific application requirements:

- **Tables**   Tables store data as *records* (each row is a record) of information related to a single tracked thing, just like XML elements store data related to a single item. Records store pieces of information as *fields* (another name is *attributes* or *properties*), and each field has a specific data type.

- **Queries**   *Queries* are data retrieval and modification tools (technically, database interactions). They can pull records based on specific criteria, and they can also modify, eliminate, and add records. Queries are often used for pulling or modifying many records at once, but they're also useful for working with individual records.

- **Forms**   Like HTML forms, *database forms* are the user interface of database applications. They are used to access data by adding, editing, deleting, or searching for individual records. Database forms are also useful for performing navigation functions. When user input is necessary on a Web site, forms may be used as a substitute for the forms inside a database application.

- **Reports**   In a database application, *reports* are mainly used as a device to achieve nicely formatted printed results, while on a Web site, results are usually displayed in a Web page.

10

Ask the Expert

Question: If I create a database with Microsoft Access to use on my Web site, how does the person who uses or manages the Web site work with the database? What's the most efficient way to manage data online, particularly when many of the management functions are going to be performed offline?

Answer: You can create and work with databases that are going to serve a Web site in several ways. The easiest is to create the database file and load it into a published folder on the Web site. Then use either a connection string or a DSN (discussed later in the section on the ADO Connection Object) to access the database from your scripts.

You can provide users with a method for searching the data (and, perhaps, entering their own data) with scripts. An easy way of managing data is to enable admin users (probably someone designated by the owners or managers of the Web site) to download the database file and work with it directly through the DBMS program it was created in—in this case Microsoft Access. You need to create a workable user interface in Access, so users can easily perform their functions, and you need to make sure users know how to upload the database once they're done.

There is a drawback to this method: During the time an admin user is working with the database offline, online users may have added more data. The admin user would have to download the most recent database file before uploading the offline version, with the hope that no data is lost in between. For simple applications, or for applications in which online users don't have the ability to add or modify data, this might be workable.

For many applications, uploading and downloading the database file simply isn't feasible, so you'd need to create all admin functions online as well (password protected, of course). Then admin personnel can manage the data while still online. If another offline application requires the online data (to maintain integration between online and offline inventory counts, for example), however, you'd need to build some function to update the online and offline data periodically or perhaps even in real time.

Question: And where does XML fit in?

Answer: Building a Web site application means connecting to data stores, often databases. So, for example, if you have an online application that calculates taxes, you might store and retrieve tax tables. If the IRS makes a change to its tax tables, however, you would have to update your tax table records in your internal database.

Suppose the IRS offered access to tax tables online. Then you could write a query to poll the IRS's online tax tables periodically. But suppose you needed data that was available from a number of online sources? You might have to write queries for extracting data in a variety of formats, each with its own unique requirements. And if you need to submit processed data to those sites as well (such as completed tax returns) or engage in a dialog with those sites, the programming requirements could grow dramatically.

If your site and all the others are capable of exchanging data in an XML format, the programming requirements become much more manageable. You would still have to build queries for selected data (XML elements and attributes), but reformatting the data would be eliminated to a large degree. And maintaining your queries would probably also be easier.

10

Queries and SQL

Desktop RDBMSs such as Microsoft Access 2000 have built-in tools for accomplishing routine tasks, such as the creation of queries. One of the tools included with Access 2000 is called QBE (Query-By-Example). The QBE screen offers a view of the fields of data to be retrieved as a grid, with a line beneath each field for specifying criteria to be used to select records from a given table or a set of related tables. To build a query using QBE in Access 2000, you select the tables from which records are to be retrieved, select the fields (columns) to be included, and enter criteria for any fields you like (for example, you might specify only records in which the last name field contains "Smith"). Once you choose tables and fields and enter criteria, you can choose from several query types:

- **Select Query**   Selects records based on the criteria you enter

- **Delete Query**   Deletes records matching the criteria you enter

- **Append Query**   Appends records (from the included tables) matching your criteria into another table

- **Update Query**   Updates all records matching your criteria to a new value for any field you choose

- **Make-Table Query**   Makes a new table from all the records matching your criteria

Access and Structured Query Language (SQL)

When you create a query in Access 2000 with the QBE, Access is automatically writing SQL code in the background. You can view this code by choosing View | SQL View. As you are creating your database, you can easily create queries in Access and then view the appropriate SQL using this feature. The SQL created is specific for Microsoft Access, however, and may take a bit of tweaking to work in your ASP scripts or with other data sources.

For example, suppose you build a database to manage invoices for classes you've taught. One of the things you might want to do is determine the total amount due for classes in a particular period. In Access, once you build the query, you can switch to SQL view and see the result, shown here:

```
SELECT ClassesTaught.MonthYear,
 Sum(ClassesTaught.TotalDue) AS SumOfTotalDue
FROM ClassesTaught
GROUP BY ClassesTaught.MonthYear
HAVING (((ClassesTaught.MonthYear)
=[Forms]![ClassesTaught]![Combo26]));
```

The fields MonthYear and TotalDue are to be retrieved, with TotalDue summed up (all the TotalDue values for a month are added) from the table ClassesTaught. The month and year field criteria are retrieved from an Access form named ClassesTaught, in a combo box named Combo26. Notice how Access adds parentheses to the SQL. These should be removed from SQL statements before being placed in your scripts. And the criteria value from the

Access form should be replaced by a criteria value from a Web page (typically) when the SQL is used in an ASP script.

Forms as a User Interface

In databases, forms are mostly used for one of two purposes: for entering and editing data in tables or for navigating the application. Access 2000 has several manual and automated methods for creating forms and also includes a database utility function called the *Switchboard Manager* that makes creating navigation forms easy. The most important thing to remember when you create forms is that you make them easy to understand and use for the specific task at hand. If only three of the fields will enable the user to do the job, for example, you needn't include every field from a table in a form.

Note

We don't cover forms in detail here (at least not the forms you can create in a DBMS), because you'll probably develop those forms as Web pages made from XML documents. XHTML forms, with links and buttons, contain the same kinds of capabilities as ordinary database forms.

1-Minute Drill

● Most RDBMSs contain what kind of function that helps you write SQL statements?

● Why is SQL important?

ActiveX Data Objects

ActiveX Data Objects (ADO) are ASP components that work with databases and data stores. ADOs were specifically designed to work well with ASP scripting because it's common for Web sites to require database support. On the back-end, you can use nearly any database application, whether it's Microsoft Access 2000, SQL Server, or any other ODBC-compliant database (such as Oracle).

● Most RDBMSs contain a conversion function for going from a visual query view to a SQL query view, such as Access's QBE.
● SQL stands for Structured Query Language, which is an industry standard used by most of the RDBMSs on the market.

Many containers of data (other than databases) exist—from spreadsheets and word processing documents to e-mail clients and plain text files. For that matter, any data in any format, online or offline, can be considered a data source.

Data Consumers and Data Providers

Objects that store data are called *data providers*, while applications that use data are called *data consumers*. ADO is one part of a two-layer architecture for retrieving data, consisting of ADO and Object Linking and Embedding (OLE) DB. OLE DB is the mechanism that directly interacts with the data store, whatever it might be, and ADO talks to OLE DB. This means you can program for ADO and OLE DB can take care of the technical details.

OLE DB Providers

ADO is installed with this set of OLE DB providers:

- **Jet OLE DB 4.0**   For Microsoft Access databases

- **DTS Packages**   For SQL Server Data Transformation Services

- **Internet Publishing**   For accessing Web servers

- **Indexing Service**   For index catalogs

- **Site Server Search**   For the Site Server search catalog

- **ODBC Drivers**   For accessing ODBC data sources

- **OLAP Services**   For the Microsoft OLAP Server

- **Oracle**   For accessing Oracle databases

- **SQL Server**   For accessing Microsoft SQL Server databases

- **Simple Provider**   For accessing simple text files

- **MSDataShape**   For accessing hierarchical data

- **Microsoft Directory Services**   For Windows 2000 Directory Services

- **DTS Flat File**   For the SQL Server Data Transformation Services flat file manager

The ADO 2.5 Object Model

ADO 2.5 has built-in objects for connecting to and working with data. The syntax for using ADO objects from ASP and VBScript is pretty simple and straightforward. Basically, you make a database connection, run commands if you like, and retrieve recordsets.

Like their functions, the ADO objects have easy-to-remember names: Connection, Command, and Recordset objects. The Connection object includes an Errors collection, the Command object has a Parameters collection, and the Recordset object has a Fields collection. These collections can be accessed using typical dot notation, such as this:

```
Recordset.Fields("firstname")
```

Providers also make available a unique Properties collection. This collection, which can also be accessed, provides information about the ability of each provider. For example, some providers do not offer the ability to make modifications. And as another example, a database may have special security settings that a simple text file doesn't need.

The Connection Object

The *Connection object* lets you connect to data stores with OLE DB. To create a connection, you need to specify the data provider, security parameters, and other parameters. It's easy to create a connection with the Connection object (and in fact it's quite common to do so), but keep in mind that Connection objects are also implicitly created whenever you use the other ADO objects, such as Command and Recordset. And, like the Command object, the Connection object can also be used to run commands against a data store.

The Command Object

The *Command object* was designed to run commands against a data store. It has more command capability and is also more flexible than the Connection object. For example, you may be very specific about how the commands you're running are formed, and the Command object provides a better interface and programming structure for your commands.

10

The Recordset Object

The *Recordset object* is like a table in a database in that it exposes each record, and via the Fields collection, it exposes specific fields within those records to your scripting commands. Using VBScript, you can address records, fields, and values to make changes, find certain records, delete records, add new records, and perform other tasks. Methods are also available to filter records, count records, and determine whether you are at the beginning or end of the records in a recordset.

1-Minute Drill

- What ADO object is like a table in a database?
- What ADO object is best for running commands against a database?

The Connection Object

Using ASP and VBScript, you can start an instance of the Connection object whenever you need to make a connection to a database. It can be used to run SQL statements as well. The SQL statements you run might be typical SELECT queries (to pull records based on specific criteria) or they can be INSERT or DELETE queries. Since some of the data providers differ in the capabilities they provide, the collections, methods, and properties discussed in the following section may not be available.

Hint

Requesting certain object properties (such as a particular kind of cursor, which we'll discuss shortly) involves setting certain values within your script. VBScript can use these values or value representations (called *ADO Constants*) with common names. To make it easier to include these representations, you should include a file named adovbs.inc in all your scripts and make sure to add the file to any folders in which scripts are located. In adovbs.inc, the constant names and the values they represent are listed. When you include this file in your script files, the constants are available to the script. Find the file (it's probably already loaded on your system), and then copy it in to the appropriate folder(s) (the folders that contains your script).

- The Recordset object is like a table in a database because it enables you to work with individual records as though the table were open in front of you.
- The Command object is the best ADO object for running commands against a database, but you can use the Connection object in a limited way.

Making a connection to a data store requires certain data, such as driver type, username/password, and path and filename of the data store file. There are several ways to provide this data:

- Use a connection string

- Use a Data Source Name (DSN)

- Use a separate file with the connection string in it

In the next examples, we show acceptable connection strings. The first example is for Microsoft Access:

```
Driver={Microsoft Access Driver (*.mdb)}; DBQ=the path and file name
Provider=Microsoft.Jet.OLEDB.4.0; Data Source=the path and file name
```

Here's an example for Microsoft SQL Server:

```
Driver={SQL Server}; Server=the server name; Database=the database name;
UID=the user ID; PWD=the password
```

If you are going to set up a DSN in Windows 2000, follow this procedure:

1. In the Start menu, open the Administrative Tools section of the Programs menu.

2. Choose Data Sources (ODBC) to open the ODBC Data Source Administrator. In older operating systems (Windows NT), this function was found in the Control Panel.

Connection Object Methods

ADO objects have properties that provide information and methods to work with them. The Connection object has properties useful for managing transactions and for a variety of other database operations. Following is a list of a few of the most important methods to get you started:

- **Open** Opens a connection to a data source and accepts arguments such as a ConnectionString, UserID, and Password.

- **Execute** Executes, via the CommandText argument, queries in the form of either SQL statements, stored procedures, or simply a call to a

10

particular table. It also accepts options, such as the number of records affected and the direction for evaluating the CommandText argument.

● **Close**   Closes the Connection object, but doesn't remove it from memory.

Cursor Types

If you are working in a table in a database, the current record has focus and you can make changes to it, even though you can also see other records. A cursor in a recordset is like the cursor on the current record in a database table. It lets you work with the current record and can be used to navigate among the records. When a recordset is first opened, the cursor will be located either on the first record (if records exist and no particular order was specified)) or at a point called BOF/EOF (Beginning Of File, End Of File) if no records exist. Note that the test for BOF or EOF is often used to determine whether or not you've reached the last record in a Recordset object.

Several types of cursors are available for the popular RDBMSs, and cursor type may be specified in your scripting code (using an ADO Constant, if you like):

● **Forward Only**   The default cursor type. Enables forward movement through the recordset only. The ADO Constant is adOpenForwardOnly.

● **Static**   Enables movement forward and backward through the recordset. Doesn't show changes made by other users. The ADO Constant is adOpenStatic.

● **Dynamic**   Enables movement in both directions and shows changes made by other users. The ADO Constant is adOpenDynamic.

● **Keyset**   Enables movement in both directions and shows changes made by other users. Added records aren't visible and deleted records remain in the set. The ADO Constant is adOpenKeyset.

Coding the Cursor Type   The cursor type can be set using a Command object, and you need to use the Open method for the recordset to set the cursor type. Several arguments may be used for the Open method, including the Source (Customers in the following example) and the Cursor Type (adOpenDynamic in the following example). The code for setting the cursor type could look similar to this:

```
myRs.Open = Customers, , adOpenDynamic
```

1-Minute Drill

- Which cursor type is the default cursor type?
- Which cursor type is the most flexible?

The Recordset Object

Recordset objects also have properties and methods similar to those you might find in a database table. For example, in a database table, you can move from one record to the next, to the last or first record, or to a specifically numbered record. You can also filter and sort records in a database table. These same capabilities are found with the Recordset object properties and methods.

Recordset Methods

The available Recordset object methods are shown here:

- **Open**   Opens a recordset, with options for cursor type, source, and other properties

- **Close**   Closes a recordset

- **AddNew**   Adds a new record in a recordset and specifies the values to be entered in each field

- **Move**   Moves the cursor forward or backward through the recordset a specified number of records

- **MoveFirst**   Moves the cursor to the first record in a recordset

- **MoveLast**   Moves the cursor to the last record in a recordset

- **MoveNext**   Moves the cursor to the next record in a recordset

- **MovePrevious**   Moves the cursor to the previous record in a recordset

- **Delete**   Deletes the specified record from the recordset

- **Update**   Saves changes you made to the current record in a recordset

- **UpdateBatch**   Updates the records affected (specified by an ADO constant for current, filtered, or all records) for changes you make to these records

10

- A Forward-Only cursor is the default cursor type when you connect to a database.
- The Dynamic cursor is the most flexible cursor type.

- **NextRecordset**   Returns the next recordset when you place commands returning more than one recordset in your command or stored procedure

- **Requery**   Updates the data in into your recordset, based on re-executing the original query statement

- **Resync**   Refreshes the data in the Recordset object from the underlying database

- **Clone**   Creates a duplicate of the current Recordset object

- **GetRows**   Puts records from a recordset into an array

- **Supports**   Returns a value indicating what functions the data provider supports

- **CancelUpdate**   Cancels changes you've made to records, as long as you use it before the final Update method call

- **CancelBatch**   Cancels batch updates to records in a recordset

Recordset Properties

Recordset properties provide information about the recordset retrieved, such as the size and composition of the recordset, and such things as the source and status of a recordset. Here are the supported properties:

- **BOF**   Indicates the record pointer for the cursor is located at the beginning of the recordset. This is before the first record.

- **EOF**   Indicates the record pointer for the cursor is located at the end of the recordset. This is after the last record.

- **RecordCount**   Indicates the number of records in the current recordset.

- **MaxRecords**   Used to set the number of records to return with a recordset.

- **PageSize**   Sets or returns the number of records that make up a page of records for the current recordset.

- **PageCount**   Indicates the number of pages of records in the current recordset, based on the PageSize setting.

- **Bookmark**   Returns or sets a bookmark, which uniquely identifies a specific record in the current recordset.

- **AbsolutePosition**   Specifies the ordinal or numeric position of a record within the current recordset or returns an ADO constant, which indicates the position is unknown or BOF or EOF.

- **AbsolutePage**   Specifies the page for the current record.

- **ActiveConnection**   Indicates the connection object to which the recordset belongs.

- **CacheSize**   Indicates the number of records in the recordset cached locally in memory.

- **CursorType**   Tells you what kind of cursor the recordset has.

- **EditMode**   Indicates the editing status of the current record, which can be none, in-progress, or addnew.

- **Filter**   Enables you to filter records based on criteria, changing the viewable contents of the current recordset.

- **LockType**   Reflects the lock type in force when the recordset was retrieved.

- **MarshallOptions**   Available only for client-side recordsets and used to optimize performance when sending records back to the server.

- **Source**   Indicates the source of the records in the recordset.

- **State**   Indicates whether the recordset is open or closed.

- **Status**   Indicates the status of the current record regarding batch update operations.

1-Minute Drill

- Which Recordset object method exposes the functions provided by the data provider?

- What does it mean if the Recordset BOF property is True?

- The method of the Recordset object that tells you the functions the data provider provides is the Supports method.
- If the Recordset BOF property is True, this means you have reached a record position before the first record.

10

Recordset Navigation and Manipulation Operations

You use Recordset object methods and properties to maneuver in a recordset and to make updates and changes. It's important that you become familiar with the various connection and command parameters that affect the kind of recordsets retrieved, because some of the Recordset methods and properties may be unavailable—unless they're supported by the provider and specified in the commands used.

Creating and Using Recordsets

Before we can begin working with records retrieved in a Recordset object, you need to make a connection, perhaps run some commands, and retrieve some records. Of course, you'll need an Access or SQL Server database with plenty of records in it to try this out, and you'll need to make a DSN for the connection to go through.

Note

You can use the database files on the Osborne Web site (at www. osborne. com), rather than enter your own data, if you want your operations to match the code in the book exactly.

Now let's write some code that makes the connection and returns a recordset that can be worked with—meaning a dynamic cursor type. Try this on your server:

```
Set myConn = Server.CreateObject("ADODB.Connection")
myConn.Open "mod10dsn"
Set myRs = Server.CreateObject("ADODB.Recordset")
With myRs
        .Source = "Customers"
        .ActiveConnection = myConn
        .CursorType = adOpenDynamic
        .LockType = adLockOptimistic
        .Open
End With
```

In this example, the Connection object was used to open a connection via your "mod10dsn" DSN. Then the Recordset object and the *With* command were used to set the Source, ActiveConnection, CursorType, and LockType for your recordset.

To view the properties of the recordset, you can use code like the following:

```
Response.Write "The AbsolutePage Property of the Recordset is <B>"
 & myRs.AbsolutePage & "</B><BR>"
```

Navigating Through the Recordset   To traverse records in an open recordset, first check to determine whether any records were returned. After checking with the EOF property, use the Move methods of the Recordset object to navigate. To start, use code like this:

```
If myRs.EOF Then
                Response.Write "No records found in this table"
          Else
                myRs.MoveFirst
                Response.Write "The Customer First Name is " &
myRs.Fields("FirstName") & " and the Last Name is " &
myRs.Fields("LastPrice")
          End If
```

To move to the next, previous, and last records, the code is essentially the same as in the previous example, substituting in the MoveNext, MovePrevious, and MoveLast methods for the MoveFirst method. If you end up outside the recordset, the BOF or EOF properties may become *True*, so use some additional code (after the rst.MovePrevious, for instance) for next and previous, which checks for this condition. Here's an example:

```
If myRs.BOF OR myRs.EOF Then
                Response.Write "At BOF or EOF"
             Else
                Response.Write "The Customer First Name is "
 & myRs.Fields("FirstName") & " and the Last Name is " &
myRs.Fields("LAstName")
                End If
```

To move to a specific record in the recordset, use this code with a variable named vMoveNumber (or whatever you want to name your variable):

```
MyRs.Move vMoveNumber
```

In this case, vMoveNumber is a number contained in a variable representing the record number to move to. You can allow the user to insert this information via an HTML form. You could write an entire user interface, allowing the user to navigate records in a recordset, in this way.

10

1-Minute Drill

● What programming construct might be used to check for recordset conditions, such as EOF?

● What programming construct allows you to use code to iterate through each record?

Ask the Expert

Question: What happens when multiple users open a recordset using the same table? Is there any way of preventing one user from overwriting the changes made by another user?

Answer: Recordsets contain a snapshot of data currently found in a table. They must be locked to update values accurately when users make changes. Often, many users are accessing a Web site database at the same time, so appropriate locking is essential. Problems with multiple users are called *concurrency problems*. Most recordset concurrency problems are the same as those of an ordinary, networked database application. A variety of lock types are available to solve or reduce the impact of these problems. The Requery method is also available to refresh the contents of the recordset as often as necessary.

Question: All data providers are not the same, and I might need to know when certain properties are unavailable. Is there some way to do this or get around having to double-check every time a database connection is made?

Answer: Not really, but it may not be as bad as it seems. You'll probably be familiar with the data stores you are going to be using, so that should help. And you should consider programming an object that automatically performs the checks for you if you're going to be dealing with unfamiliar data stores. An object programmed with Visual Basic or Visual C++ is going to run a lot faster than a manual process of making the checks inside scripting code.

● You can use the "If recordset.EOF Then" structure to check for no records returned.
● You can use the "Do While Not recordset.EOF" structure to visit all the records.

XQuery

XML documents carry structure as well as data, especially when they may be validated against a DTD or schema. But they are text documents, and quickly retrieving or modifying only the specific parts an XML document that are important to you can be difficult. In addition, suppose a requirement exists to retrieve or modify parts of an XML document based on specific or complex criteria? For these reasons, an XML query language is under development.

Some controversy exists as to the need for a separate query language, however, considering the extensive query capabilities built-in to XSLT (discussed in Module 11) and because XQuery is still in the working draft stage (it has the status of working draft as of February 2001). Perhaps later, there will be a single, converged query language for all query-related uses developed by the W3C.

The XQuery Language

The XQuery language is being created under the following requirements:

- **Syntax**   Convenient to read and write, and must be written in XML

- **Declarativity**   Must be declarative

- **Protocol Independence**   Independent of any protocols with which it's used

- **Error Conditions**   Defines standard error conditions that may occur during query processing

- **Updates**   Compatible with future updates

- **Instances**   Defined for finite instances

- **Uses XML Information Set**   Uses information provided in Information Set items

- **Data types**   Represents data types from XML 1.0 and XML Schema

- **Collections**   Represents collections of documents and collections of simple and complex values

- **References**   Supports references inside a document and between documents, and traverse references

- **Schema**   Supports queries even when no schema is available

10

- **Namespaces**   Aware of namespaces

- **Operations**   Supports operations on all data types

- **Text/Element Boundaries**   Able to query text conditionally, even across elements

- **Quantifiers**   Supports universal and existential quantifiers

- **Hierarchy and Sequence**   Supports operations across hierarchy and sequence of documents

- **Combination**   Combines information within a document and across documents

- **Aggregation**   Groups and summarizes information from related elements

- **Sorting**   Sorts results

- **Composition**   Supports operations composed of expressions, including queries

- **Null Values**   Includes support for null values

- **Structural Preservation**   Preserves hierarchy and sequence structure

- **Structural Transformation**   Transforms existing structures and creates new structures

- **Identity Preservation**   Preserves identities

- **Literal Data**   Supports operations on literal data

- **Names**   Performs operations on names

- **Schemas**   Provides access to the XML schema or DTD

- **Schema PSV Infoset**   Performs operations on the post-schema-validation infoset

- **Extensibility**   Supports the use of externally defined functions on all data types

- **Environment Information**   Provides access to environment information

- **Closure**   Queries must be closed or defined purely in terms of XML Query Data Model

The XML Query Data Model

The XML Query language is predicated on the XML Query Data Model. As you learned in Module 9, a data model defines the structure of information contained in a particular format, and several data model types can be used. XQuery uses a formally defined data model.

The XML Query Data Model is defined as "a node-labeled, tree-constructor representation" that includes the concept of "node identity." The data model includes a definition of the structure of tree nodes, functions to build tree nodes, and functions (called *accessors*) that allow access to tree nodes. Tree nodes are referred to as *node types*, *schema type* is used to refer to an XML Schema type, and *unit type* is used to refer to either a node or a schema type.

Using MSXML 3.0 and Databases

Once you load the MSXML 3.0 tools (discussed in Module 6), it's easy to start working with these tools, XML documents, and ASP and ADO objects for connecting to databases. For example, the following (Microsoft) ways get XML data on the server:

- Use ADO to get XML information directly from any database that supports ADO.

- Read data from a database or other source and construct an XML tree using the (Microsoft) Document Object Model (DOM).

- Load an XML file using the *load* method of the XML control.

- Build a string and use the *loadXML* method to load it into the XML control.

- Build an XML text string without building an XML document object on the server.

In the following project, you use the capabilities of Microsoft's implementation of the DOM, as well as ASP and ADO, to work with XML documents.

Proj10-1.zip

Project 10-1: Retrieving XML Data

Part of most Web site/database applications involve retrieving data from a database, manipulating that data, and then perhaps sending it somewhere or inserting some of it back into the database. When XML is involved, it's convenient to have tools that can manipulate XML documents and data just as easily as ordinary records from a database or text content.

10

Step-by-Step

Initially, let's focus on building an XML tree structure with the DOM.

1. In your first code example, pull data from a database and use it to construct an XML document. The code might look like this:

```
<% Response.ContentType = "text/xml" %>
<?xml version="1.0" encoding="windows-1252" ?>
<%
if (xmldoc.childNodes.length = 0) then
  set root = xmldoc.createNode("element","CustomerData","")
  xmldoc.appendChild(root)
  SQL = "SELECT CustomerID, CompanyName,"
  SQL = SQL & " FROM Customers"
  set Conn = Server.CreateObject("ADODB.Connection")
  Conn.Open("mod10dsn")
  set rst = Conn.Execute(SQL)
  ocount = 0
  rst.MoveFirst
  while (not rst.EOF and ocount < 10)
  set onode = xmldoc.createNode("element","Customers","")
  xmldoc.documentElement.appendChild(onode)
  for i = 0 to rst.Fields.Count - 1
  set child = xmldoc.createNode("element",rst.Fields(i).Name,"")
  child.text = rst.Fields(i)
  onode.appendChild(child)
  next
  pcount = 0
  set isnode = xmldoc.createNode("element","Customer","")
  onode.appendChild(isnode)
  SQLa = "SELECT FirstName, LastName FROM Customers"
  SQLa = SQLa & rs("CustomerID")
  set rst1 = Conn.Execute(SQLa)
  rst1.MoveFirst
  while (not rst1.EOF and pcount < 3)
  set inode = xmldoc.createNode("element","Customer","")
  isnode.appendChild(inode)
  for i = 0 to rst1.Fields.Count - 1
  set child = xmldoc.createNode("element",rst1.Fields(i).Name,"")
  child.text = rst1.Fields(i)
  inode.appendChild(child)
  next
  rst1.MoveNext
  pcount = pcount + 1
  wend
  rst.MoveNext
  ocount = ocount + 1
  wend
end if
Response.Write(xmldoc.xml)
%>
```

> Sets up an element named CustomerData and puts it on the root of the document

> For each record, creates a new element named Customer and appends it to the document, filling it with the data from the recordset; then goes to the next record

> Writes out the finished document in XML format

In this example, the XML tree is built—one node at a time—using the *createNode* and *appendChild* methods of the DOM, with the text property filling in the values. For each record returned, nodes are created representing customers and their data.

2. Now load an XML document from a file. The code could be written like this:

```
xmlObj = Server.CreateObject("msxml2.DOMDocument")
xmlObj.load(Server.MapPath("basicXMLDoc.xml"))
```

In this example, the MapPath method changes the relative path of the file to an absolute path.

3. Use this type of method for outputting XML text data directly:

```
<% Response.ContentType = "text/xml" %>
<?xml version="1.0" encoding="windows-1252" ?>
<CustomersData>
<%
SQL = "SELECT CustomerID, CompanyName, FirstName, LastName" &
      " FROM Customers " &
      "ORDER BY LastName"
set Conn = Server.CreateObject("ADODB.Connection")
set rst = Server.CreateObject("ADODB.Recordset")
Conn.Open("cust")
set rst = Conn.Execute(SQL)
rst.MoveFirst
while (not rst.EOF)
%>
  <Customer>
    <CustomerID> <%= rst("CustomerID") %> </CustomerID>
    <CompanyName> <%= rst("CompanyName") %> </CompanyName>
    <FirstName> <%= rst("FirstName") %> </FirstName>
    <LastName> <%= rst("LastName") %> </LastName>
  </Customer>
<%
    rst.MoveNext
wend
rst.close
conn.close
%>
</CustomersData>
```

This method of building XML documents avoids the overhead of creating DOM document objects because the text is directly written into the tags by the Response object from the Recordset object.

10

XML and IE 5.0 Data Islands

Internet Explorer 5.0 allows authors to include *data islands* in the output of XML documents. These are areas in which the data from XML elements is inserted into bound data fields. One benefit is that these work even if the user has disabled scripting.

XML data can be inserted from an inline XML document or an external XML file, or by using the $Text element, a special element understood by IE 5.0 and later browsers. Inline XML is inserted using the XML element:

```
<XML ID="xmlData">
<?xml version="1.0" ?>
<Customer>
<CustomerName>John Doe</CustomerName>
</Customer>
</XML>
```

External XML document files are referenced with the *src* attribute of the XML element, as shown here:

```
<XML ID="xmlData" SRC="myXMLDoc.xml"></XML>
```

The *datasrc* and *DATAPAGESIZE* Attributes

Certain HTML elements, such as the table element, may include a *datasrc* attribute understood by Internet Explorer 5.0 and later, and this attribute may be bound to data from an XML document via the *id* attribute of the XML element, as shown in the next example:

```
<HTML><HEAD></HEAD><TITLE>XML Data Sources</TITLE>
<BODY>
<XML ID="Customers">
<?xml version="1.0" ?>
<Customers>
<Customer>
<CustomerName>John Doe</CustomerName>
</Customer>
<Customer>
<CustomerName>Mary Smith</CustomerName>
</Customer>
</Customers>
</XML>
<table datasrc="#Customers">
<tr>
```

```
<td><div datafld="CustomerName"></div></td>
</tr>
</table>
</BODY>
</HTML>
```

The *DATAPAGESIZE* attribute can be used in the starting table tag to restrict the number of records shown in the table, using code such as this:

```
<table datapagesize="10" datasrc="#Customers">
```

The $Text Data Field

A field named $Text is automatically created whenever you use the XML Data Source object (the *datasrc* attribute) in IE 5.0 and later. It contains the concatenated items in the record. Simply referring to it in the code will insert it into your table, like so:

```
<td><div datafld="$Text"></div></td>
```

Of course, because it is concatenated, you may or may not find the data very useful.

☑ *Mastery Check*

10

1. Of what value are database application programs when working with XML and databases?

   A. Their automatic functions make it easier to define data structures.

   B. They often include SQL code-writing functions.

   C. They are efficient data storage and retrieval containers.

   D. All of the above

2. What sequential steps might you take to build a database application using a typical RDBMS, such as Microsoft Access?

   A. Build the tables, build the queries, build the forms, and build the reports.

✓ Mastery Check

    B. Build the forms, build the reports, build the queries, and build the tables.

    C. Build the functions, enter the data, and test it.

    D. None of the above

3. Active Server Pages and VBScript were already introduced as a means of interacting with XML documents. What additional Microsoft technologies did you use in this module to work with both XML documents and databases?

    A. Data Interaction Language (DIL)

    B. Active Data Objects (ADO)

    C. Active Data Interaction (ADI)

    D. None of the above

4. What is the function of the Connection object?

    A. The Connection object connects disparate XML documents, so their content can be placed into a database format.

    B. The Connection object retrieves data as a set from databases.

    C. The Connection object enables a connection to a database via an ODBC driver.

    D. None of the above

5. What is the function of the Command object?

    A. The Command object allows commands to be executed against a database.

    B. The Command object allows commands to be run against an XML document generated from a database.

    C. The Command object allows commands to be run against a script retrieving data from a database.

    D. None of the above

☑ *Mastery Check*

6. What is the function of the Recordset object?

A. The Recordset object creates a connection to a database.

B. The Recordset object contains records retrieved from a database.

C. The Recordset object allows commands to be run against a database.

D. None of the above

7. What type of cursor allows only forward movement through a set of records, and what method would be used to move forward one record at a time?

A. The Forward-Only cursor allows only forward movement through a set of records, and the MoveNext method would be used to move forward from one record to the next.

B. The Keyset cursor allows only forward movement through a set of records, and the MoveNext method would be used to move forward from one record to the next.

C. The Static cursor allows only forward movement through a set of records, and the MoveNext method would be used to move forward from one record to the next.

D. None of the above

8. Name the properties that indicate the number of records in a recordset and whether you're at the beginning or end of a recordset.

A. The Start, End, and RecordCount properties

B. The Begin, End, and RecordCount properties

C. The BOF, EOF, and RecordCount properties

D. None of the above

9. When connecting to a database from an ASP script using ADO, either a connection string or a DSN must be used to provide the information to make the connection. What information is included in the connection string or the DSN?

10

☑ *Mastery Check*

A. The maker of the database, the type of data it contains, and the username and password for the database

B. The driver for the database, the path to the database, and, if necessary, the username and password for the database

C. The driver for the database, the filename for the database, and, if necessary, the username and password for the database

D. None of the above

10. What process might be used to retrieve data from a database and provide it in an XML document format?

A. Retrieve the data from the database; iterate through the records; and for each record, create the XML elements, attributes, and content for those records as an XML document.

B. Retrieve the data from the database as a text file and use the XMLConvert method to convert it into an XML document.

C. Load an empty XML document into memory and fill it with data retrieved from the database using the XMLFill method.

D. None of the above

11. For users of Internet Explorer 5.0 and above, what method might be used to provide XML data if scripting has been disallowed?

A. XML data delivery

B. Data Islands and the XML element

C. Specialized HTML that works for all browsers

D. None of the above

12. What methods can be used to include XML data in a Web page viewed in Internet Explorer 5.0 and above?

A. Inline XML or references to an XML file, using the XML element

B. The XML element and binary XML data retrieval

☑ *Mastery Check*

    C. The XML element and XML source generation

    D. None of the above

13. What technique can be used to bind XML data to HTML Web page structures, such as tables?

    A. Reference the XML data inline in the table element using the *xmlsrc* attribute.

    B. Reference the XML data from a URL using the *xmlsrc* attribute.

    C. Reference the ID attribute value of the XML element using the *datasrc* attribute.

    D. None of the above

14. If a table is being used to view XML data in Internet Explorer, what attribute of the table may be used to restrict the number of records displayed, and how many records will be shown if this attribute is set to 3?

    A. The DATAPAGESIZE attribute, and 3

    B. The DATARESTRICT attribute, and 3

    C. The DATAPAGESIZE attribute, and 30

    D. None of the above

15. What content is provided by the $Text data field and how is it generated?

    A. The $Text data field concatenates the content for a given record, automatically.

    B. The $Text data field concatenates the content for a given record when the onrecord event is triggered.

    C. The $Text data field concatenates the text content of all records, automatically.

    D. None of the above

10

Module 11

XML Presentation and XSL

The Goals of This Module

- Learn about and practice CSS2
- Understand the difference between XML and rendered documents
- Learn about XSL style sheets
- Learn about XSLT transformations
- Create an XML document for transformation
- Create a style sheet to transform the XML document
- Practice transformations
- Examine the formats to which transformations can be made

Agreement is nearly universal that XML vocabularies are an ideal way to structure data, but often data needs to move between XML vocabularies or across multiple data structures. And presenting information appropriately depends as much on the media by which the data is delivered as the data itself. Therefore, while XML is regarded as a fundamental way to store information, the efficient and appropriate presentation of that information, being variable depending on the medium in which it's displayed or rendered, requires a flexible transformation mechanism. The eXtensible Style Sheet Language (XSL) provides such as mechanism. This module covers use of XSL, XSLT (eXtensible Style Sheet Language Transformations), and XPath, three components of XSL dedicated to transforming and rendering XML documents.

Before delving into XSL and XSLT, let's look at Cascading Style Sheets Level 2 (CSS2). This style sheet language is now commonly used for HTML and XHTML documents. This language may already be familiar to you. In some respects, how it works is similar to the workings of XSL and XSLT, although CSS2 documents aren't XML documents, as XSL and XSLT style sheets are.

Cascading Style Sheets

XML documents can be associated with style sheets written in Cascading Style Sheets Level 2, in addition to XML-based style sheet languages, such as XSL/XSLT. In this section, how CSS2 works—as a foundation to the functions of XSL/XSLT—is described. When preparing XML documents for output as HTML/XHTML documents, CSS2 may be appropriate for style purposes.

CSS2 style sheets are more flexible and offer more precise layout and style control for these document types. Although HTML/XHTML elements and attributes often perform style functions, many of these are deprecated and may be unusable in the coming years. The term "Cascading" in Cascading Style Sheets Level 2 refers to the fact that multiple style sheets may be applied to a single document, with a set of rules for how each sheet is applied.

One of the reasons style sheet languages are popular is that using them separates style information from data and information structures. For example, if you have a series of documents that all require similar formatting, changing styles within each document individually would be more difficult and time-consuming than simply changing one style sheet document that's associated with every XML document.

And style sheet languages such as CSS2 can conditionally format documents according to the media in which the document will be displayed. XSL takes this ability even further, with a variety of functions that not only can perform conditional processing, but can select among XML elements as well as perform processing functions such as calculations.

HTML Documents and Style Sheets

In CSS2, style sheet commands consist of a selector that matches document elements and a declaration that declares what style property is affected and the value that property should take for the selected elements. In XSL, elements are selected using XPath syntax, and those elements are formatted using a template mechanism. The following code shows how a style sheet can be connected or associated with an HTML document when the style sheet is an external file:

```
<HTML><HEAD><TITLE>Using CSS2 Stylesheets</TITLE>
<LINK href="mystylesheet.css" rel="stylesheet" type="text/css">
</HEAD>
<BODY bgcolor="#FFFFFF">
<P class="pstyle">This paragraph has blue text.
<P>This paragraph does not.
</BODY></HTML>
```

In this example, the code in the LINK element links the HTML document to an external style sheet file named "mystylesheet.css". The *rel* attribute is set to "stylesheet" to make this a persistent style sheet. Setting the *type* attribute to "text/css" informs the browser of the style sheet language being used. The code in the style sheet file is shown here:

```
P.pstyle {
color : blue;
}
```

11

In the CSS2 code, the capital *P* is the selector for all paragraph elements (<P>) in the HTML document. The dot notation (.) syntax is used to associate this selector with a name (pstyle). Following that is the declaration (or property-value) part of the style instruction, showing the affected property is color, and the value for the affected property is "blue". What this means is all paragraph elements in the HTML document will be assigned a color value of blue, so all text in these paragraph elements will be blue.Within the HTML document, only paragraphs that have the *class* attribute set to the name in the dot-notation syntax, pstyle, are affected by the style instruction. If the requirement was for all paragraph elements in the document to have blue text, then leaving off the dot-notation syntax would have applied the color property to all paragraph elements.

CSS2 Selectors

In CSS2, elements are matched using selectors that have the same name as their HTML element counterparts. CSS2 also includes functionality for selecting elements based on a number of more flexible methods, such as wildcard searches. This flexibility has obvious benefits, such as making it easy to specify elements indirectly rather than by name. As an example, asterisks may be used to specify a match on all elements and are, therefore, called *universal selectors*. Named selectors are called *type selectors* because they match a specific element by type (such as paragraph, image, and so on). Some other kinds of selectors are *descendant selectors* (such as italicized text within headers), *child selectors* (child elements of a given element, such as LI elements in an OL element), selectors that match up to particular attributes (even capable of matching attributes by their value), and of course selectors that use dot notation to match by *class* or *id* attribute values.

In CSS2 code, the pound sign (#) is used to differentiate *class* attribute name dot-notation syntax from the syntax appropriate for the *id* attribute name, like so:

```
<HEAD>
 <STYLE type="text/css2">
<!--
    #anidstyle { color : blue}
-->
</STYLE>
</HEAD>
<P id="anidstyle">Paragraphs with this id have this style</P>
```

CSS2 Syntax

The structure of CSS2 instructions in code follows a pattern of selector (possibly including wildcards or class names), and within curly braces, the declaration property and property value (one or more, separated by and ending with semicolons), as shown in the following example:

```
H3 { color : red; font-style : italic;}
```

In this example, the properties and their values appear within curly braces, properties and values are separated by colons, and the property/value pairs end with semicolons. Property/value pairs constitue declarations (or rules). They can be written on the same line or on separate lines.

Setting the Style Sheet Language

Because more than one style sheet language may be used with HTML, XHTML, or XML documents, setting the style sheet language is required. In HTML documents, this can be accomplished using the META element (among a variey of methods). META elements aren't displayed in a rendered document, but they are used to convey information about the document, such as what style sheet language is being used, as shown here:

```
<META http-equiv="Content-Style-Type" content="text/css2">
```

When a style sheet language specification appears in a META element, this setting has precedence over other settings. The default style sheet language setting for HTML documents is "text/css".

Inline Element Style References

Most HTML elements support an attribute named *style,* which allows document authors to insert style instructions directly into HTML elements. Many properties of HTML elements can be modified with the *style* attribute by using the style formats appropriate to the element into which they're being inserted. In the next code example, the style of a single list item is modified with the *style* attribute:

```
<ul>
   <li>Option 1</li>
   <li>Option 2</li>
   <li style="font-weight : bold;">Option 3 Bold</li>
   <li>Option 4</li>
</ul>
```

11

In the case of inline element *style* attributes, no selector is necessary, obviously, because the declaration is already inside the element it will affect. The rest of the syntax remains the same, however.

The HTML STYLE Element

Another way to apply style instructions to an HTML document is to use the STYLE element—the equivalent of putting a style sheet inside the document. Style settings can be coded in the same way as when an external file is used, but for small numbers of pages or simple style sheets, STYLE may be a faster method. STYLE elements are often placed in the HEAD element of an HTML document, and several STYLE elements can be used, as shown here:

```
<HEAD>
 <STYLE type="text/css2">
  <!--
   H2 {text-align : left}
   P { color : blue}
  -->
 </STYLE>
</HEAD>
```

Notice several interesting things about the code shown in the example. First, the actual style sheet instructions are placed inside HTML comment delimiters inside the STYLE element starting and ending tags. This is because CSS2 code may include instructions that wouldn't be properly parsed by a browser. In addition, when a declaration is made with only one property and property-value pair, there's no need to use the semicolon at the end of the pair.

The STYLE Element DTD

The STYLE element definition appears in the HTML/XHTML DTD maintained by the W3C, at **www.w3.org**. Here's an excerpt from that DTD, showing the parameters of the STYLE element as defined:

```
<!ELEMENT STYLE - - %StyleSheet
        -- style info -->
<!ATTLIST STYLE
  %i18n;
        -- lang, dir, for use with title --
  type        %ContentType;
  #REQUIRED -- content type of style language --
  media       %MediaDesc;
    #IMPLIED  -- designed for use with these media --
  title       %Text;
        #IMPLIED  -- advisory title --
  >
```

Both starting and ending tags are required for the STYLE element, and the *type, media,* and *title* attributes are supported. The *type* attribute tells the browser what type of style sheet language is going to be used, the *media* attribute specifies the media type to which the style applies, and the *title* attribute lets the author set a title for that style.

Using Style with DIV and SPAN Elements

Blocks of HTML elements may be contained in DIV elements—to group them together—while inline elements may be contained in SPAN elements. Both of these element types are useful for applying styles across a group of elements. A common method for accomplishing this is to set the class or ID value of these elements to the appropriate name associated with a selector in a STYLE element or external style sheet. The next example shows how this method works for SPAN elements:

```
<html><head><title>STYLE Element using SPAN</title>
<style>
<!--
span.textspan { color: #FF0000; font-size: 24pt; font-variant: small-caps }
-->
</style>
</head><body>
<p>Text inside the
 <span class="textspan">SPAN element</span>
 is red, 24 points, and small caps</p>
</body></html>
```

Style applied to the DIV element works essentially the same way, as shown here:

```
<html><head><title>STYLE Element using DIV</title>
<style>
<!--
div.textdiv { color: #FF0000; font-size: 24pt;
 font-variant: small-caps }
-->
</style>
</head><body>
<div class="textdiv">
<p>The text in this DIV element is red,
 24 points, and small caps</p>
</div>
</body></html>
```

11

Setting Style Properties Conditionally for Media Types

The STYLE element has a *media* attribute, as you saw in the DTD. The purpose of this attribute is to allow for conditional selection based on the media type of the end device rendering the document. The browser (or other device) loads only stylesheet information that applies to the media specified. The specification details values approved for use in the *media* attribute, called *media descriptors*. Following is a list of the approved values (note that these values aren't yet considered a formal part of a recommendation, so they may change):

- **All**   States these style instructions can be rendered on any device
- **Aural**   States these style instructions can be rendered on speech synthesizers
- **Braille**   States these style instructions can be rendered on braille tactile feedback devices
- **Embossed**   States these style instructions can be rendered on paged braille printers
- **Handheld**   States these style instructions can be rendered on handheld devices
- **Print**   States these style instructions can be rendered on paper and is also useful for documents viewed in Print Preview mode
- **Projection**   States these style instructions can be rendered on projectors
- **Screen**   States these style instructions can be rendered on color computer screens
- **Tty**   States these style instructions can be rendered on media using a fixed-pitch character grid
- **Tv**   States these style instructions can be rendered on television-type devices

The next example shows two STYLE elements, each containing instuctions for different media types:

```
<HEAD>
 <STYLE type="text/css2" media="tv">
    P { font-size: 28pt}
 </STYLE>
```

```
<STYLE type="text/css2" media="handheld">
  P { font-size: 10pt}
</STYLE>
</HEAD>
```

External Style Sheet Files

As mentioned earlier, the LINK element can be used to reference external style sheet files, which makes style sheets easier to use and maintain. The LINK element must be inside the HEAD element of the HTML document, and multiple style sheet files may be referenced. Inside the LINK element, a URL references the style sheet by placing the URL value in the *href* attribute of the LINK element. Like the STYLE element, the *type* attribute of the LINK element tells the browser what type of style sheet can be expected (text/css2, for example). The *rel* and *title* attributes tell the browser whether the style sheet is persistent, preferred, or alternate:

- **Persistent** Style instructions are meant to be applied, regardless of any other style settings applied. To be persistent, the *rel* attribute must be set to persistent and the *title* attribute must not be present in the LINK element.

- **Alternate** Gives users the ability to choose from among several style sheets. To make this setting, the *rel* attribute must be set to "alternate stylesheet" and the *title* attribute value is the name for the alternate style sheet.

- **Preferred** The preferred style has been set and the browser should use that style, unless the user forces another style to be used. This setting is created when the *rel* attribute is set to "stylesheet" and the *title* attribute is set to the name for the preferred style sheet.

The *media* attribute can be used to assign a media type for external style sheets, and they're loaded only if the end device is appropriate for such media.

11

Using Cascading Style Sheets

As mentioned, the term *cascading* refers to the ability of some style sheet languages to accommodate multiple style sheets and instructions in a single HTML document. The term *cascading* comes from the concept of sets of formatting characteristics being applied in precedence according to a set of rules, thereby "flowing" into the document in order. Styles are applied as style sheets are loaded, but the last sheet has the final say. If styles in earlier sheets aren't found in later sheets, the original styles will apply, but styles found in later sheets override those in the earlier sheets. For example, a paragraph style applied by the first sheet among a set of sheets is overridden by a paragraph style found in the last sheet.

To show how this might work in practice, the following example includes several LINK elements, each connecting to a different external style sheet file. The first LINK element is connected to "a.css" while the second is connected to "b.css". Both of these style sheets are marked as "alternate" with the *rel* attribute, so if the user picks that alternate, both style sheets' style instructions will be mixed, with the second style sheet's instructions taking precedence. The third LINK element connects to another style sheet entirely (the file named c.css). The last LINK element is connected to a basic style sheet named base.css that's persistent, so the styles in it are applied in all cases.

```
<LINK rel="alternate stylesheet"
 title="alt" href="a.css" type="text/css2">
<LINK rel="alternate stylesheet"
 title="alt" href="b.css" type="text/css2">
<LINK rel="alternate stylesheet"
 title="alt2" href="c.css" type="text/css2">
<LINK rel="stylesheet" href="base.css"
 type="text/css2">
```

The CSS2 Formatting Model

In CSS2, formatting is accomplished by the construction of what is called a "box" for each formatted object. Think of the box as a container for the object (whether a character of text, a paragraph, an image, or any object that can be rendered). How the boxes are constructed is referred to as the *Box model*. Within a box, the element being rendered is positioned, and surrounding the box are layers called the border, padding, margin, and so on. Each part of the surrounding layers has a top, bottom, left, and right edge, and dimensions for width and height in pixels.

The rendered content within a box (text, images, table, and other elements) drives the size of the box by forcing the layers inward or outward. The Box model allows authors to address individual layers as formatting properties, such as RM for right margin, RP for right padding, and BB for bottom border. The final size for a box depends on how many pixels are assigned to each formatting property. Note that margins are always forced to be transparent, but borders can have a color.

Using CSS2 to Position Elements

In addition to allowing color and sizing to be specified, CSS2 also allows the exact pixel-for-pixel placement of elements onscreen. The screen can be thought of as a grid of pixels, with pixels in the x dimension forming width and pixels in the y dimension forming height. This gives CSS2 two-dimensional positioning accuracy that may be impossible to achieve with standard HTML. However, with CSS2 a third dimension, called the z dimension, can be assigned. Although it doesn't make a true 3-D representation on the screen, it does allow some elements to overlap or appear in front of or behind other elements. And when used with HTML element events and common scripting languages, dynamic positioning of elements onscreen can give the appearance of animation.

The first step is to assign appropriate sizes for the boxes that will contain elements on a page. Next, the way the boxes flow can be set, giving a default positioning or an explicitly set position. Methods for setting positioning are referred to by the following terms:

- **Normal Flow**   Includes block formatting of block boxes, inline formatting of inline boxes, and the positioning of compact and run-in boxes

- **Floating Boxes**   Boxes float to the right or left, and other content, such as text, may wrap around a box

- **Absolute Positioning**   Allows boxes to be positioned directly at any point onscreen and take no notice of any other boxes, whether or not they overlap

The screen on which boxes are positioned may be what is called the *containing box,* meaning the containing box at the highest level is the screen itself; at lower levels is the box containing the box in question. From the smallest element on up, each element or set of elements may make a containing box for the elements it holds or affects positioning for.

11

Boxes are positioned using properties called *position* and *float*. When these properties are set, the position property may be assigned values ranging from *static* (for normal flow), *relative* (in which boxes are offset from their normal flow position), *absolute* (in which boxes take a specific position according to their *x* and *y* dimensions), and *fixed* (in which the position of boxes never varies, even when the screen is scrolled). The float property affects how other elements (text, in particular) wrap around boxes.

In the following code example, style instructions are used to position elements onscreen:

```
<<HTML><HEAD><TITLE>Positioning Properties</TITLE>
<STYLE type="text/css">
<!--
 BODY { height: 10in }
 #head {
   position: absolute;
   width: 100%;
   height: 12%;
   top: 0;
   right: 0;
   bottom: auto;
   left: 0px;
; clip:      rect(   )}
 #menu {
   position: absolute;
   width: 15%;
   height: 25px;
   top: 12%;
   right: auto;
   bottom: 100px;
   left: 0;
; clip: rect(   ) }
 #content {
   position: absolute;
   width: auto;
   height: auto;
   top: 12%;
   right: 0;
   bottom: 0;
   left: 15%;
; clip:      rect(   )}
 #foot {
```

```
    position: absolute;
    width: 100%;
    height: 100px;
    top: 200px;
    right: 0;
    bottom: 0;
    left: 0;
; clip:  rect(   ) }
-->
</STYLE>
</HEAD>
<BODY>
<DIV id="head">The head of the document</DIV>
<DIV id="menu">The menu of the document</DIV>
<DIV id="content">The content of the document</DIV>
<DIV id="foot">The foot of the doucment</DIV>
</BODY></HTML>>
```

The *z* Index and Absolute Positioning

The *x* and the *y* dimensions are used to position boxes in two dimensions, but a third dimension is also available for positioning boxes in front of or behind other boxes. No capacity exists for ordinary three-dimensional perspective, but boxes may overlap if their boundaries intersect.

If an object isn't positioned absolutely (or as fixed), it find its place on the page solely by its interactions with other boxes. But an object that's positioned absolutely may have *x, y,* and *z* index coordinates set and may, therefore, fall above or below other boxes and may overlap. While the *x* and *y* dimensions are referring to pixels, percentages, or some other measure of the available screen space, the *z* dimension is a sequential set of numeric values in which boxes with higher *z*-index values are "in front of" boxes with lower *z*-index values. No particular starting or ending number must be used and no particular increment is required.

11

eXtensible Style Sheet Language

XSL is an XML-derived language for transforming XML documents from one XML vocabulary to another, or from XML documents into what are called *rendition objects*. XSL uses XSLT for the transformation process, and formatting objects in the "fo" namespace for the final formatting in a browser or other end device. XSL uses XPath (discussed in Module 6) to select elements and attributes for transformation. The result of transformation may be plain text, XHTML, or any other XML vocabulary.

The XSL Specification

The specification for XSL is a style sheet language, and *XSL documents* are style sheets in which the content of XML documents may be interpreted stylistically, meaning styles (such as colors, fonts, and so forth) may be defined as well as page layout, and proceeding to other media formats entirely. To transform a document, a style sheet processor is required. In brief, the transformation process consists of a series of steps, from the initial transformation into what is called a result tree, and then on to the formatted results presented as a rendered document in a Web page or printed on paper (or some other media formatted result). Producing the initial result tree is called tree transformation and is performed by the style sheet processor; the formatting step may be completed by a browser or some other end device.

During the transformation process, components of XML documents may be filtered, rearranged, and modified, so the resulting structure (the result tree) is quite different from how it began. Often, a style sheet contains information that allows a basic XML document to support a wide variety of media types or information structures. For example, think of DVD movies. Are they movies, books (of a sort), computer games (of a sort), or what? They contain elements of each, and the playback mechanisms and programmatic functionality embedded make them a little of each, depending on the interests and sophistication of the user. XSL style sheets offer this kind of functionality to XML documents.

The style sheet also provides formatting information, although the end device performs the formatting. The nodes of the result tree contain formatting information in the form of properties, such as indentation, spacing, and hyphenation control.

Tree Transformations

When an XML document is transformed into a result tree, this is called *tree transformation*. The result is termed an element and attribute tree, and the objects in it are primarily part of the formatting object namespace. By convention, this namespace has a prefix of *fo*, although any prefix may be used. Formatting objects in the result tree are represented as elements, while the properties of those objects are represented as sets of XML attribute-value pairs. The content of a given formatting object is the same as the content of the XML element.

XSL style sheets contain the tree construction rules used to produce the transformation of an XML document. These tree construction rules are composed of a pattern applied to elements in the source tree (to see which ones match) and a template for constructing the appropriate part of the result tree.

The Formatting Process

The formatting process is conducted by a browser or other end device by interpreting the result tree in a way appropriate for display or rendering on the end device. A result tree intended for display on a browser might include HTML or XHTML elements and attributes because browsers are programmed to format these elements properly.

Formatting Objects   XSL supports a number of formatting objects, found in the "fo" namespace. This example of a style sheet fragment shows how the formatting object namespace is declared

```
<?xml version='1.0'?>
<xsl:stylesheet
xmlns:xsl="http://www.w3.org/1999/XSL/Transform"
xmlns:fo="http://www.w3.org/1999/XSL/Format"
version='1.0'>
```

Formatting objects allow document authors control over such issues as pagination, layout, and styling. Formatting object types represent formatting methods, rather than a specific style. A given formatting object may be subject to formatting methods supplied by itself and other formatting objects, as in the layout of a page in which paragraph and image objects are subject to page layout methods, as well as methods defining their interaction with each other.

Formatting object properties specify formatting for a given object, such as color and size. The browser or other end device doing the formatting may also specify how objects are rendered. When the result tree is formatted, a series of geometric areas is generated, termed the *area tree*. Geometric areas in the area

11

tree each have a position on the page, as well as information regarding the contents of the area and any borders, padding, or background styles. Final rendering brings the area tree to life as a finished page or Web page.

Formatting Process Steps   The production of a rendered document starts with *objectification,* which is taking the result tree and converting the tree elements into formatting object nodes and the attributes into property specifications. The result of this step is a *formatting object tree.* For example, each character in the result tree is replaced by *fo:character* nodes in the formatting object tree.

The next step in the formatting process produced a refined formatting object tree, basically refining properties into *traits.* The process expands any properties written in the shorthand version, maps them to corresponding properties, and computes values based on expressions as necessary.

The last step in formatting is the generation of the area tree. The refined traits generated in the last step control how the individual areas are generated and, from there, the browser can create the final rendered Web page.

1-Minute Drill

● How is a result tree created?

● What is a formatting object tree?

The xml-stylesheet Processing Instruction

In many cases, style sheets are separate documents and they can be associated with an XML document just as CSS2 style sheets can be associated with an XHTML document. To connect an XML document to a style sheet, the xml-stylesheet processing instruction may be used, as shown in this example:

```
<?xml-stylesheet href="mystyle.css" type="text/css"?>
```

If an xml-stylesheet PI is used, it must be included in the prologue of the document.

● A result tree is created via tree transformation from the original XML document.
● A formatting object tree is an objectified result tree in which elements are converted to formatting objects and attributes are converted to formatting object properties.

XSLT

XSLT is the part of XSL that performs tree transformations. XSLT transformations are called *transforms* or *style sheets,* and they are well-formed XML documents in their own right.

An XSLT document contains the rules inserted by the document author for transforming a source tree (the original XML document) into a result tree. Transformation is accomplished by the association of patterns with template constructs. Elements from the source tree are matched or selected according to a pattern, and then the result tree is generated by those elements within the parameters of the associated template. In XSLT, XPath is used to select elements to be transformed, to process elements conditionally, and to write expressions for generating text values.

1-Minute Drill

● What is the difference between XSL and XSLT?

● What language is used to select elements for transformation?

Style Sheet Structure

An XSLT style sheet's general structure includes a version and namespace declaration, as well as any XSL elements that apply, such as those listed in the structure examined in Table 11-1.

XSL Elements	Function
<xsl:stylesheet version="1.0" xmlns:xsl="http://www.w3.org/1999/XSL/Transform">	This is the style sheet version declaration, as well as the connection to the XSL namespace, using the xsl prefix.
<xsl:import href="..."/>	The import element allows the style sheet to import other style sheets. Importing a style sheet may override the semantics of existing style sheet.

Table 11-1 General Components of an XSLT Style Sheet

11

● XSL is the overall style sheet language specification, while XSLT is the part that performs the transformations.
● XPath is the language used to select elements for transformation.

XSL Elements	Function
`<xsl:include href="..."/>`	The include element allows the style sheet to include other style sheets. Including a style sheet doesn't change its semantics.
`<xsl:strip-space elements="..."/>`	This element causes white spaces to be stripped from any elements whose name matches one of the names in the *elements* attribute.
`<xsl:preserve-space elements="..."/>`	This element causes white spaces to be preserved in any elements whose name matches one of the names in the *elements* attribute.
`<xsl:output method="..."/>`	This element is used to control how the result tree is output, for example, as an XML document.
`<xsl:key name="..." match="..." use="..."/>`	This element is used to declare keys for any node that matches the pattern entered in the *match* attribute, using the expression entered in the *use* attribute as the value for the key.
`<xsl:template match="...">`	This element specifies a template rule, with the *match* attribute specifying the nodes to be matched.
`</xsl:template>`	The ending tag for the template element.
`<xsl:template name="...">`	This element specifies elements to apply the template rule to, by name.
`</xsl:template>`	The ending tag for the template element.
`</xsl:stylesheet>`	The ending tag for the style sheet element.

Table 11-1 General Components of an XSLT Style Sheet (*continued*)

Proj11-1.zip

Project 11-1: Using XSLT

So far, you've learned the basics of how XSL and XSLT are related, and how they use the various trees, namespaces, and objects to conduct their business. Now you're ready to see how you might construct actual style sheets in practice.

Let's start with an already created xml document, the Customer and Orders document, created back in Project 2-2. This document has elements for Customers, Orders, and so on but contains no formatting information. So, to produce a pleasing display in a browser, instead of only the raw data, you need to produce a style sheet and connect it.

Step-by-Step

1. The first few lines of the Project 2-2 file, with an xsl-stylesheet element added, look like this:

```
<?xml version="1.0" encoding="UTF-8"?>
<?xml-stylesheet href="mystyle.xsl"
 type="text/xsl" media="screen"?>
<!--This document tracks Customers and their orders-->
<!DOCTYPE Customers PUBLIC "Project2-2DTD.dtd"
"http://www.e4free.com/XMLBeginnersGuide/Module02/
Project2-2DTD/Project2-2DTD.dtd">
<Customers>Here are our customers
<Customer customerid="cid111"
 email="jd@e4free.com" fulladdress="123
 MySTreet MyCity, MyState, 90000">John Doe
<Orders>
```

2. Create the "mystyle.xsl" file for your style sheet. You need to decide how to
   locate and select elements from this document using pattern matching. Use
   the output element's *method* attribute to make the output HTML.

   The code to do this might look like this:

```
<?xml version="1.0"?>
<xsl:stylesheet xmlns:xsl="http://www.w3.org/
1999/XSL/Transform" version="1.0">
<xsl:output method="html"/>
```

3. Now use the slash (/) pattern-matching symbol from XPath to match the
   root node, and then lay out an HTML template. The xsl:value-of element's
   select attribute selects nodes named Customers and places the content
   found there in between the HTML TITLE tags.

```
<xsl:template match="/">
<HTML>
<HEAD>
<TITLE><xsl:value-of select="//Customers"/></TITLE>
```

4. Continue the HTML template, using more xsl:value-of elements to make your
   Customer, Orders, and Order elements into headings.

```
</HEAD>
<BODY>
<h1><xsl:value-of select="//Customer"/></h1>
<h2><xsl:value-of select="//Orders"/></h2>
<p><xsl:value-of select="//Order"/></p>
```

11

```
</BODY>
</HTML>
</xsl:template>
</xsl:stylesheet>
```

5. To process through the orders, you want to add in the rest of the Project 2-2 XML document and create transformations appropriate for it. First, here's the XML document code for Customers:

```
<Order>
<OrderDetails OrderNumber="onid111"
 OrderDate="1/12/01" OrderTotal="0.00"/>
<OrderItems>
<OrderItem SKUNumber="1212"
 ItemNumber="1212-1" ForOrder="onid111">
<ItemCost>500</ItemCost>
<ItemPrice>1500</ItemPrice>
</OrderItem>
</OrderItems>
</Order>
</Orders>
</Customer>
<Customer customerid="cid222"
 email="js@e4free.com"
 fulladdress="234 Your Street,
 Your City, YourState, 90000">Jane Smith<Orders>
<Order>
<OrderDetails OrderNumber="onid222"
 OrderDate="1/12/01"/>
<OrderItems>
<OrderItem SKUNumber="2121"
ItemNumber="2121-2" ForOrder="onid222">
<ItemCost>200</ItemCost>
<ItemPrice>1200</ItemPrice>
</OrderItem>
</OrderItems>
</Order>
</Orders>
</Customer>
</Customers>
```

Working with data like this could be a problem, but XSLT has a function that lets you step through the data, element by element and region by region. In fact, you can apply your template to each section of XML elements, regardless of how many times they appear in the XML document, even though you enter the template only once.

6. Total the sales for each region and display the total on the page. Create a style sheet file with the following code in it, and name it **Mod11.xsl**.

```
</BODY>
</HTML>
</xsl:template>
</xsl:stylesheet>
<table>
<tr>
<th>Customer\Orders</th>
<xsl:for-each
  select="//Customer/Orders/Order[1]/OrderItem/ItemPrice">
<th>CustomerID<xsl:value-of select="@customerid"/></th>
</xsl:for-each>
<th>Total Orders</th>
</tr>
<xsl:for-each select="//Customer/Orders">
<tr >
<th style="text-align:left">
<xsl:value-of select="name"/></th>
<xsl:for-each select="OrderItems">
<td style="text-align:right">
<xsl:value-of
  select="format-number(ItemPrice,'###,###')"/>
</td>
</xsl:for-each>
<td style="text-align:right;font-weight:bold;">
</td>
</tr>
</xsl:for-each>
</table>
```

> This code starts an HTML page for output from the template, and also gets the template element going, and then it builds a table structure for the template.

7. Save and close the style sheet, and then open your XML document in Internet Explorer. You should see Customers, Order, and the total for ItemPrice in each order in an HTML table.

11

Using XSL Elements

The XSL parser performs its work using XSL elements and attributes forming a pattern and a template. The xsl:for-each element allows the selection of each element in the XML document that matches the criteria specified, while applying the template sequentially to each of the matched elements. The *select* attribute in the xsl:for-each element uses the XPath syntax to find the appropriate XML elements from the hierarchy of elements present. The beginning of the template portion, with the <td> element, begins to set the format of the output as an HTML table cell, while the xsl:value-of element and its accompanying *select* attribute value of @customerid retrieve the value of the *customerid* attribute from the XML document's Customer element and place it inside the cell.

Calculation Functions of XSL

XSL also has functions that allow calculations on values found in XML documents. For example, the following code retrieves the ItemPrice values for Order Items in your XML document and sums them for display inside the table you built. The format-number value in the *select* attribute also formats the number to have a comma in the thousands place:

```
<xsl:value-of
  select="format-number(sum(OrderItems/ItemPrice),
'###,###')"/>
```

Conditionally Formatted Elements

Many times, rendered documents make more sense when formatting changes (such as color, font weight, and other visual cues) as values change. For example, if a sales team in one area of the country is outperforming (or underperforming) sales goals by a wide margin, highlighting this data can make this easier to catch and investigate. XSL allows conditional formatting with conditional statements. The xsl:param element is used to set a parameter; name it (using the *name* attribute); and make it select elements, attributes, or values from your XML document based on their values. First, you create your parameter using code such as this:

```
<xsl:param name="TotalItemPrice" select="4"/>
```

Now, a parameter variable named TotalItemPrice can be used as the lowest price for any items sold. To create the conditional test, the xsl:choose element is used in conjunction with the xsl:when element and the xsl:otherwise element. The xsl:choose element creates a conditional block, in which the *test* attribute of the xsl:when element checks to determine whether the value of your parameter is met. If it is met, formatting is handled in one way and, if not, formatting is handled in another way, as demonstrated in the following code:

```
<td><xsl:attribute name="style">
<xsl:choose>
<xsl:when test="number(@ItemPrice &gt;=
  $OrderTotal)">color:blue;</xsl:when>
<xsl:otherwise>color:red;</xsl:otherwise>
</xsl:choose>
text-align:right;
</xsl:attribute>
<xsl:value-of
  select="format-number(@ItemPrice,'###,###')"/>
</td>
```

Here, the test is applied to the numerical value of ItemPrice to determine whether any items were sold below the base price. If so, those items appear in red, while all other items appear in blue. This makes it easy to catch and double-check why items are being sold below the base price.

Mixing XML Documents

Building a finished, rendered document with XML and XSL sometimes means mixing data from one XML document with another. There's an XSL function for including other XML documents during processing, named the *document( )* function. This function accepts absolute or relative URLs as its argument, and the URL may be a plain string or a node that works out to a URL. An XML document may be at the other end of the URL. The entire document is then loaded into the current document, so it gives the appearance of one large XML document.

For example, suppose a requirement existed to produce a footer section with copyright and slogan attached to many rendered documents. The

11

first step is to produce such as document as a text file in XML format, as shown here:

```
<footer>
<copyright>Copyright 2001</copyright>
<slogan>Slogan goes here</slogan>
</footer>
```

This code would be saved as a separate text file, named "footer.xml". Next, in your style sheet file, an xsl:variable would be created, using code such as this:

```
<xsl:variable name="otherfile"
        select="document('footer.xml')"/>
```

Finally, the following code might be placed inside the style sheet file, so the code would be processed, and the contents of the other file (footer.xml) would be inserted just above the end of the document being rendered. This code might look like this:

```
<xsl:value-of select="$otherfile//footer"/>
```

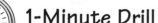

1-Minute Drill

● How does the *select* attribute of the xsl:for-each element retrieve XML elements, and what does it do each time it finds one?

● What elements are required for conditional processing?

● The *select* attribute sets criteria for finding XML elements, so each element in an XML document that matches the criteria is retrieved. When a matching element is found, the template is applied, and then the process begins again, until no more elements are found. After all elements have been found, the for-each element ceases to process and the next lines of the style sheet are actuated.

● The xsl:choose element starts the conditional processing process, the xsl:when element sets the parameters for testing (using the *test* attribute), and the xsl:otherwise element tells the formatting device what to do when test conditions aren't found.

Ask the Expert

Question: The workings of XSL and XSLT resemble scripting functions found in VBScript and other common scripting languages. What's the advantage of using XSL and XSLT?

Answer: The primary advantages are XSL and XSLT use a standard format, XML, as the basis for their own structures. Therefore, they should be easier to work with and maintain in the long run, as well as being compatible across companies, industries, and organizations. Another advantage is that XSL documents can be manipulated and stored as XML documents, so all the XML development tools now available (or being built) will be available to work with these style sheets.

Question: How are the Box model in CSS2 and the Formatting Objects DTD in XSL related?

Answer: The Formatting Objects DTD has many components that are similar in structure and function to the Box model in CSS2. The properties available, the values those properties may assume, and the flow characteristics are often similar. The advantage, of course, is that the model may be extended at any time without changing the basic elements and attributes allowed in the Formatting Objects DTD.

11

☑ *Mastery Check*

1. What is the difference between Cascading Style Sheets Language and XSL?

    A. Cascading Style Sheets Language is designed for HTML documents, while XSL is designed for XML documents.

    B. XSL includes XSLT, a transformation language.

    C. XSL uses XPath to select elements, while CSS2 uses selectors.

    D. All of the above

2. What process is used by XSLT to transform XML documents into a format suitable for viewing in browsers?

    A. All XML elements are converted to XHTML table, table row, and table data elements. The text content of those XML elements is written into the XHTML table data elements for display.

    B. XML elements are selected from the XML document using the XPath language, and these elements are transformed according to rules in the XSL style sheet.

    C. XML elements are selected using the XPath language, and these elements are converted into their corresponding XHTML elements.

    D. None of the above

3. What terms are used to describe the XML document before and after it's transformed, and why?

    A. The XML document is described as the base document, and the transformed document is described as the finished document. This is because these terms denote the base from which the transformation is made and the end product of the transformation.

    B. The XML document is described as the source tree, and the transformed document is described as the result tree. This is because these terms denote the source structure from which the transformation is made and the result structure of the transformation.

☑ Mastery Check

C. The XML document remains an XML document throughout the transformation process, but the names of the elements are changed for display purposes. Therefore, the document is described as the XMLSource and XMLDisplay document, depending on its stage of transformation.

D. None of the above

4. What does an XSL style sheet contain?

A. References to the original XML source document and conversion rules for the results tree

B. Tree construction rules

C. Transformation parameters and source tree definitions

D. None of the above

5. How may style sheets be associated with XML documents?

A. Through the use of a processing instruction whose target is xml-stylesheet

B. Through the use of an annotation whose data type is style sheet

C. Through the use of an XML comment in the epilogue

D. None of the above

6. What data must be present in the xsl-stylesheet element of an XSL style sheet?

A. The transform attribute and the version number

B. The version number and the XML namespace

C. A reference to the XSL namespace and the version number

D. None of the above

11

✓ Mastery Check

7. What is prefix for the XSL namespace, and what is the URL?

A. The prefix is xsl, and the URL is
http://www.w3.org/1999/XSL/Transform

B. The prefix is xslt, and the URL is
http://www.w3.org/1999/XSL/Transform

C. The prefix is xsl, and the URL is http://www.w3.org/1999/XSL/XSLT

D. None of the above

8. What are the purposes of the xsl:include and xsl:import stylesheet elements?

A. The xsl:include element includes additional XML documents in the
XSLT processing, while the xsl:import element imports specific
elements and attributes.

B. The xsl:include element includes other style sheets, while the xsl:import
element imports other style sheets, the difference being that definitions
and template rules in the imported style sheet have a lower precedence.

C. The xsl:include element includes additional XML documents in the XSLT
processing, while the xsl:import element imports other style sheets.

D. None of the above

9. What are formatting objects, and what is their prefix and URL of their
namespace?

A. Formatting objects are the result of transforming an XML document
using tree transformation rules, ending with elements and attributes
from the formatting objects (fo) namespace, having a prefix of fo, and a
URL of http://www.w3.org/1999/XSL/Format.

B. Formatting objects are built into the XML document, so the end
result is an objectified version of the original XML document. The
prefix for formatting objects is fo, and the URL of the namespace
is http://www.w3.org/1999/XSL/Format.

☑ *Mastery Check*

    C. Formatting objects are rules that tell the browser how to interpret certain XML element for rendering. The prefix of the formatting objects namespace is fo, and the URL is http://www.w3.org/1999/XSL/Format.

    D. None of the above

10. In addition to being able to select certain elements and attributes from an XML document for transformation, XSL also allows conditional processing. What are some of the conditional processing structures provided?

    A. xsl:do and xsl:select

    B. xsl:if and xsl:choose

    C. xsl:if and xsl:choose

    D. None of the above

11. What is the area tree, and how is it generated?

    A. The area tree is a location in memory where the formatted XML document is stored, prior to rendering. It's generated via processing by the formatter.

    B. The area tree is a description of all nodes in the tree transformation and is generated via processing by the formatter.

    C. The area tree consists of a tree structured set of area nodes, including the root node. Except for the root node, all nodes are areas defined as rectangular boxes, typically one for each unique object in the formatting object tree.

    D. None of the above

11

Module 12

XML, WAP, and Ecommerce

The Goals of This Module

- Examine ecommerce fundamentals
- Learn how XML facilitates ecommerce
- Review the Wireless Application Protocol (WAP)
- Learn about Wireless Markup Language (WML)
- Create an XML document for Wireless Application Protocol
- Transform an XML document into WML
- Learn about XML Ecommerce initiatives

The word *commerce* typically evokes a vision of commercial transactions— buying and selling, often with capitalist overtones. And yet, commerce is basic to all of us, whether we live in a communist country or work for non-profit organizations. Even in societies where trade and barter are the primary form of exchange, commerce still applies.

Ecommerce denotes the exchange of information required in electronic commerce, but it seems to have taken on the specific connotation of transactions conducted over the Internet. So, for example, if you call someone or mail her a letter to make a deal, that seems to be ordinary commerce. But if you email her, or buy her products from a Web site, that is called ecommerce.

Realistically, commerce is commerce. Perhaps it would be best simply to think of commerce as a subset of the communications we engage in to conduct our lives, defined by a relationship to the process of buying and selling.

Ecommerce

So why is ecommerce so important? Maybe a better definition for the *e* in ecommerce would be efficient, rather than electronic, because ecommerce makes commercial transactions more convenient, faster, less prone to error, and less costly.

Suppose you are in the market to buy a house. Just a few years back you would call a real estate agent, provide a list of features and areas you desired, wait for the agent to produce a list of appropriate homes, physically visit those homes, fill out miles of paperwork, apply for a loan, and so forth. Today, you can visit the home online (even before you call an agent), fill out and submit much of the paperwork online, receive offers for a loan in hours, and so forth. Many of the physical shopping, approval, and review steps have been made more convenient, faster, and less costly—although there is still progress to be made. Except for some temporary dislocations for folks whose jobs were to process paperwork by hand, everyone benefits, the time and costs are reduced, and the economy works more efficiently. This is the promise of ecommerce.

The first wave of ecommerce business seemed to focus on business to consumer sales (B2C), while subsequent companies made their mark with business-to-business models (B2B). Now there are numerous variations with acronyms that run the gamut. Acronym growth in this area is partly hype and partly a scramble to define all the ways commerce is conducted and made more efficient by electronic means.

Rather than trying to define ecommerce in terms of who is selling to (or buying from) whom, perhaps the focus should be on what kinds of integration are taking place. For example, consider automated retail sales for some consumer sites, in which the site operates much like a vending machine to offer products anonymously, accept payments, and dispense (or deliver) products. In ecommerce, the vending machine would also reorder products as inventory gets low, making for a pretty well-rounded and low-maintenance business.

But suppose prices for products stocked in your vending machine varied from vendor to vendor, and you wanted your vending machines to search out the best prices or request bids for supply? Adding more intelligence to your vending machine's automation code would only be half the battle; the other half would be finding ways to communicate with the myriad suppliers of vending machine products.

XML offers a way to standardize communications, but in each industry, groups are forming to develop competing XML vocabularies, and whether true standards will emerge is still an open question. In this module, you explore an XML-based language, Wireless Markup Language (WML), that stands to assist greatly in making commercial transactions convenient and efficient.

Wireless Application Protocol

Although circumstances are rapidly changing, wireless access to the Internet is still a pretty slow and spotty service in most cases. In many countries, wireless systems have evolved to allow many highly popular services, such as the ability to buy (and pay for) items from vending machines, via a cell phone, and via ubiquitous messaging services. In the United States, wireless services are a bit behind the times, but they're catching up rapidly.

Because the wireless services in the U.S. are still somewhat slow (meaning low bandwidth), special protocols have been adopted to compress and reformat Web pages and email messages. WAP is one popular protocol for such purposes, created and promoted by the WAP Forum (at www.wapforum.org), a group of industry leaders.

12

Wireless Markup Language

Wireless Markup Language is an XML-based cousin of HTML that is designed for creating Web pages usable on the tiny, monochrome screens of cell phones. The version described here can be found at the WAP forum at www.wapforum.org, in a specification named "WAP 191 Wireless Markup Language Specification." WML can be written by hand, like HTML, and has an easy-to-pick-up structure.

Writing WML Code

WML is XML-based, and so writing WML documents follows many of the syntactic constructs of XML, such as a DTD, elements and attributes, and so forth. WML documents contain many common XML document components, listed here:

- **Entities**   Character references, such as numeric and named character entities, are allowed within WML documents. These entities begin with an ampersand and end with a semicolon, and they must be escaped when used in ordinary text data.

- **Elements and attributes**   WML elements use start and end tags, and of course must be properly formed and not overlapping. Attributes contain more information about elements, and their values must be quoted. Both element and attribute names must conform to the XML names specification and are case sensitive.

- **Comments**   Comments use <!-- and --> as delimiters, cannot be nested, and are not processed.

- **Variables**   WML documents can be parameterized with variables. Variables start with the dollar sign, followed by an identifier (possibly in parentheses, if the identifier name contains white space). They can be used to substitute values into the code. Variables can be used in PCDATA values as well as attribute values with a vdata type.

- **CDATA sections**   CDATA sections are the same as any XML CDATA sections, using the delimiters <![CDATA[and]]>. Any text (often scripting) inside CDATA delimiters won't be parsed.

- **Processing Instructions**   WML does not support processing instructions, except those defined in the XML specification.

WML Data Types

WML uses XML data types to define character data, such as these:

- **CDATA**   Used for attribute values

- **PCDATA**   Used in elements, and may contain character references such as numeric or named character entities

- **NMTOKEN**   A name token, as defined by the XML specifications

- **Length**   CDATA, used in attribute values to specify pixels numerically, or as a percentage, for height or width of screen consumed by a particular object

- **Vdata**   Used in attribute values to contain a string for variable reference

- **Flow**   Used to convey card-level information about the flow of elements displayed

- **Href**   Used in attributes to convey URLs, either absolute or relative

- **Boolean**   Used for true/false values

- **Number**   Used for integers of 0 or greater

WML Attributes

As with HTML elements, several attributes apply to all WML elements. For example, the *id* and *class* attributes are called *core attributes*, and they perform essentially the same functions as their HTML counterparts. The *id* attribute gives an element a unique identity within a single deck (decks are discussed again in a moment), while the *class* attribute associates an element with others in the same class. Note that class names are case sensitive, and if several different class names are given for an element's *class* attribute, a single element can belong to multiple classes.

WML Events and Navigation

In WML is a system for events similar to that for the DOM, with a do event element and an onevent event element. Events can be connected to tasks, and when the event is triggered the task is executed. Tasks include going to a URL, submitting data, and so forth.

WML Decks and Cards

Instead of Web pages and a Web site, WML documents are termed *cards* and *decks*. A single WML file consists of one or more cards, and a group of cards is considered a deck. On each card there may be content and usually a series of navigation controls (such as links). Like navigating between Web pages, it is usually possible to navigate to and from cards and among decks in WML pages.

12

WML Document Structures

Like any XML document, WML documents must contain certain structures to be considered well-formed. For example, a document prologue is required. The following section discusses the various WML document components.

The Prologue   WML documents are designed to be validated against the WML DTD. They must contain an XML declaration and the appropriate DOCTYPE declaration, as shown in the following code:

```
<?xml version="1.0"?>
<!DOCTYPE wml PUBLIC "-//WAPFORUM//DTD WML 1.3//EN"
"http://www.wapforum.org/DTD/wml13.dtd">
```

The wml Element   The DTD for WML documents shows the wml element defined as wml with the head?, template?, and card+ elements following in sequence. The attribute list for the wml element includes the *xml:lang* attribute (NMTOKEN, implied) and the core attributes. All other elements in WML documents are child elements of this element.

The DTD defines the head, template, and card elements as being permissible in the wml element. The only attribute available for the wml element (other than the core attributes) is the *xml:lang* attribute, and it allows for the inclusion of a token (such as EN) to specify the language for the document. The following is a deck containing two cards, each represented by a card element. After loading the deck, a user agent displays the first card. If the user activates the do element, the user agent displays the second card.

```
<wml>
<card>
<p><do type="accept">
<go href="#secondcard"/>
</do>
You have come to the first card</p>
</card>
<card id="secondcard">
<p>And now you are at the second card</p>
</card>
</wml>
```

The WML head Element   The DTD for the head element is defined next, and includes the access and meta elements. Like an HTML document, the head element is a container for information about the deck (the meta element), as well as access-control elements (the access element). It includes the core attributes *id* and *class*.

The WML access Element   The access element has an empty content model, and includes the *domain* and *path* attributes. These attributes define what domain and path are followed when access actions are initiated. Only one access element is allowed per deck, and if no access element is defined, any other deck may access the current deck.

   The *domain* and *path* attributes enable authors to control what other decks may access the current deck. For example, if a user attempts to navigate to a deck, an access element will test the domain from which the user is coming to see whether that domain is allowed to access the current deck.

The WML meta Element   The meta element has an empty content model and contains information about the document. It has the core attributes *id* and *class*, and it also has a set of additional attributes. Each meta element is made up of a name-value pair, with the name being given by the *name* attribute and the value being given by the *content* attribute. If the *http-equiv* attribute is used instead, the name-value pair should be interpreted as an HTTP header. The *scheme* attribute defines the form or structure that should be used to interpret the value in the *content* attribute. The *forua* attribute tells whether the element is for the user agent.

The WML template Element   The DTD for the template element includes the navigation elements do and onevent, as well as the cardev events and core attributes. The cardev events include onenterforward (occurring when a user enters the card using a go task), onenterbackward (occurring when a user enters a card using a prev task), and ontimer (occurring when a timer expires). Any events specified in a template element apply to all cards in a deck.

12

The WML card Element   Cards are defined with the card element, and each card can contain content, such as other elements. In cards, the onevent and timer elements are included, as well as the do, p, and pre elements. Attributes include *title*, *newcontext*, *ordered*, *xml:lang*, and the cardev events and core attributes. The onevent element is for capturing events, and the timer element is for responding to time periods (we discuss the timer element later). The p element creates paragraphs, and the do element is for initiating actions.

The *title* attribute simply makes a title for the card, to tell the user the purpose of the card. The *newcontext* attribute is a Boolean value that tells the browser to reinitialize the card. The *ordered* attribute is also Boolean, and it may be used to place and order on the layout of the card elements. The default order is as a linear sequence of elements.

The WML do Element   The do element provides the user with the ability to initiate actions. When a do element is activated, its task is executed. The do element can be rendered as a button or as some other recognizable object onscreen. If set into a card, the do element appears at the location specified. If set inside a template element in the deck, the do element will appear on each card in the deck.

The *type* attribute values tell the browser what the do element should do. For example, the *accept* action indicates acceptance of a choice, the *prev* action tells the browser to navigate back to a previous card, the *help* action makes a request for help, the *reset* action clears or resets the card, the *options* action asks for more options, and the *delete* action deletes an item.

The *label* attribute applies a label to a do element, while the *name* attribute gives it a name. Do elements with an *optional* attribute set to "true" may be ignored by the browser.

The next example shows a card element in a deck, with text displayed to the user, and a do element for initiating an "Accept" action.

```
<wml>
<do type="accept" label="Accept">
</do>
<card>
<p>
Do you accept these terms?
</p>
</card>
</wml>
```

WML Control Elements

Control elements are used on forms like controls in HTML forms (such as text fields, drop-down lists, radio buttons, and so on) to provide a means for users to interact with and provide feedback to a WML-based site.

The input Element   The input element may be either a text or password area, depending on the setting of the *type* attribute. The input element forms a text entry spot in a WML document. In addition to the core attributes and a *tabindex* attribute, the input element is required to have a *name* and may have a *size*, *maxlength*, and *title*. It may also have an initial or default *value*, with a VDATA data type. If the *format* attribute is specified, it sets an input mask for entry, meaning data values entered must conform to the format specified in the *format* attribute, such as telephone numbers required to contain only digits, be a specified length, and perhaps have dashes at certain locations. Other available attributes include *emptyok*, which has a Boolean value indicating whether the field may be left blank.

Here's an example of this element. To create a text input element that is named "FullName", has a size of 20 characters, a maximum length of 25 characters, an initial value of "John Doe", and must be filled in, code such as the following would be applicable:

```
<input name="FullName" type="text"
 size="20" maxlength="25" value="John Doe"
 emptyok="false"/>
```

The WML select Element and Drop-down Lists   You've all worked with drop-down lists in application programs as well as Web pages. WML uses a set of tags similar to those in XHTML to produce drop-down lists or selection lists. The options included in the lists are made with the Option element (or the Optgroup element), and the Select element is the container. The attributes available to the Select element include *name*, *value*, *iname*, and *ivalue*, which control what name-value pair is returned to the WML site. *Tabindex*, *xml:lang*, and *title* all work as with an input element, while the *multiple* attribute is a Boolean that specifies whether multiple choices are allowed.

When multiple choices are allowed, the value in the name-value pair returned to the WML site is a list of tokens separated by semicolons, in any order the browser finds convenient.

12

The option Element   An option element enables users to select a single option from the list. In addition to the core attributes, an option element may have a *value*, a *title*, and an *xml:lang* attribute. The option element has an associated event—the *onpick* event, which is triggered when the option is selected from the list.

The timer Element   The purpose of the timer element is to provide a mechanism for timing out if activity does not take place within a certain timeframe. A timer starts when a card is entered and is stopped when the card is left.

 The timer may have a *name* (useful for scripting functions) and must have a *value*. The value is set in tenths of a second, and the timer counts down from the initial value to zero, at which point an intrinsic event named *ontimer* is fired. No more than one timer per card is allowed. The following code example will create a timer and send the user to another card if no activity happens before the timer runs out:

```
<wml>
<card ontimer="/otherpage">
<timer value="500"/>
<p>
This card has a timer set to 50 seconds!
</p>
</card>
</wml>
```

The tabindex Attribute   The *tabindex* attribute is useful for expressing the order to which controls are tabbed. A sequence of numbers, with any starting, ending, or increment, serves to express the tab order. The higher the tab index number, the later in the tab order an element with a *tabindex* attribute becomes. If no tab order value is assigned, the browser will assign one by default.

1-Minute Drill

● How are WML pages composed?

● What is the function of the timer element?

● WML pages are referred to as decks, and decks contain cards, so a single WML file creates a deck with one or more cards.

● The function of the timer element is to enable the author of the WML page to set a timeout and thereby initiate an action if no activity has taken place in a particular card within the timeout period.

Proj12-1.zip

Project 12-1: WML and ASP Scripts

To build a Web application using WML, you need to use ASP scripts in the background, as well as a database. What you're going to build here is a small application that lets users log in, search for products, and perform other tasks. You'll build a database for these interactions with usernames and passwords, so you can filter out invalid users who might be trying to break in.

You can use Microsoft's SQL Server to build a few tables (such as Employees, Customers, and Products) to hold the records containing usernames, passwords, and a few other key pieces of data. In the database, you must create these three tables and make the fields CustomerID, username, password, companyname, Phone, firstname, and lastname for the Customers table; and the fields employeeid, username, password, FirstName, LastName, and PhoneExt for the Employees table. Also, the Products table must have a field for names of products (ProductName), qtyinstock for quantity in stock, ProductID, and ProductPrice.

To make the database accessible, you'll build a connection string to make the connection. Each time a database connection is made, you use the connection string.

Step-by-Step

1. Build the login function. Use a WML document connected to the DTD located at www.phone.com, which is for the WML 1.1 version. Name this file **login.wml**.

```
<?xml version="1.0"?>
<!DOCTYPE wml PUBLIC "-//PHONE.COM//DTD WML 1.1//EN"
"http://www.phone.com/dtd/wml11.dtd" >
<wml>
<card id="MyLogin">
<do type="accept" label="Login">
<go href="UserValidate.asp?
userid=$(userid)&amp;password=$(password)"/>
</do>
<p>
<b>My Login</b>
<br/>
User ID:
<input name="userid" maxlength="10" type="text" emptyok="false"/>
<b>My Login</b>
<br/>
Password:
<input name="password" maxlength="10" type="password" emptyok="false"/>
</p>
</card>
</wml>
```

> Sets up the variables for userid and password, and then creates the input areas for these variables

12

2. Now create the UserValidate script using ASP. Start by specifying the language (VBScript), and set the script to contain the contents in a buffer until it's done processing. Next, write the WML document (as an XML document, of course), and search the database for a valid user record using the username and password that were entered. If a valid username is found, the user is redirected to the MyDbaseMain.asp page; otherwise, the user sees a message that says the user is not a valid user. Name this file **UserValidate.asp**.

```
<%@ Language=VBScript %>
<%
Response.Buffer = true
Response.ContentType = "text/vnd.wap.wml"
%>
<?xml version="1.0"?>
<!DOCTYPE wml PUBLIC "-//PHONE.COM//DTD WML 1.1//EN"
"http://www.phone.com/dtd/wml11.dtd">
<wml>
<card>
<p>
<%
Dim strUID
Dim strPass
Dim strNextURL
Dim cnMyDbase
Dim rstU
Dim strConn
Dim strSQL
strConn =
  "Provider=SQLOLEDB;Data Source=MyDbase;"
strConn= strConn & "Initial
Catalog=MyDbase;Trusted_Connection=Yes;"
strUID = Request.QueryString("userid")
strPass = Request.QueryString("password")
strSQL = "SELECT FirstName FROM Employees "
strSQL = strSQL & "WHERE username =
  '" & strUID & "' AND "
strSQL = strSQL & "password = '" & strPass & "'"
Set cnMyDbase = Server.CreateObject("ADODB.Connection")
With cnMyDbase
  .ConnectionString = strConn
  .Open
end with
Set rstU = Server.CreateObject("ADODB.Recordset")
With rstU
  .ActiveConnection = cnMyDbase
  .Open strSQL
end with
```

Dimensions the variables, and then creates the connection string and the SQL query string

Makes the connection and then retrieves the recordset

```
Set cnMyDbase = Nothing
If not rstU is Nothing then
If rstU.RecordCount > 0 then
strNextURL = "AdministratorMain.asp"
strNextURL = strNextURL & "firstname=" &
rstU.Fields("FirstName").Value
Response.Redirect(strNextURL)
else
Response.Write "You are not a valid user."
end if
end if
Set rstU = Nothing
%>
</p>
</card>
</wml>
```

> Sends valid users to another URL and invalid users a message

3. Create a file named AdministratorMain.asp. In this file, the administrator for the system is presented with a series of choices to search for, including Customers, Employees, and Products. Each URL that may be referred to is associated with a variable, and that variable fills the do element; so if the user accepts the choice, he or she will be taken to the appropriate card.

```
<%@ Language=VBScript %>
<%
 Response.Buffer = true
 Response.ContentType = "text/vnd.wap.wml"
%>
<?xml version="1.0"?>
<!DOCTYPE wml PUBLIC "-//PHONE.COM//DTD WML 1.1//EN"
 "http://www.phone.com/dtd/wml11.dtd">
<wml>
<card title="AdministratorMain">
<p>
<b>Administrator Main Menu</b>
<br/>
<%
Dim strFName
strFName = Request.QueryString("firstname")
Response.Write "Welcome " & strFName
Response.Write "<br/>"
%>
</p>
 <do type="accept">
<spawn href="$(card)">
<catch/>
</spawn>
```

> Welcomes the user by first name

12

```
</do>
<p>
<select name="card">
<option value="wml/EmpSearch.wml">
Employee Search</option>
<option value="wml/ProdSearch.wml">
Product Search</option>
<option value="wml/CustSearch.wml">
Customer Search</option>
</select>
</p>
</card>
</wml>
```

Creates options to choose from

4. Create a file named EmpSearch.wml. This file enables the user to enter an employee's first and last names. When the data is entered, the data and the user are referred to an ASP script that performs the database search.

```
<?xml version="1.0"?>
<!DOCTYPE wml PUBLIC "-//PHONE.COM//DTD WML 1.1//EN"
 "http://www.phone.com/dtd/wml11.dtd" >
<wml>
<card id="EmployeeSearch">
<do type="accept" label="Find">
<go href="http://www.e4free.com/
XMLBeginnersGuide/EmpSearch.asp?
fname=$(fname)&amp;lname=$(lname)"/>
</do>
<p>
<b>Employee Search</b>
<br/>
First Name:
<input name="fname" maxlength="10"
 type="text" emptyok="false"/>
<b>Employee Search</b>
<br/>
Last Name:
<input name="lname" maxlength="10"
 type="text" emptyok="false"/>
</p>
</card>
</wml>
```

Sets up variables for fname and lname

5. Create a file named EmpSearch.asp. This script performs the search of the database for an employee's first and last name. For each employee appearing in the resulting recordset, the first name, the last name, and the phone extension are printed back to the user onscreen.

```
<%@ Language=VBScript %>
<%
Response.Buffer = true
Response.ContentType = "text/vnd.wap.wml"
%>
<?xml version="1.0"?>
<!DOCTYPE wml PUBLIC "-//PHONE.COM//DTD WML 1.1//EN"
 "http://www.phone.com/dtd/wml11.dtd">
<wml>
<card>
<p>
<%
Dim strFName
Dim strLName
Dim cnMyDbase
Dim rstE
Dim strConn
Dim strSQL
strConn = "Provider=SQLOLEDB;Data Source=MyDbase;"
 strConn = strConn & "Initial Catalog=MyDbase;Trusted_Connection=Yes;"
strFName = Request.QueryString("fname")
strLName = Request.QueryString("lname")
strSQL = "SELECT * FROM Employees "
strSQL = strSQL & "WHERE FirstName = '" & strFName & "' AND "
strSQL = strSQL & "LastName = '" & strLName & "'"
Set cnMyDbase = Server.CreateObject("ADODB.Connection")
With cnMyDbase
 .ConnectionString = strConn
 .Open
end with
Set rstE = Server.CreateObject("ADODB.Recordset")
With rstE
 .ActiveConnection = cnMyDbase
 .Open strSQL
end with
Set cnMyDbase = Nothing
If not rstE is Nothing then
Dim I
 For i = 0 to rstE.RecordCount - 1
  Response.Write cstr((i + 1)) & "."
  Response.Write rstE.Fields("FirstName") & " "
  Response.Write rstE.Fields("LastName") & " "
  Response.Write "<br/>"
  Response.Write "X" & rstE.Fields("PhoneExt")
  Response.Write "<hr/>"
  rstE.MoveNext
 Next
End if
```

After performing the search, writes back to the user the first name, last name, and phone extension of any employees found in the recordset

12

```
Set rstE = Nothing
%>
</p>
</card>
</wml>
```

6. Create a file named CustLogin.wml. This WML page enables customers to log in to the system, so they may initiate searches for products (if they are valid users). They must already have registered and have a username and password. If they are valid customers, they are directed to a deck that gives them the option to search for products and purchase if they desire. The CustValidate.asp file (to be created in step 9) validates the users before allowing them to go on to the CustomerMain.asp script, but this script won't be included in this project.

```
<?xml version="1.0"?>
<!DOCTYPE wml PUBLIC "-//PHONE.COM//DTD WML 1.1//EN"
 "http://www.phone.com/dtd/wml11.dtd" >
<wml>
<card id="CustomerLogin">
<do type="accept" label="Login">
<go href="http://www.e4free.com/
XMLBeginnersGuide/CustomerValidate.asp?
custid=$(custid)&amp;password=$(password)"/>
</do>
<p>
<b>Customer Login</b>
<br/>
Customer ID:
<input name="custid" maxlength="10"
 type="text" emptyok="false"/>
<b>Customer Login</b>
<br/>
Password:
<input name="password" maxlength="10"
 type="password" mptyok="false"/>
</p>
</card>
</wml>
```

7. Create a file named CustSearch.wml. This file provides the administrator with a screen for entering customer names to search for and activating the search.

```
<?xml version="1.0"?>
<!DOCTYPE wml PUBLIC "-//PHONE.COM//DTD WML 1.1//EN"
 "http://www.phone.com/dtd/wml11.dtd" >
<wml>
<card id="CustomerSearch">
<do type="accept" label="Find">
<go href="http://www.e4free.com/
```

```
XMLBeginnersGuide/Module12/CustSearch.asp?
custid=$(custid)&amp;name=$(name)"/>
</do>
<p>
<b>Customer Search</b>
<br/>
Customer ID:
<input name="custid" maxlength="10"
 type="text" emptyok="false"/>
<b>Customer Search</b>
<br/>
Customer Name:
<input name="name" maxlength="10"
 type="text" emptyok="false"/>
</p>
</card>
</wml>
```

8. Now create a file named CustSearch.asp. This file enables the administrator to search for customers by name, in much the same way as the administrator can search for employees.

```
<%@ Language=VBScript %>
<%
Response.Buffer = True
Response.ContentType = "text/vnd.wap.wml"
%>
<?xml version="1.0"?>
<!DOCTYPE wml PUBLIC "-//PHONE.COM//DTD WML 1.1//EN"
 "http://www.phone.com/dtd/wml11.dtd">
<wml>
<card>
<p>
<%
Dim strCID
Dim strCName
Dim cnMyDbase
Dim rstC
Dim strConn
Dim strSQL
strConn =
 "Provider=SQLOLEDB;Data Source=MyDbase;"
strConn = strConn & "Initial
Catalog=MyDbase;Trusted_Connection=Yes;"
strCID = Request.QueryString("custid")
strCName = Request.QueryString("name")
strSQL = "SELECT * FROM customers
 WHERE customerid = '"
strSQL = strSQL & strCID & "' AND "
strSQL = strSQL & "companyname =
 '" & strCName & "'"
Set cnMyDbase =
```

```
  Server.CreateObject("ADODB.Connection")
With cnMyDbase
 .ConnectionString = strConn
 .Open
end with
Set rstC =
  Server.CreateObject("ADODB.Recordset")
With rstC
 .ActiveConnection = cnMyDbase
 .Open strSQL
end with
Set cnMyDbase = Nothing
If not rstC is Nothing then
Dim I
For i = 0 to rstC.RecordCount - 1
 Response.Write cstr((i + 1)) & "."
 Response.Write "<b>"
 Response.Write rstC.Fields("companyname")
 Response.Write "</b>"
 Response.Write "<br/>"
 Response.Write rstC.Fields("Phone")
 Response.Write "<hr/>"
 rstC.MoveNext
Next
End if
Set rstC = Nothing
%>
</p>
</card>
</wml>
```

> Writes back to the user the company name and phone number of any customers found in the recordset

9. Next, create a file named CustValidate.asp. This script validates customers when they try to log in, much like the UserValidate.asp script validates administrative users (although you don't create the CustomerMain.asp file for this project).

```
<%@ Language=VBScript %>
<%
Response.Buffer = true
Response.ContentType = "text/vnd.wap.wml"
%>
<?xml version="1.0"?>
<!DOCTYPE wml PUBLIC "-//PHONE.COM//DTD WML 1.1//EN"
 "http://www.phone.com/dtd/wml11.dtd">
<wml>
<card>
<p>
<%
Dim strCID
```

```
Dim strPass
Dim strNextURL
Dim cnMyDbase
Dim rstC
Dim strConn
Dim strSQL
strConn =
 "Provider=SQLOLEDB;Data Source=MyDbase;"
strConn= strConn & "Initial
Catalog=MyDbase;Trusted_Connection=Yes;"
strCID = Request.QueryString("custid")
strPass = Request.QueryString("password")
strSQL = "SELECT CompanyName,
 CustomerID FROM Customers "
strSQL = strSQL & "WHERE CustomerID =
 '" & strCID & "' AND "
strSQL = strSQL & "Password = '" & strPass & "'"
Set cnMyDbase =
 Server.CreateObject("ADODB.Connection")
With cnMyDbase
 .ConnectionString = strConn
 .Open
end with
Set rstC =
 Server.CreateObject("ADODB.Recordset")
With rstC
 .ActiveConnection = cnMyDbase
 .Open strSQL
End with
Set cnMyDbase = Nothing
If not rstC is Nothing then
If rstC.RecordCount > 0 then
 strNextURL =
"http://www.e4free.com/XMLBeginnersGuide/
Module12/CustomerMain.asp?
 strNextURL = strNextURL & "companyname=" &
 rstC.Fields("companyname")
 strNextURL = strNextURL & "&;custid=" &
 rstC.Fields("CustomerID")
 Response.Redirect(strNextURL)
else
 Response.Write "You are not a valid customer!"
end if
end if
Set rstC = Nothing
%>
</p>
</card>
</wml>
```

12

10. Create a file named ProdSearch.wml. This file creates a screen that lets the administrator enter product ID and product name to find in the database.

```
<?xml version="1.0"?>
<!DOCTYPE wml PUBLIC "-//PHONE.COM//DTD WML 1.1//EN"
 "http://www.phone.com/dtd/wml11.dtd" >
<wml>
<card id="ProductSearch">
<do type="accept" label="Search">
<go href="http://www.e4free.com/
XMLBeginnersGuide/ProdSearch.asp?
prodid=$(prodid)&amp;name=$(name)"/>
</do>
<p>
<b>Product Search</b>
<br/>
Product ID:
<input name="prodid" maxlength="10"
 type="text" emptyok="false"/>
<b>Product Search</b>
<br/>
Product Name:
<input name="name" maxlength="10"
 type="text" emptyok="false"/>
</p>
</card>
</wml>
```

11. Now create a file named ProdSearch.asp. This script performs the database search using data gathered from the administrator. For each product found, the name, price, and the number of units in stock are returned to the user.

```
<%@ Language=VBScript %>
<%
Response.Buffer = true
Response.ContentType = "text/vnd.wap.wml"
%>
<?xml version="1.0"?>
<!DOCTYPE wml PUBLIC "-//PHONE.COM//DTD WML 1.1//EN"
 "http://www.phone.com/dtd/wml11.dtd">
<wml>
<card>
<p>
<%
Dim strPID
Dim strPName
Dim cnMyDbase
Dim rstP
Dim strConn
```

```
Dim strSQL
strConn =
 "Provider=SQLOLEDB;Data Source=MyDbase;"
strConn= strConn & "Initial Catalog=MyDbase;Trusted_Connection=Yes;"
strPID = Request.QueryString("prodid")
strPName = Request.QueryString("name")
If strPID <> "" Then
 strSQL = "SELECT * FROM Products WHERE "
 strSQL = strSQL & "ProductID = " & strPID
Else
 strSQL = "SELECT * FROM Products WHERE "
 strSQL = strSQL & "ProductName
 LIKE '" & strPName & "%'"
End If
Set cnMyDbase =
 Server.CreateObject("ADODB.Connection")
With cnMyDbase
 .ConnectionString = strConn
 .Open
end with
Set rstP = Server.CreateObject("ADODB.Recordset")
With rstP
 .ActiveConnection = cnMyDbase
 .Open strSQL
end with
Set cnMyDbase = Nothing
If not rstP is Nothing then
Response.Write cstr(rstP.RecordCount)
 & " Products Found"
Response.Write "<br/>"
Dim I
For i = 0 to rstP.RecordCount - 1
 Response.Write cstr((i + 1)) & "."
 Response.Write "<b>"
 Response.Write rstP.Fields("ProductName")
 Response.Write "</b><br/>"
 Response.Write "Product Price:"
 Response.Write rstP.Fields("ProductPrice")
 Response.Write "<br/>"
 Response.Write "Qty in stock:"
 Response.Write rstP.Fields("qtyinstock")
 Response.Write "<hr/>"
 rstP.MoveNext
Next
End if
Set rstP = Nothing
%>
</p>
</card>
</wml>
```

12

✓ Mastery Check

1. What is ecommerce, and how is it different from ordinary commerce?

   A. Ecommerce refers to the execution of business transactions electronically, while ordinary commercial transactions are often manually executed.

   B. Ecommerce refers to the electronic transmission of data, while ordinary commercial transactions are performed via traditional means such as the telephone and postal mail.

   C. Ecommerce refers to email communications, while ordinary commercial transactions are conducted using regular mail.

   D. None of the above

2. What is the difference between WAP and WML?

   A. WAP is a protocol for securing wireless devices, while WML is a markup language optimized for building documents for wireless devices.

   B. WAP is a protocol for transmitting WML documents, while WML is a markup language optimized for building documents for wireless devices.

   C. WAP is a protocol for encrypting WML documents, while WML is a markup language optimized for building documents for wireless devices.

   D. None of the above

3. WML is an XML language. This means that what?

   A. WML elements and attributes must be lowercase.

   B. WML elements and attributes must be uppercase.

   C. WML documents must be well-formed.

   D. None of the above

4. What core attributes apply to all WML elements?

   A. ID and class

   B. ID and style

☑ Mastery Check

C. ID and name

D. None of the above

5. How are WML documents structured?

   A. WML documents are structured as sets of pages, so that each document may contain one or more pages and each page may contain one or more links to other pages.

   B. WML documents are structured as decks, and each deck may contain one or more cards.

   C. WML documents contain scrollable menu choices formatted as menus, and each menu may contain one or more choices.

   D. None of the above

6. What data is required to be present in the prologue of a WML document?

   A. The XML declaration, version number, and DOCTYPE declaration

   B. The WML declaration, version number, and DOCTYPE declaration

   C. The XML declaration, WML version number, and the DOCTYPE declaration

   D. None of the above

7. What WML element contains the entire document, and what WML element contains the contents of a card?

   A. The xml element and the content element

   B. The html element and the card element

   C. The wml element and the card element

   D. None of the above

12

Part IV

Appendixes

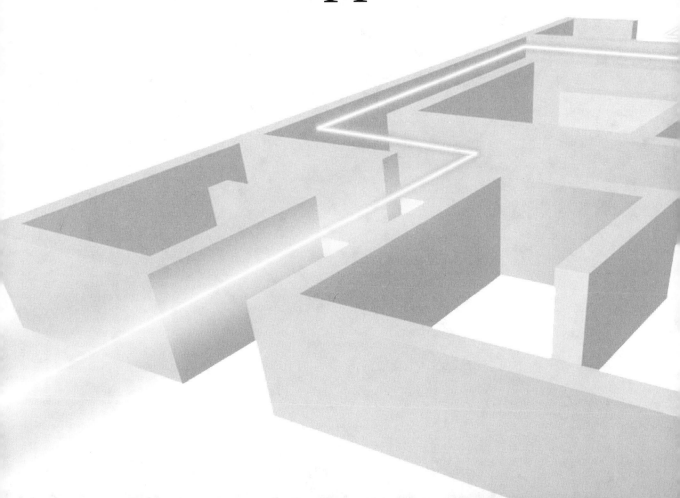

Appendix A

Answers to Mastery Checks

Module 1: The History of XML

1. How does XML differ from HTML?

B. HTML is a language; XML is a technology for making languages.

2. What components do HTML and XML languages have in common?

Both HTML and XML languages have elements and attributes in common, the main difference being that XML elements and attributes can be made up at will by the XML language author, while HTML elements and attributes are predefined.

3. Name four differences between XHTML and HTML.

Unlike in HTML, in XHTML, all element and attribute names must be in lowercase, all elements must be properly nested (not overlapping), all elements must be properly closed with a closing tag, and attributes cannot be minimized.

4. What is the relationship of a DTD to an XML document, if the document references the DTD?

B. The DTD defines some or all of the allowable elements and attributes for the document.

5. What is the process by which XML documents are transformed into a finished product for rendering in a browser?

XML documents are first read by the XSL processor and transformed from the original document tree (formed by the DOM) into what is called a result tree, which contains only those elements appropriate for the media on which the document is to be displayed and additional formatting elements and style instructions. Next, the document is rendered by the browser or other user agent using the formatting elements and style instructions.

6. What signs mark the beginning and ending of an HTML command; and what are the signs called?

B. The greater-than and less-than signs; a tag

7. What two parts always make up an attribute?

C. The name of the attribute and the value of the attribute.

8. When an attribute is minimized, what does that mean? How is it different from an attribute that is not minimized?

Attributes always come as a name value pair. However, when an attribute is minimized, the value of the attribute may be left off. It is still there, but it is supplied automatically by the browser. For example, consider the *selected* attribute for the INPUT element when the type is "radio". This attribute should be written *selected="selected"*, but in HTML the equal sign and the value of the attribute may be left off and are automatically supplied by the browser when the page is loaded, so that the radio button created is in the selected state when the page loads.

9. What is a new XML application?

A. A new XML language

10. Who may create new XML applications?

A. Anyone

11. In what case must HTML elements and attributes be written?

C. It doesn't matter

12. What are elements and attributes in XML documents?

C. Elements are important parts of a document, and attributes represent properties of those elements

13. What does it mean that elements may not overlap?

A. The start tag of an element that is inside another element must be written after the start tag of the element it is inside, and the end tag of the inside element must be written before the end tag of the outside element.

14. What is a CDATA section, in XHTML?

A. CDATA stands for Character Data, and it refers to a section of content defined by the CDATA delimiters, in which scripting content is placed.

A

Within a CDATA section, scripting commands that would not ordinarily be unprocessed by the browser are left alone.

15. What is a data model?

B. A conceptual representation of the way data flows and interacts in your problem area

Module 2: XML Basics, Syntax, and DTDs

1. What is an XML vocabulary?

C. Terms applicable to a particular industry that have been codified as an XML DTD or schema

2. What are XML names, how are they defined, and what restrictions are placed upon them?

C. Names for XML components such as elements and attributes, written from the ASCII character set, may not start with uppercase or lowercase *xml* or digits.

3. What is a content model?

The term *content model* refers to whether or not an element may contain text data or other elements. It's just a technical way of describing what content is allowed within an element, if any.

4. What is the root of an XML document called? Is this the same as the *root element*? What does *root* mean, and what does it mean to be the *root element* of an XML document?

The root of an XML document is called the *document root*, but the root element springs *from* the document root, so they are not the same thing. The term *root* refers to the top *object* in a hierarchy of objects, such of the objects in an XML document. The root element of an XML document is the top *element* (or bottom element, depending upon which view you prefer); all other elements in the document are child elements of the root element.

5. What would the DOCTYPE declaration look like for an XML document with an internal DTD defining a root element named "Car" in which any content can appear?

    A. `<!DOCTYPE Car [<!ELEMENT Car ANY>]>`

6. What is the purpose of the attribute types ID, IDREF, and IDREFS?

    E. A and B above. ID is suitable for using with an element where the element must be unique across the entire document. IDREF makes a single reference from one element to another with an ID attribute of the same name. IDREFS makes a reference to multiple other elements via ID attribute names in a single element. ID, IDREF, and IDREFS attributes allow linking from one element to another, allowing the formation of relationships from one element to another, when the elements are not in a parent-child relationship.

7. What elements might you use to build an XML DTD for tracking recipes within a cookbook?

    In order, from root to child elements: Recipes, Recipe, Ingredients, Ingredient

8. What attributes might be appropriate for some of the elements you've created in question 7?

    For Recipe: Name, Author, Date. For Ingredient: Brand, Price. For the amount of an ingredient, it might be wise to use a child element of Ingredient named Amount, so that the same ingredient could be used twice in different amounts.

9. What symbol would be used in a DTD to allow a particular element to appear within another element one or more times?

    C. The plus sign (+)

10. What term, when included as part of an ATTLIST attribute declaration, makes it so an attribute is optional?

    A. #IMPLIED

A

11. What is a CDATA section?

B. A special area in a document delimited by CDATA delimiters, in which character data that is not part of the allowed Unicode characters may appear

12. What is meant by the CDATA data type in a DTD, as applied to an attribute?

A. Character data

13. What is a notation, and what form does it take?

A. It's an identifier of the type of content contained in unparsed character data, and it takes the form *data type/specific type*. For example, a set of data that forms a JPEG image would have a notation *image/jpeg*.

14. What is contained in the prolog of an XML document?

C. The DOCTYPE declaration, comments, and processing instructions

15. What attribute data type might be used to identify an element uniquely across an entire document?

B. The ID type

Module 3: XML Schema

1. What is one of the major advantages of using an XML Schema rather than a DTD to create valid XML documents from?

D. All of the above

2. What is a schema?

D. All of the above

3. How are elements declared in an XML schema?

E. B and C only. With the <element/> element and a name; and with the <element/> element, a name, and a type

4. What are primitive data types? Name two.

   B. Primitive data types are not derived from any other type; they are basic data types built into XML Schema, such as string and decimal.

5. The difference between a simple type and a complex type is that the simple type contains no elements as part of its content. To derive a simple type from a primitive data type, you would use either a restriction or an extension.

6. What is the type anyType, and what kind of data type is it?

   C. It is the default data type, and it may be any data type.

7. What is the value space of a data type?

   C. The range of values possible

8. What are data type facets?

   D. B and C above: Properties of data types, such as length; restrictions on the values a data type may assume

9. What kind of data type is timeDuration, and how is it coded?

   The data type timeDuration is a primitive data type because it is not derived from any other data type. It is coded as the letter *P* followed by a number, the letter *Y*, a number, the letter *M*, a number, and the letter *D*. The *P* stands for period; the *Y* stands for year; the *M* stands for month; the *D* stands for day; and the numbers represent the amount of years, months, and days in the duration.

10. From what data type is the data type integer derived, and how is the derivation accomplished?

   C. The integer data type is derived from the data type decimal and is made by setting the scale facet to 0.

11. What method can be used to determine the elements, attributes, and data types required for constructing a schema using the XML Schema recommendation?

   D. A combination of the methods in A, B, and C

A

12. How is an XML schema different from an ordinary XML document, according to what we've learned so far?

B. The format and structure of an XML schema is the same as for an ordinary XML document, but an XML schema depends upon the XML DTD for Schemas for the definition of elements, attributes, and data types.

13. What XML Schema element is used to begin the declaration of a new data type with content consisting only of other elements?

B. complexType

14. What XML Schema elements may be used to declare elements, attributes, and their data types?

D. Either A or C

15. What is the purpose of the "sequence" element in XML Schema?

B. It forces the elements in a data type into a particular sequence.

Module 4: XML Namespaces and Advanced Schemas

1. What is an XML namespace?

B. A set of names representing a specific XML vocabulary

2. What is the value of using namespaces with XML documents?

A. Namespaces allow a single XML document to reference the same component names from multiple DTDs or schemas.

3. What method might be used to reference a namespace?

B. Include the *xmlns* attribute, set to a URL reflecting the location of the DTD to which the namespace refers.

4. What is a qualified name?

   B. A name having a prefix and local name separated by a colon

5. What is an NCName?

   C. A Non-Colonized Name

6. From what set of names do NCNames derive?

   B. Any names conforming to XML Names, minus the colon

7. What is the purpose of the prefix in a qualified name?

   A. Any element or attribute in an XML document to which the prefix is attached is referenced to the DTD for the namespace of the prefix.

8. What is the default namespace?

   D. None of the above

9. If a namespace is attached to an element by a prefix, what is the effect on non-prefixed child elements?

   C. The namespace affects all child elements of the element to which the namespace is attached, no matter what level.

10. If a namespace is attached to an element by a prefix, what is the effect on nonprefixed attributes in its child elements?

   A. Nothing

11. What are schema, element, and attribute in XML Schema, and what is their purpose?

   A. These are XML Schema elements, and they declare the schema and any elements and attributes allowed within an XML document based upon it.

12. What is the purpose of the *minOccurs* and *maxOccurs* attributes in XML Schema?

   B. They specify the minimum and maximum number of times an element may occur.

A

13. What is the purpose of the *complexType* element in XML Schema?

    B. It defines a data type that includes elements and possibly simpleType data types as well.

14. What is the rule regarding attributes and the namespaces they may be attached to?

    B. No two attributes may have the same name in a single element, and they also may not have prefixes attached that point to the same namespace reference.

15. What is the purpose of the *base* attribute in XML Schema?

    B. It sets the base data type from which a new data type is derived.

Module 5: XML Graphics Basics and SMIL

1. What is the basic format of image files?

    B. Encoded binary data

2. What image file format supported by most browsers can be animated, interlaced, and can have a transparent background?

    C. Graphics Interchange Format (GIF)

3. What is a color space and what color space is currently used by browsers?

    A. A range of colors, RGB

4. What does the term "color depth" refer to?

    B. The number of bits required to encode a range of colors

5. If an image file is scanned from an original that is 2 inches square (at full size) at a resolution of 100 dpi, what size, in inches, would the image appear to be on a screen 12 inches wide with a horizontal resolution of 600 pixels and 8 inches high with a vertical resolution of 400 pixels?

C. The image would appear 4 inches by 4 inches on the screen.

6. What element could be used in an XHTML document to insert images and what attribute provides a text value if the image doesn't appear?

C. The IMG element, and the *alt* attribute

7. If you create an XML document that includes an image file, how might you produce finished HTML/XHTML from the XML document?

D. All of the above

8. In a SMIL document, in what element does the *region* element appear as a child, and what does the *region* element do?

A. The *region* element appears in the *layout* element, and it defines a region for one or more media objects.

9. What code would you write to define a region with a unique identifier of *a1*, appearing 10 pixels from the top of the viewport, and 6 pixels from the left of the viewport?

B. `<region id="a1" top="10" left="6"/>`

10. What elements control timing of media objects in the *body* element?

B. The *par* and *seq* elements

11. What attribute controls layering of elements in the *region* element?

A. The *z-index* attribute

12. If no explicit beginning is specified for a media object, when will the media object begin to show itself?

B. As soon as any elements of which it is a child element finish playing

A

13. What is the purpose of the *system* attributes?

C. They allow the SMIL document to query the system on which it's being played back, to select the most appropriate resource to play dependent on the user's system.

14. What is the purpose of the *switch* element, and how does it work?

C. The *switch* element switches among various *media object* elements, based on which elements are found to be acceptable, and also matching the user's system capabilities.

15. What attribute specifies a media object's location for retrieval, and what attribute specifies the region into which the object should be placed?

C. The *src* attribute specifies where the media object should be retrieved from, and the *region* attribute specifies where it should be placed.

Module 6: XML Applications, XLink, XPath, and XPointer

1. What XML documents have information sets?

C. Those that are well-formed

2. Under what circumstances might a well-formed XML document not have a meaningful information set?

B. When the document doesn't conform to the specification of the namespaces

3. What is the purpose of the "All declarations processed" property of the document information item?

A. It's a Boolean value that indicates whether the complete DTD has been read.

4. How many document information items may be present in an XML document?

C. Zero if no information set is present, otherwise one

5. How many element information items occur in the infoset of an XML document possessing an infoset, and what is the purpose of the prefix property for these items?

C. One for each element in the document. The prefix denotes the namespace prefix, if any, attached to the element.

6. When would an attribute specified in a DTD not appear as an attribute information item in the infoset of an XML document?

D. B or C: When the attribute is not found; when the attribute has an implied value (#IMPLIED)

7. Which of the following statements is a good definition of an XLink link?

A. An explicit relationship between resources or portions of resources

8. In XLink, what is a remote resource and how is it addressed?

A. A remote resource is any resource referenced, and it's addressed by a reference, such as a URL.

9. What is a traversal and what terms are used for resources involved in a traversal?

C. A traversal is the act of using or following a link for any purpose. The resources involved are called the starting resource and the ending resource.

10. What is the purpose of a location path expression, in XPath?

A. A location path expression selects for a set of nodes from the context of the XML document.

11. What is the purpose of the XPointer language?

B. XPointer provides a means of addressing the internal structures of an XML document.

A

12. What extended capabilities does XPointer bring to XPath?

D. All of the above

13. What XML development tools might make up a good set of applications for creating, modifying, and maintaining XML vocabularies and documents?

A. A validating XML parser, development environment, and XSL processor

14. From what XML language is XPointer built upon?

B. XPath

15. What is one of the primary uses for XPath and XPointer?

A. To assist in the transformation process performed by XSLT

Module 7: XML and the Web

1. What XHTML structures are used to arrange objects on Web pages for browsers that don't understand CSS2?

D. All of the above

2. What are some of the common page types found in most Web sites?

C. About, Contact, Order, Search, Privacy, and Terms

3. Why might a Web site author place all Web pages in the same folder on a Web site?

B. To simplify the management of hyperlink and image references

4. The XML Signature Syntax and Processing specification provides what capabilities?

B. The application of digital signatures to digital objects

5. What is the root element of an XML Signature document?

C. The Signature element

6. What elements make up the content of the Signature element and how many times may they occur? Place them in the correct order.

A. The SignedInfo element (once), the SignatureValue element (once), the KeyInfo element (zero or more times), and the Object element (zero to an unbounded number of times)

7. If a Web site has several security policies in force, with different policies applying to different areas on the Web site, how might these policies be represented to users?

B. A Privacy policy should be published as a P3P XML Document

8. What are the components of forms in documents, and what is the purpose of XForms?

B. Forms usually contain labels identifying the information to be supplied and fields for entering the information. XForms separates the structure of the form from the presentation of the form.

9. What are some of the abilities of XForms extensions?

D. All of the above

10. What are some of the abilities of the XForms Submit Protocol?

D. A and B above (the ability to submit the contents of a form to the server and the ability to allow a form to be half-filled out, suspended, and then resumed later)

11. What is the difference between static and dynamic Web site content?

B. Dynamic content refers to Web site content that is generated on the fly, often by scripts from data in databases

12. What would be a good description of how public key encryption works?

A. Public key encryption involves a public key and a private key. A user who wants to send an encrypted message to a recipient uses the recipient's

A

public key to encrypt the message, with the assurance that only the recipient can decrypt the message with their private key.

13. What properties are available for model items in XForms?

C. Name, read-only, required, relevant, calculate, priority, and validate

14. How would the use of P3P help people manage access to Web sites?

C. Sites could be queried automatically and, if they don't provide P3P data or don't meet the user's preset restrictions based on P3P, the site would be blocked

15. Why would a Web site author bother with XML, if all data is stored initially in a database format?

B. Transforming data into XML makes the data more accessible to other servers.

Module 8: The Document Object Model

1. Why is the DOM compared to a tree?

B. A single object is the parent of all other objects, and the objects may have one or more child objects, with some having no child objects. When drawn out as a diagram, the objects and their relationships often resemble a tree.

2. Why is working with the DOM easier than with an XML document as is?

A. XML documents are plain text and there's no easy way to address or navigate individual elements. Objects in the DOM expose properties and methods, making it easy to find and manipulate them programmatically.

3. What are some of the interfaces listed in the DOM Level 2 Core, and how are they described?

    A. Element, Attr, and CharacterData. They are described in terms of what function they perform, what attributes are available, and what methods may be used to work with them.

4. Style sheet languages allow document authors to add style to XHTML, XML, and other structured documents. What style sheet languages may be used with the DOM Level 1?

    C. All style sheet languages

5. Why must the DOM be aware of style sheets?

    A. The DOM may be used to address a particular element or set of elements and change the values of some of their attributes, including style attributes.

6. Give an example of the kind of action that might be directed toward a component of an XHTML document via a style sheet.

    C. The background color of a table cell might be set to light-blue

7. What are events, and what are they used for in XHTML Web pages?

    A. Events are things that might happen to an object on a Web page, such as the *onclick* event happening to a button object within a form on a page.

8. What is the relationship between events and the DOM in DOM Level 2?

    C. Events travel through the DOM hierarchy of objects, so that an event occurring to a button on a form in a page would travel from the page, to the form, to the button, and back up again.

9. In the Microsoft DOM, what object is used to represent elements in an XML document?

    B. The IXMLDOMElement object

10. What property contains attributes for Microsoft DOM elements, and how might this property be changed?

    C. The attributes property contains attributes of elements in the Microsoft DOM, and the setAttributeNode method is used to change this property.

A

11. What property of a DOMDocument object (in the Microsoft DOM) could be set to specify the language to be used for selecting nodes within an XML document represented in the DOM?

A. The SelectionLanguage property

12. When an object is a collection, what benefits does that structure offer?

B. Collections may have more than one item in them and can, therefore, be iterated through using a For...Next loop, without necessarily knowing the names of each item in the collections.

13. What collection of the IXMLDOMNode object contains attributes, and what property of this collection tells how many exist?

A. Attributes and leng

14. When a DOMDocument object is created, what method could be used to bring an XML document into the DOMDocument object in memory?

C. The load method

15. What properties of the IXMLDOMNode object tell its type and name?

B. The nodeType and nodeName properties

Module 9: Designing Data Models for XML

1. What are two methods of approaching the development of a data model?

C. Both A and B: Starting with what you know and building up from there; and Starting with the requirements and working backward

2. Can a database or XML document be empty and still have structure?

B. Both a database and an XML document may be empty, but may still have structure.

3. What kinds of things can be modeled with a data model?

    C. Both A and B: Physical things, such as cars, people, buildings, and so forth; Virtual things, such as orders, messages, calculations, and so forth

4. In the ER type of data model, what is an attribute?

    C. An attribute is a property of an entity

5. What values can the null value represent?

    C. Not applicable, unknown but existent, and unknown-nonexistent

6. What relationships may exist between entities?

    D. None of the above

7. In the ER type of data model, what characteristics may an attribute have?

    D. All of the above

8. What are key attributes, and how do they work?

    A. Key attributes are unique values within a set of records in a table or elements in an XML document. Their uniqueness makes them ideal for identifying individual records.

9. How are key values used to form relationships between records in a relational database?

    C. The primary-key values for one set of records may be included as the foreign-key values for another set of records. Thereafter, any record with a foreign-key value (in the second table) is connected by that value to the record in the first table with a matching primary-key value.

10. What value may not be allowed in a primary key field?

    D. All of the above

11. What is the purpose of the reserved word WHERE in SQL?

    C. It provides criteria by which to select records

A

12. What reserved word in SQL is used to delete tables from a database?

B. DROP

13. Modeling the relationships between children and their toys, which of the following might be a good data model?

A. Children and toys might be entities, and the children and toys might have a one-to-many (one child to many toys) or many-to-many relationship (where the children share toys).

14. What do the SELECT, DELETE, and INSERT SQL reserved words share in common, and how do they differ?

B. These words all form queries, but SELECT selects certain records, DELETE deletes certain records, and INSERT inserts new records.

15. What symbol is used to return all fields in a SELECT query in SQL, and what is used to return only a selected set of fields in a SELECT query in SQL?

C. The asterisk is used to return all fields, and individual field names separated by a comma are used if only selected fields are desired.

Module 10: Databases and XML

1. Of what value are database application programs when working with XML and databases?

D. All of the above

2. What sequential steps might you take to build a database application using a typical RDBMS, such as Microsoft Access?

A. Build the tables, build the queries, build the forms, and build the reports.

3. Active Server Pages and VBScript were already introduced as a means of interacting with XML documents. What additional Microsoft technologies did you use in this module to work with both XML documents and databases?

B. Active Data Objects (ADO)

4. What is the function of the Connection object?

   C. The Connection object enables a connection to a database via an ODBC driver.

5. What is the function of the Command object?

   A. The Command object allows commands to be executed against a database.

6. What is the function of the Recordset object?

   B. The Recordset object contains records retrieved from a database.

7. What type of cursor allows only forward movement through a set of records, and what method would be used to move forward one record at a time?

   A. The Forward-Only cursor allows only forward movement through a set of records, and the MoveNext method would be used to move forward from one record to the next.

8. Name the properties that indicate the number of records in a recordset and whether you're at the beginning or end of a recordset?

   C. The BOF, EOF, and RecordCount properties

9. When connecting to a database from an ASP script using ADO, either a connection string or a DSN must be used to provide the information to make the connection. What information is included in the connection string or the DSN?

   B. The driver for the database, the path to the database, and, if necessary, the username and password for the database

10. What process might be used to retrieve data from a database and provide it in an XML document format?

    A. Retrieve the data from the database; iterate through the records; and for each record, create write out the XML elements, attributes, and content for those records as an XML document.

A

11. For users of Internet Explorer 5.0 and above, what method might be used to provide XML data if scripting has been disallowed?

B. Data Islands and the XML element

12. What methods can be used to include XML data in a Web page viewed in Internet Explorer 5.0 and above?

A. Inline XML or references to an XML file, using the XML element

13. What technique can be used to bind XML data to HTML Web page structures, such as tables?

C. Reference the ID attribute value of the XML element using the *datasrc* attribute.

14. If a table is being used to view XML data in Internet Explorer, what attribute of the table may be used to restrict the number of records displayed, and how many records will be shown if this attribute is set to 3?

A. The DATAPAGESIZE attribute, and 3

15. What content is provided by the $Text data field and how is it generated?

A. The $Text data field concatenates the content for a given record, automatically.

Module 11: XML Presentation and XSL

1. What is the difference between Cascading Style sheets Language and XSL?

D. All of the above

2. What process is used by XSLT to transform XML documents into a format suitable for viewing in browsers?

B. XML elements are selected from the XML document using the XPath language, and these elements are transformed according to rules in the XSL style sheet.

3. What terms are used to describe the XML document before and after it's transformed, and why?

B. The XML document is described as the source tree, and the transformed document is described as the result tree. This is because these terms denote the source structure from which the transformation is made and the result structure of the transformation.

4. What does an XSL style sheet contain?

B. Tree construction rules

5. How may style sheets be associated with XML documents?

A. Through the use of a processing instruction whose target is xml-stylesheet

6. What data must be present in the xsl-stylsheet element of an XSL style sheet?

C. A reference to the XSL namespace and the version number

7. What is the prefix for the XSL namespace, and what is the URL?

A. The prefix is xsl, and the URL is http://www.w3.org/1999/XSL/Transform

8. What are the purposes of the xsl:include and xsl:import style sheet elements?

B. The xsl:include element includes other style sheets, while the xsl:import element imports other style sheets, the difference being that definitions and template rules in the imported style sheet have a lower precedence.

9. What are formatting objects, and what is their prefix and URL of their namespace?

A. Formatting objects are the result of transforming an XML document using tree transformation rules, ending with elements and attributes from the formatting objects (fo) namespace, having a prefix of fo, and a URL of http://www.w3.org/1999/XSL/Format.

A

10. In addition to being able to select certain elements and attributes from an XML document for transformation, XSL also allows conditional processing. What are some of the conditional processing structures provided?

B. xsl:if and xsl:choose

11. What is the area tree, and how is it generated?

C. The area tree consists of a tree structured set of area nodes, including the root node. Except for the root node, all nodes are areas defined as rectangular boxes, typically one for each unique object in the formatting object tree.

Module 12: XML, WAP, and Ecommerce

1. What is ecommerce, and how is it different from ordinary commerce?

A. Ecommerce refers to the execution of business transactions electronically, while ordinary commercial transactions are often manually executed.

2. What is the difference between WAP and WML?

B. WAP is a protocol for transmitting WML documents, while WML is a markup language optimized for building documents for wireless devices.

3. WML is an XML language. This means that what?

C. WML documents must be well-formed.

4. What core attributes apply to all WML elements?

A. ID and class

5. How are WML documents structured?

B. WML documents are structured as decks, and each deck may contain one or more cards.

6. What data is required to be present in the prologue of a WML document?

  A. The XML declaration, version number, and DOCTYPE declaration

7. What WML element contains the entire document, and what WML element contains the contents of a card?

  C. The wml element and the card element

A

Appendix B

XML Schema and DTD Syntax

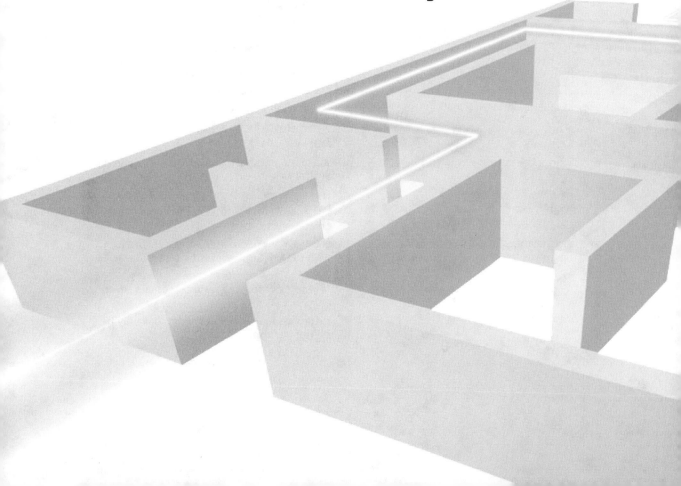

The following table is a quick reference to XML Schema and DTD syntax and construction techniques.

Regular Expression Symbols	Definition
.	any character
?	previous value occurs zero or one times
[ ]	matches any one of the values contained in [ ]
{x,y}	previous value occurs a minimum of x times, and a maximum of y
\s \S	whitespace / non-whitespace
\d \D	digit / non-digit
+	previous value occurs one or more times
*	previous value occurs zero or more times
( )	contained portion is treated as one value

Regular Expression Examples	
a\sstring	a followed by one whitespace character followed by string
a*c	any number of a's followed by one c
a?c	one or zero as followed by one c
[xy][XY]	x or y followed by X or Y
a{3,8}b	number between 3 and 8 as followed by b
a{3,}b	at least 3 as followed by b
.a	any character followed by a

Schema	Notes
<xsd:schema xmlns:xsd="[url here]">	sets the namespace xsd to the XML Schema at "[url here]"
<xsd:element name="eName" type="eType"/>	creates a new element named "eName" and has a type defined by "eType"
<xsd:list itemType="aType"/>	creates a list of type "aType"
<xsd:element name="eName2" type="xsd:integer"/>	creates a new element named "eName2" with the built-in type "xsd:integer"
<xsd:complexType name="cType">	creates a new complex type named "cType"; Complex types may contain several elements
<xsd:sequence>	begins a sequence of elements that may be part of a complex type

Schema	Notes
`<xsd:complexType name="cType2"><xsd:sequence><xsd:element name="eName3" type="xsd:decimal"/><xsd:element name="eName4" type="xsd:string"/></xsd:sequence><xsd:attribute name="aName" type="xsd:integer"/></xsd:complexType>`	definition of a complex type with a sequence of elements and an attribute
`<xsd:simpleType name="sType">`	defines a simple type
`<xsd:restriction base="xsd:string">`	restricts the valid values
`<xsd:enumeration value="val1"/>`	when used in the restriction context, this requires that the value be one of those contained in an enumeration
`<xsd:pattern value="[0-9]{2}-.{5}"/>`	when used in the restriction context, this restricts the value to the regular expression
`<xsd:annotation>`	see xsd:documentation below
`<xsd:documentation>`	add a statement for the benefit of humans or machines seeking information
`minOccurs="2"`	requires that a certain element be present 2 times in the context
`maxOccurs="3"`	requries that a certain element be present no more than 3 times
`base="someType"`	derive the type from a preexisting type "someType"

Simple Built-in Schema Type Examples

string	a string
CDATA	a string
byte	-1, 42
unsignedByte	0, 42
integer	9, -9
positiveInteger	9, 11
negativeInteger	-14
nonNegativeInteger	0, 7
nonPositiveInteger	0, -41
int	8
unsignedInt	12
long	-7389145, 1000000000

B

Simple Built-in Schema Type Examples

unsignedLong	1000000000
short	100
unsignedShort	120
decimal	7.4
float	7.453
double	7.50E+006
boolean	true, false
time	14:19:12.01
date	2001-03-19
month	2001-05
year	2001
century	20
Name	typeName (this is an XML name type)
uriReference	http://www.e4free.com
language	en-US, en-GB

Index

Z

INTERNATIONAL CONTACT INFORMATION

AUSTRALIA
McGraw-Hill Book Company Australia Pty. Ltd.
TEL +61-2-9417-9899
FAX +61-2-9417-5687
http://www.mcgraw-hill.com.au
books-it_sydney@mcgraw-hill.com

CANADA
McGraw-Hill Ryerson Ltd.
TEL +905-430-5000
FAX +905-430-5020
http://www.mcgrawhill.ca

**GREECE, MIDDLE EAST,
NORTHERN AFRICA**
McGraw-Hill Hellas
TEL +30-1-656-0990-3-4
FAX +30-1-654-5525

MEXICO (Also serving Latin America)
McGraw-Hill Interamericana Editores S.A. de C.V.
TEL +525-117-1583
FAX +525-117-1589
http://www.mcgraw-hill.com.mx
fernando_castellanos@mcgraw-hill.com

SINGAPORE (Serving Asia)
McGraw-Hill Book Company
TEL +65-863-1580
FAX +65-862-3354
http://www.mcgraw-hill.com.sg
mghasia@mcgraw-hill.com

SOUTH AFRICA
McGraw-Hill South Africa
TEL +27-11-622-7512
FAX +27-11-622-9045
robyn_swanepoel@mcgraw-hill.com

**UNITED KINGDOM & EUROPE
(Excluding Southern Europe)**
McGraw-Hill Education Europe
TEL +44-1-628-502500
FAX +44-1-628-770224
http://www.mcgraw-hill.co.uk
computing_neurope@mcgraw-hill.com

ALL OTHER INQUIRIES Contact:
Osborne/McGraw-Hill
TEL +1-510-549-6600
FAX +1-510-883-7600
http://www.osborne.com
omg_international@mcgraw-hill.com